THE CONNECTION CONUNDRUM

THE CONNECTION CONUNDRUM

Empowering Teachers to Lead a
Culture of Sustainable Connection

MATT PITMAN

Praise for *The Connection Conundrum*

"The research is clear: real human connection improves mental wellbeing and outcomes in schools. *The Connection Conundrum* is the map for any teacher who is ready to make the journey. A must-read for all educators."

Dr Mark Williams – neuroscience professor, author and speaker

"I absolutely loved *The Connection Conundrum* – it's exactly the kind of insightful and practical read that educators and school leaders need right now. Matt captures perfectly why connection and relationships aren't just 'nice-to-haves' but are fundamental at the heart of school culture. I found the book really motivating, full of down-to-earth advice and accessible. If you're passionate about making your school a place where students and staff genuinely thrive, this book is a fantastic place to start."

Al Kingsley – multi academy trust chair, author, speaker and edtech CEO

"This brilliant, practical and heartfelt resource for every school centres connection where it truly belongs: at the heart of teaching, learning and inclusion. With thoughtful insights into Universal Design for Learning, Cognitive Load Theory and restorative practices, it helps educators shift from a mindset of 'how do I manage all these needs?' to 'how can I create space for every learner to belong and succeed?' It's not about more work; it's about doing what truly matters: more human connection. A must-have for any educator committed to creating a culture where all students feel seen, valued and empowered to thrive, especially in an AI-driven world where human connection matters more than ever."

Naz Zengin – inclusive education leader, speaker and teacher

"In *The Connection Conundrum*, Matt Pitman invites us to reimagine school as a place of deep, lasting connection. He offers practical tools to rebuild trust, strengthen relationships and cultivate belonging. Grounded in research but easy to engage with, the book encourages both reflection and action. It reminds us that connection is foundational to student engagement, teacher wellbeing and school-wide success. It's a quiet call to slow down, look up and lead with intention. Every educator must read this."

Mathew Green – assistant principal, podcast host and teacher

"*The Connection Conundrum* is an absolute must-read for every educator! This book focuses on the importance of connection as the foundation to everything that occurs in the classroom. Matt Pitman uses the metaphor of climbing a mountain to encapsulate the work required to not only build but sustain a culture of connection, belonging and collaboration with our learners. This practical book highlights that connection and belonging must be purposefully planned for, implemented and sustained over time. The message is clear: every classroom teacher can have a positive impact on school culture, starting with the learners in their classroom."

Alice Vigors – school principal, author and teacher

"*The Connection Conundrum* comes at a critical juncture in education. In a world dominated by discussions around AI and the increasing loss of human connection due to digital devices, this book is the kind of practical, professional reading that all teachers need to read. It provides a set of timeless, functional waypoints for teachers to flourish and build stronger connection in our schools."

James Vella – eLearning leader and teacher

Published in 2025 by Amba Press, Melbourne, Australia
www.ambapress.com.au

© Matthew Pitman 2025

All rights reserved. No part of this publication may be reproduced, stored in a retrieval system or transmitted in any form by any means, electronic or mechanical, including photocopying, recording or by any information storage or retrieval system without written permission from the author or publisher except for brief inclusion of quotations in review.

Cover design: Tess McCabe
Internal design: Amba Press
Editor: Rica Dearman

ISBN: 9781923403260 (pbk)
ISBN: 9781923403277 (ebk)

A catalogue record for this book is available from the National Library of Australia.

Contents

Acknowledgement of Country		vii
Acknowledgements		viii
About the author		ix
A note for school leaders		xi
Introduction		1

Part 1: The call to climb — 9

Chapter 1	Standing before the range *The nature of change and the influence of a teacher*	11
Chapter 2	Calling the explorer *The Connection Journey and the mountainous metaphor*	20
Chapter 3	Charting the first route *The 4Cs and how to leverage them for sustainable connection*	30

Part 2: Base camp — 39

Chapter 4	Packing the essentials *Building trust and safety*	41
Chapter 5	Mapping the journey *Setting goals and inspiring motivation*	56

Part 3: Trailhead — 73

Chapter 6	Exploring new horizons *Fostering empathic curiosity and inclusivity*	75
Chapter 7	Navigating together *Building classroom community*	89

Part 4: The first climb — 105

Chapter 8	Guiding the way *Connecting learning to purpose*	107
Chapter 9	Finding your rhythm *Differentiating for meaningful learning*	121

Part 5: Facing the valleys — 139

Chapter 10	Weathering storms *Traversing classroom challenges*	141

Part 6: The summit and the next mountain — 167

Chapter 11	Planting the flag *Reflecting on progress and growth*	169
Chapter 12	Acting with courage *Celebrating progress and inspiring greater change*	183

Conclusion — 199
References — 204

Acknowledgement of Country

I begin this book by acknowledging the Wurundjeri Woiwurrung people of the Kulin Nation, the Traditional Custodians of the land on which this book was written. I pay my respects to their Elders, past, present and emerging, and extend this respect to all First Nations peoples, whose lasting connection to Country and community continues to inspire.

In writing this book, I've also had to face a regret: my last book didn't include an Acknowledgement of Country. Caught up in the excitement of writing, I missed the opportunity to honour the Traditional Owners and their enduring wisdom. It's a mistake I've carried with me and am determined not to repeat.

I'm no expert, but I know that Indigenous Australians have much to teach us about connection. Their practices of deep listening, community celebration and nurturing interdependence are powerful models for the relationships we build in schools. They remind us that connection isn't just about bringing people together; it's about creating collective bonds that make us stronger.

At its core, education is about these bonds: between students, staff, families and the wider world. As you explore connection in this book, I invite you to learn from the wisdom of First Nations peoples and let their perspectives inform the connections you create in your classroom. Let this acknowledgement be more than words – it's a commitment to respect inclusion and community spirit in schools and beyond.

Acknowledgements

This book exists because of my wife, Marina.

Her support made this possible, not just in spirit, but in the most practical, generous and selfless ways imaginable. She sacrificed her time, took on bedtime routines and gave up countless weekends so I could hide away and write. She sat with my endless questions, clarified thoughts and lifted me through the inevitable dips in motivation. Though this is my second book and it came together quicker than I expected, it only came into being because my two girls created the space for it to happen. I love you both, thank you so much.

Thank you also to the wonderful team at Amba Press, especially Alicia Cohen, for your steady guidance and belief in the work. I'm equally grateful to Naz, Alice, James, Mathew, Al and Mark for generously reviewing drafts and challenging me to shape this into its best possible form.

It takes a village to raise a child. I think it's fair to say it takes a similar kind of village to bring a book into the world. I am forever appreciative.

About the author

Matt Pitman is a husband, father, teacher and educational leader based in Melbourne, Australia. He's known for fostering connection, community and innovative learning environments across Catholic, government and independent schools.

Early in his career, Matt led curriculum teams and developed impactful programmes to enhance student learning and development. Over time, his focus expanded to positive education and student wellbeing, driving initiatives that meet the evolving needs of young people today. His collaborative approach, working closely with students, parents and staff, has been central to his success.

Matt's academic pursuits reflect his commitment to education: he holds multiple master's degrees in educational leadership, student wellbeing and evidence-based teaching. As a doctoral candidate, his research centres on building stronger school connections – an ethos that underpins his work.

Matt has been recognised nationally for his innovative leadership and impactful contributions to education, with multiple awards highlighting his commitment to equipping young people to thrive in an interconnected world.

He's also the author of *The Connection Curriculum*, a practical guide for educators on using sustainable connection to drive academic success and improve wellbeing. Available now from Amba Press.

A note for school leaders

Dear school leaders,

I want to begin by acknowledging the incredible demands and complexities of school leadership. The challenges you face are significant, and I know that at times they can feel insurmountable. This book isn't about dismissing or minimising those challenges but about recognising an opportunity to strengthen our schools by leaning into the expertise and innovation already present within your staff.

This book exists because teachers across schools have asked for it. They have spoken openly with me about the challenges they face and the moments when action feels urgent, even if it doesn't align perfectly with current priorities. Teachers see the disconnects, the barriers and the missed opportunities for connection every day – and they want to do something about it. They want to work alongside leaders, not in opposition, to build stronger, more connected school communities, now.

Leadership is vital, and when leaders act with purpose and vision, they inspire collective action. But when circumstances prevent leaders from taking the first step, teachers must feel empowered to act. This isn't about bypassing leadership but about ensuring the momentum of connection and progress isn't lost. This book is an invitation to teachers to harness their unique position in schools and lead the way, when necessary, always with the goal of supporting the shared mission of education.

The hope is that this book becomes a tool for all of us – a resource that strengthens the partnership between teachers and leaders. The book is written for the teachers, but the lessons within are for all of us. Together, through trust, collaboration and connection, we can navigate the complex challenges of education and build schools where everyone thrives.

From a current leader, with respect and a shared commitment to our schools,

Matt

conundrum /kəˈnʌndrəm/ (*noun*)

1. **A confusing and difficult problem or question**

    Example: Teachers face the conundrum of how to differentiate instruction effectively in a classroom with widely varying abilities.

    (Knowles, 2005)

Introduction

A summit of connection

On Christmas day in December 2016, I found myself at Everest Base Camp. Being winter, and the off-season, it wasn't populated by tents, gear and climbers as you may have seen in photos and videos; it was desolate but for the few small groups who had made the trip from Lukla Airport. It was a harsh but strikingly beautiful environment. Somehow empty, yet so fulfilling.

At 5,364 metres above sea level (17,598 feet), it sits far below the peak of Mount Everest at 8,849 metres above sea level (29,031 feet) and I distinctly remember looking up at the peak, which seemed so close and thinking, *"I want to keep going."* So, I did my research, quickly realised the costs and recognised this probably wouldn't be a summit I'd be attempting any time soon, if at all.

It did, however, send me quickly down a rabbit hole of research, which continues today, covering the Himalayan region, the history, the tragedies and the connections that are formed at that very site I was fortunate to visit and spend a few (very cold) hours at. To summit Mount Everest demands connection – an incredible team effort where relationships are built, a sense of belonging is created and shared meaning drives each expedition. While each climber may seek the summit for different personal reasons, it's the team, a community, that makes the climb possible, together.

Yet even the best-prepared teams can be undone by Everest's unpredictable weather. Like education, success depends on timing and adaptability.

In 1953, Tenzing Norgay and Sir Edmund Hillary had achieved what many had deemed impossible: the first successful ascent of Mount Everest (Hunt, 1954). But their story isn't just about physical endurance and triumph over the mountain; it's also a powerful testament to the importance of human connection. From entirely different worlds – Hillary, a beekeeper from New Zealand, and Tenzing, a Sherpa guide from Nepal – they forged a partnership rooted in trust, respect and collaboration not just with each other, but the wider expedition team.

Their climb was gruelling, with freezing winds cutting through their resolve and the thin air making every step a monumental effort (Hunt, 1954). But the greatest challenge wasn't the mountain itself, it was the necessity to place unwavering trust in one another. In the harshest conditions, their connection became their lifeline, proving that even the most daunting peaks can be conquered through shared purpose and collaboration (Hunt, 1954).

Their journey reminds us that extraordinary achievements are rarely individual triumphs; they're the result of connection, collaboration and the willingness to overcome challenges together. While schools may seem far removed from the slopes of Mount Everest, the challenges we face in education often mirror the steep, daunting climb faced by those who summit great peaks.

The challenges that manifest in the daily quest for balance between supporting diverse learners, fostering inclusive environments and building meaningful curriculum – these are our own Everest. But there isn't just one peak to summit, there is an entire mountain range. One peak followed by another, some of them obscured by clouds or inclement weather until the very last moment.

> "While on top of Everest, I looked across the valley towards the great peak Makalu and mentally worked out a route about how it could be climbed. It showed me that even though I was standing on top of the world, it wasn't the end of everything. I was still looking beyond to other interesting challenges." – Sir Edmund Hillary

Like those who climb the world's highest peaks, educators must prepare to navigate difficult terrain, unpredictable conditions and moments of doubt every single day. Because of this, the imperative to foster whole-school connections in our schools, universities and wider educational institutions has never been more urgent. Like climbers on Mount Everest, we face a narrowing window of opportunity; delays in addressing student disconnection risk losing cohorts to the relentless pressures of scores, ranks and superficial achievements.

The storm of disengagement is closing in, and postponing action will only necessitate more arduous efforts to find a safer, more navigable path in the future. By prioritising meaningful connections, we can guide our students safely through the tempest, ensuring they reach their full potential without being swept away by the storm. This book invites you to embrace connection as the foundation for your journey, equipping you to lead your students and colleagues towards a shared summit while the window is open.

Just as no climber reaches the top alone, no school can thrive without strong, sustainable connections. The path may be steep, but it is through collaboration and shared meaning that we can create schools where everyone – students, teachers and leaders alike – can flourish.

I believe *you* can be the lead on this expedition.

Our communities *need* you to be.

What is The Connection Conundrum?

Much like the treacherous slopes of Mount Everest for climbers, the challenges in schools faced by educators can feel overwhelming. They range from students disengaged from learning and avoiding school (Wang & Eccles, 2013) (see Figure 1) to teachers stretched thin by the pressures of their roles (Bottiani et al., 2019) and wider school communities divided by competing priorities (Epstein, 2018). These distract from the decision on what we want and need our schools and education system to be.

Figure 1: Level of school attendance by year level group, 2015-2022

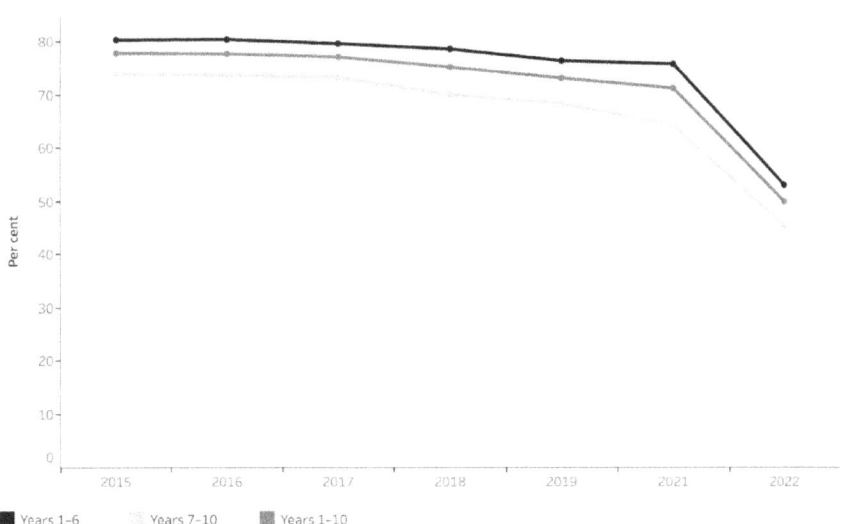

(AUSTRALIAN INSTITUTE OF HEALTH AND WELFARE (AIHW), 2023)

Are schools about the *people* or are they about the *results*?

Can they be *both*?

Should they be?

While we wait and debate, disconnection is mounting in classrooms across the world, revealing itself in student apathy, behavioural struggles and strained relationships among staff (Reinke et al., 2013; Simonsen & Myers, 2025; Wubbels et al., 2014). According to the Organisation for Economic Co-operation and Development (OECD, 2019), more than 50% of teachers report high levels of stress, with burnout and attrition rates steadily increasing across the globe for several different reasons. Australia is no different (see Figure 2).

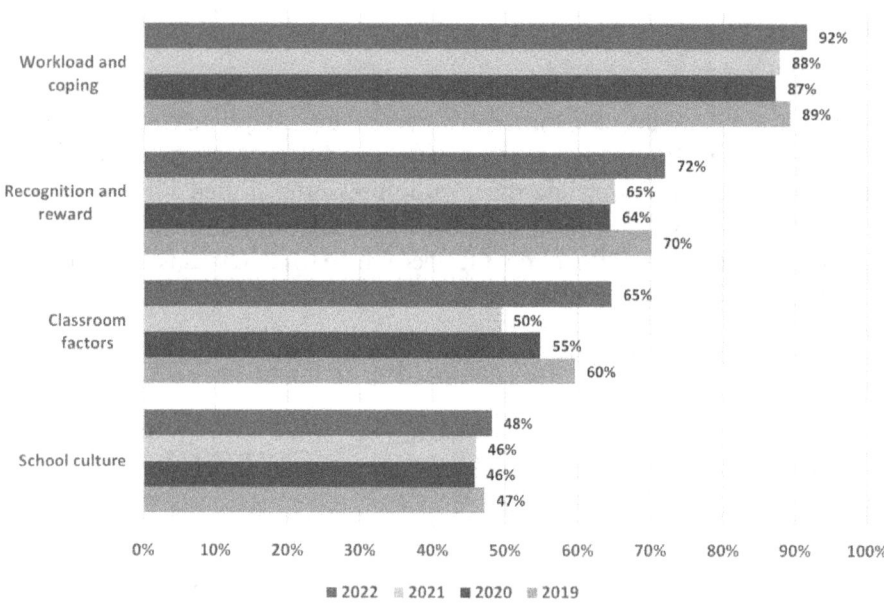

(AUSTRALIAN INSTITUTE FOR TEACHING AND SCHOOL LEADERSHIP (AITSL), 2023)

Student disengagement compounds the problem, with Goss et al. (2017) reporting that in any year, 40% of students feel unmotivated, unproductive or disconnected in school. And yet, much like climbers who recognise the summit's significance but hesitate to take the next step when the time is right, schools often treat connection as a 'nice-to-have' rather than the essential foundation it truly is.

Connection isn't just another item on the to-do list; it's the thread that ties everything together. Research consistently shows that strong teacher-student relationships are among the most significant predictors of academic success and emotional resilience (Hamre & Pianta, 2006; Roorda et al., 2017; Sabol & Pianta, 2012). That belonging positively enhances academic success, wellbeing, motivation, resilience, social skills and emotional stability while reducing dropout rates (Allen et al., 2018; Murphy & Zirkel, 2015; Walton & Brady, 2017), and that learning attached to meaning is responsible for enhancing academic motivation, achievement and engagement, while fostering a sense of purpose and relevance in students' education (Christidamayani & Kristiano, 2020; Yeager & Dweck, 2020).

Despite this, because connection is, in many ways by our current standards, intangible, seemingly unmeasurable, and requires time and trust, it often takes a backseat to short-term fixes and external pressures (Hofkens et al., 2023; Reinke et al., 2013). The challenge I put to you with the tools and strategies in this book is to help make connection more tangible and, most importantly, a visible part of your culture.

This is the heart of what I call The Connection Conundrum: despite knowing that there is growing disengagement, absenteeism and disconnection across staff, students and families, a focus on connection, which is fundamental to student success, community wellbeing and a thriving school culture, remains overlooked in favour of other priorities.

The irony is striking.

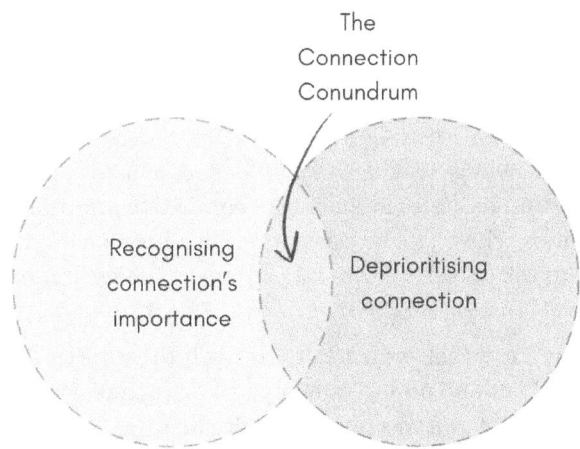

The key to addressing this conundrum lies in recognising that connection isn't a distraction from the 'real work' of education – it *is* the work. Connection transforms classrooms from spaces of mere compliance into communities of thriving learners, enabling teachers to reach students not just academically, but emotionally and socially (Hofkens & Pianta, 2022). It's what turns schools into places where every person – student, teacher and leader alike – *wants* to be.

The Connection Conundrum isn't an impossible puzzle, but it's one that requires some persistence, dedication and action to solve. This book, along with my previous book, *The Connection Curriculum*, calls you to be the impetus for the necessary change and is designed to give you everything you need to get going while the timing is right.

The change needed towards a sustainably connected community is indeed difficult, potentially confusing and extremely intricate, but all a good conundrum needs is someone willing to sit down and start working through it. There is too much at stake to wait, and this isn't a puzzle that can go back in the box to tackle later.

The time for action is now. With the tools and the knowledge at your disposal within this book, you're not just a participant but a catalyst for change. Each step you take, no matter how small, brings us closer to a world where connection thrives and communities flourish. The solution begins with you because this is a puzzle that, once solved, will reshape *everything* for the better.

Are we prepared to do what it takes?

Teachers, I've come to understand through experience, are at the heart of this work, as they're closest to the students and the (actual) present needs of the school. They see what's working and what's not. And yet, I believe, their ability to drive meaningful change is often overlooked or undervalued.

For many educators, the frustration of waiting for leadership (system or school) to act is a familiar feeling. Teachers see the impact of disconnection every day, but while leadership hesitates in the mix of competing priorities, the weight of change falls to those closest to the classroom. Still, there is a moment we all face when we have to ask ourselves: *"Are we prepared to do what it takes?"* And too often, the answer is a hesitant, *"Sort of. Maybe. I think so."*

Here is the reality: I truly believe teachers are ready to do the work, but too often, senior leadership can't be on the same page consistently. Since my first book *The Connection Curriculum* was published, I've heard from many teachers and middle leaders who are passionate about creating sustainable, whole-school connection, yet feel frustrated that their enthusiasm isn't matched by their senior leadership teams. This leaves teachers in a difficult position. They know change is needed. They're willing to action it. But they're stuck wondering, *"If no one else will step up, how do I move forward on my own?"*

The answer lies in *doing*.

As mentioned at the top of the book, this isn't an all-out attack on senior leadership; I happen to be in this type of position within a school, and I know first-hand that the burden of the job (particularly administratively) in recent years is exorbitant. The point here is that real change doesn't have to start with leadership or permission from the system, it can start with anyone, and it can start now. Small, intentional steps can build momentum, inspire colleagues and show what's possible (Erenrich & Wergin, 2017; Hargreaves, 2023; Kahan, 2010).

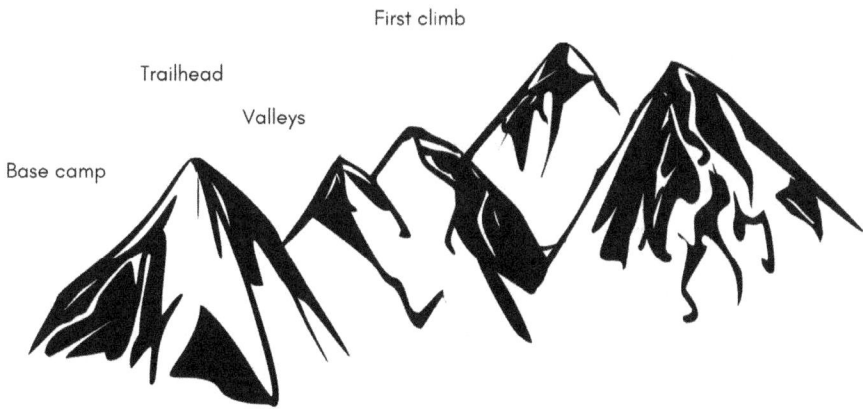

This book, its six parts and twelve chapters, isn't about waiting for permission, but acting with intention. It's about empowering everyone to lead when formal leadership can't (yet). For the teacher shouting into the void, the aspirational middle leader building momentum and anyone tired of waiting for 'someday', this book is here to climb with you.

It's time to head for the summit.

connection conundrum /kəˈnɛk.ʃən kəˈnʌndrəm (*noun*)

1. A challenge in schools where the increasing need for connection is acknowledged but deprioritised in favour of focusing on outcomes, data or compliance, despite its foundational role in improving these very areas

   Example: The leadership team struggled with the connection conundrum, focusing on lifting results without first listening to the staff or addressing disconnection within the school.

PART I
THE CALL TO CLIMB

Embracing the opportunity for connection

> "The journey of a thousand miles begins with one step"
>
> – LAO TZU

Every great journey begins with a spark, a call, a yearning. For Sir Edmund Hillary, it was a fascination with mountains that grew into an unshakable pull towards Everest. For Tenzing Norgay, it was a deep-rooted connection to the Himalayas, tied to his Sherpa heritage. The call to climb isn't just about ambition or conquest, it's about listening to that quiet, insistent voice within that says, *"This is yours to do."* The mountain, after all, doesn't care if you climb it. The call is about what happens when you hear it and decide to answer.

Standing at the base of the mountain isn't the same as staying there. Part 1 of this book is about answering the call to climb, choosing to step forward, rethink connection and take the first steps towards something stronger, deeper and more enduring. We begin in *Chapter 1: Standing before the range*, examining why change in education is so difficult and why teachers, despite systemic barriers, remain the most powerful force for transformation. Next, *Chapter 2: Calling the explorer* introduces The Connection Journey, challenging the idea that connection is a single destination and instead presenting it as a dynamic, evolving process. Using the metaphor of a mountain range, we explore how relationships, belonging and meaning serve as guiding landmarks along the way, shaping how we navigate the peaks and valleys of connection. Finally, *Chapter 3: Charting the first route* provides a tangible framework for this journey, the 4Cs, offering a practical structure for fostering connection in classrooms and beyond.

Every climb begins with a decision to move forward, to challenge the status quo, to embrace the adventure ahead. The call to climb has been made.

The question is, will you take the first step?

CHAPTER I
Standing before the range
The nature of change and the influence of a teacher

As climbers stand before a mountain range, they're met with both awe and uncertainty, much like educators confronting the ever-changing terrain of their students' lives. Change in schools is necessary, yet it's often met with resistance, weighed down by tradition, systemic inertia and the overwhelming demands placed on teachers. This chapter explores the complexity of educational change, shedding light on why transformation is so difficult and how connection, between students, teachers, leaders and the wider community, can be the key to unlocking meaningful progress.

At the heart of this discussion is the idea that teachers aren't just passive participants in school reform; they're the changemakers best positioned to lead transformation from within. Yet for change to be sustainable, educators need trust, agency and a culture that values collaboration. By understanding the forces that make change so challenging and embracing the power of connection as a driver of transformation, teachers can navigate the peaks and valleys of their own journey; creating classrooms and, ultimately, schools, where relationships, belonging and meaningful learning thrive.

The challenge of change in schools

Why is change so difficult?

Despite its necessity, change in schools is difficult. Efforts often stall due to resistance, short-term thinking or lack of sustained support (Aldridge & McLure, 2024; Fullan, 2016). It's because of these three things, that despite the best intentions of (some) educators, (some) leaders and (a few) policymakers, efforts to improve teaching and learning are often victim to chasing fads, short-term initiatives or lacklustre efforts (Aldridge & McLure, 2024; Reeves, 2009).

Schools, by design, aren't the most flexible of environments. They're complex living systems, deeply rooted in routines, traditions and established norms (Hargreaves & Fullan, 2012), all of which bring stability, but I'd wholeheartedly argue, have become significant barriers to meaningful change. Not least of these barriers is the treatment of the humble classroom teacher.

Those who are closest to the realities of classrooms are frequently left to carry the weight of change, especially when leadership is hesitant, unwilling or unsure of what supports to commit to it (Harris, 2019). To understand why we have this struggle, and before we dive into the nature of the changes required for sustainable connection, it's essential to reflect on these complex forces that make change so difficult in education.

The weight of tradition

Systemic inertia, shaped by longstanding traditions and structures, is a significant barrier to change. While these routines offer comfort and stability, they often stifle innovation and resist disruption (Fullan, 2016; Kotter, 2012) tending to favour continuity over transformation, as change can feel too risky (Burner, 2018).

Systemic inertia is particularly tricky, because it's slow moving and grows deep roots within an organisation (Fullan, 2016) (see Figure 3). Schools that have been operating for decades will have significant structural and environmental barriers to change, simply because of their storied histories. Newer schools are often impacted also, but from the perspective of attempting to develop a community, rather than maintain one.

As a result, teachers attempting to introduce new practices in schools today may find themselves met with scepticism from colleagues or leaders who are wary of the unknown or reluctant to challenge *"the way we've always done it"*. And I must admit, I understand why.

There are several significant demands on schools and their communities, none the least are those from higher levels of governance, who often, with good intention (I must believe) introduce policies and mandates that often exacerbate the inertia. There seems to be little flexibility in the mould, but don't be disheartened, we just need to shift the way we lead.

In *Leading Change*, author John Kotter (2012) states:

> "Never underestimate the magnitude of the power of the forces that reinforce the status quo."

As a teacher, you're uniquely positioned to break through the habits and routines that no longer serve your students or the school community. By prioritising connection, you can create moments that transform your classroom.

Figure 3: Why change is so challenging

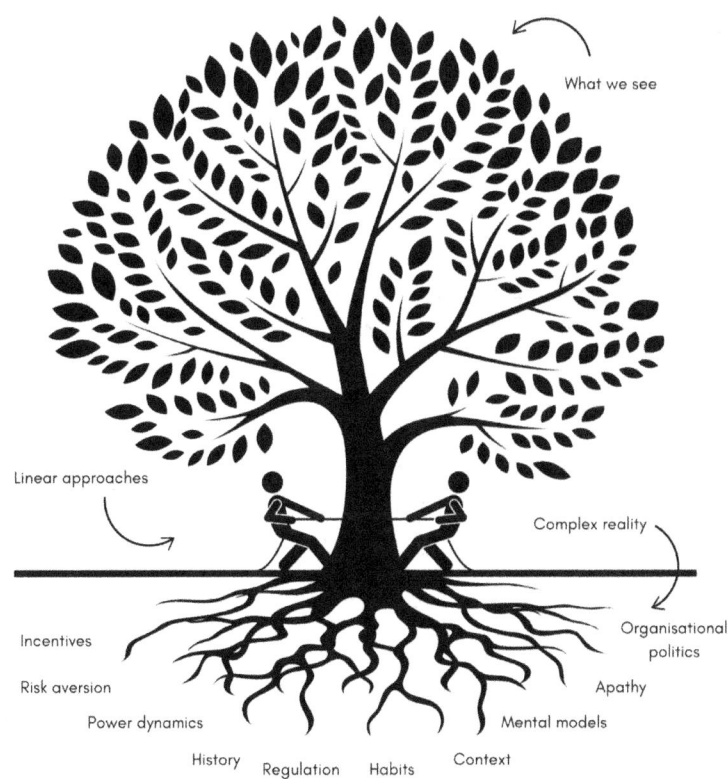

(ADAPTED FROM SYSTEMS INNOVATION, 2023)

Leadership matters, but many leaders hesitate. Teachers often bear the burden of change without enough support.

Without strong leadership, teachers are often left to initiate and sustain change on their own, which can feel challenging and overwhelming (Pantié et al., 2022). Leadership that fosters connection, between colleagues, across teams and within the broader school community, create the supportive conditions essential for teacher-led school improvement (Muijs & Harris, 2006). In the absence of these conditions, whether it be administrative backing, professional development or time for collaboration, teachers may struggle to build the momentum needed to carry their ideas forward.

While leadership provides the structural foundation for change, addressing the broader complexities of school environments and the emotional challenges teachers face is equally essential.

The complexity of school environments

Beyond leadership and structure, the very nature of schools makes change complex. Schools are shaped by many voices, including students, parents and staff. Building connection helps align them and support change.

Fullan (2016) emphasises that change isn't just about implementing a new program or policy; it's about shifting mindsets and transforming cultures. For teachers, this work takes time and energy, both of which are in short supply amid the daily demands (both perceived and real) of classroom teaching.

Additionally, change initiatives in education often lack continuity (Brown et al., 2023; Bryk & Schneider, 2002; Priestley et al., 2015). Teachers grow sceptical after repeated short-term reforms. Sustainable change demands consistency.

Turn right at the rock and if you pass a hard place, you've gone too far...

Change requires teachers to step outside their comfort zones, let go of familiar practices and embrace uncertainty – a challenge compounded when such change hasn't been modelled previously. Building trust and connection within school communities can act as a buffer, providing teachers with the emotional security to navigate these unsettling transitions (Hargreaves, 2001).

When teachers take risks to try something new, they need a culture of trust and support. Without this trust, whether in leadership, in colleagues or in the process of change itself, efforts to innovate are likely to flounder (Bryk & Schneider, 2002).

Connection, therefore, is central to change. Teachers not only need to feel supported by their leaders but also need opportunities to collaborate and share ideas with one another. These connections not only address emotional and relational barriers but also build the foundation for trust and innovation that makes change sustainable.

The key to transformation

Ultimately, despite these challenges, it's teachers who often stand at the forefront of change, and we need to shift more recognition to this reality. Teachers are the ones who understand their students' needs most intimately and who see, first-hand, what works in their classrooms. Because of this positioning, they're the agents capable of driving transformation, even in environments where leadership may be hesitant, however, we cannot expect this agency to form automatically.

Teachers need opportunities to experiment, build confidence and lead change. Priestley et al. (2015) argue that fostering teacher agency requires creating conditions that empower educators to reflect on and take ownership of their practice.

Further research highlights that empowering teachers to lead from the classroom drives innovation and meaningful school improvement (Harris et al., 2017). When educators are trusted to make decisions and assume leadership roles, they become catalysts for sustainable change (Lieberman et al., 2016).

However, again, fostering teacher agency requires a foundation of trust between teachers and school leadership. Trust enables educators to confidently engage in transformative practices and ensures their professional voices are valued (Stoll, 2015). Additionally, schools that cultivate a culture of collaboration and intellectual curiosity enhance teacher agency and develop future leaders (Chapman & Muijs, 2014).

Without trust and agency, teachers are likely to disengage, stalling innovation and progress (Priestley et al., 2015; Hargreaves & Fullan, 2012). Providing opportunities for teachers to lead could unlock meaningful changes in our schools. Change in schools remains difficult, partly because teachers aren't trusted to lead from the classroom.

This lack of trust must be addressed if we're to move forward towards more connected school communities. Teachers must be empowered to take on leadership roles within their schools. Fostering trust and creating the necessary conditions for teacher agency are essential steps to effect meaningful change in education.

Spheres of influence

The original influencers

When it comes to change, especially change linked to connection, I need you, teacher, to understand how valuable and influential you are.

Teachers are close to the centre of any school community, wielding influence that extends far beyond their classrooms (see Figure 4). Consider any former student who greets you with an enthusiastic smile, or conversely, a menacing stare. Different sides of the coin, but evidence to the lasting influence working in the classroom has.

> In *The Connected Species: How the Evolution of the Human Brain Can Save the World*, author Dr Mark Williams (2023) summarises this perfectly:
>
> "We learn from those we connect with, and we need that connection to learn." (p. 62)

Figure 4: The influence of a connected teacher

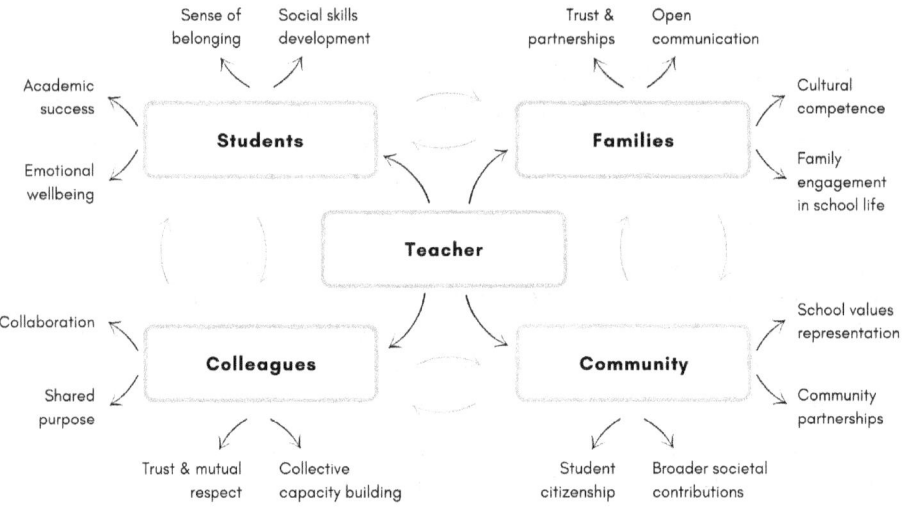

Teachers are central figures in a network that shape the school's culture, connecting students, colleagues, families and the broader community. Their role as educators is vital, but it's their ability to cultivate relationships, foster a sense of belonging and create meaning in their interactions that often determines the overall strength and cohesion of the school environment (Osterman, 2023). These aspects are often not explored specifically, which needs to change.

Connection isn't just a by-product of teaching – it's the foundation of a thriving learning community.

The classroom relationships we all strive to create are fine, but connection is much, much more powerful. Before we get into that, we need to understand the overlapping spheres of influence a teacher will impact upon within a school, and in doing so, highlight the need to empower teachers as catalysts for connection.

Influence on students

Teachers have a profound and immediate impact on students. Research shows that strong teacher-student relationships are essential for academic success, emotional wellbeing and long-term engagement (Fabris et al., 2024; Göktaş & Kaya, 2023). When students feel seen, heard and genuinely valued, they're more likely to thrive, not only in their learning but also in their personal growth (Australian Education Research Organisation [AERO], 2023a). Teachers who model empathy, respect and active listening help students develop meaningful connections and a sense of belonging, reinforcing their identity as valued members of a learning community (AITSL, 2021; Bryk & Schneider, 2002).

Influence on the wider school

The influence of teachers extends far beyond their own classrooms. Meaningful connections with students can spark a wider culture of engagement and inclusion across the school (AERO, 2023a). At the same time, teachers shape professional culture through collaboration, building trust and shared purpose among colleagues (Ronfeldt et al., 2015). This sense of belonging within the teaching community fosters resilience, professional satisfaction and a collective commitment to student success (Akinyemi et al., 2020; Killion, 2015).

Influence on families and the community

Teachers also play a pivotal role in connecting schools with families. As the most regular point of contact, they shape how families perceive and engage with the school (Yulianti et al., 2021; Mora-Ruano et al., 2019). When these relationships are built on respect and trust, families feel more included and empowered to contribute to their child's learning journey (AITSL, 2024). Beyond the school gates, teachers represent the values of the school in their communities. Whether through partnerships, local events or service projects, they help students see themselves as part of something larger, contributing to both community cohesion and personal meaning (AERO, 2023a).

Given the breadth and depth of their influence, teachers are uniquely positioned to foster meaningful connections at every level of the school community. These connections, whether with students, colleagues, families or the wider community, transform schools into places where relationships drive engagement, belonging and shared meaning.

> **Reflect on your influence**
>
> It's easy to overlook the relationships we help shape in the everyday rhythm of teaching. Yet your influence, invisible at times, is a powerful force in building connection within your school community.
>
> Take a quiet moment to consider the connections you've nurtured. The questions below aren't a checklist, but an invitation to reflect on the human side of your work.
>
> 1. **With students**
>   - Do my students feel safe, supported and valued?
>   - How have I helped a student feel more connected to their peers or the wider school?
>   - What behaviours do I model that encourage kindness and relationship-building?
>
> 2. **With colleagues**
>   - How do I contribute to a culture of trust, openness and collaboration?
>   - When was the last time I offered support or shared an idea with a colleague?
>   - Have I helped others strengthen their own professional relationships?
>
> 3. **With families**
>   - Do I create space for honest, respectful communication with parents and carers?
>   - How do I build trust and invite families into the learning process?
>   - Have I encouraged family engagement through events or personal outreach?
>
> 4. **With the community**
>   - In what ways do I connect classroom learning with the world beyond school?
>   - Have I helped students contribute to their community in meaningful ways?
>   - Are there partnerships I've developed that enrich our school's sense of connection?
>
> Now, pause and look back at your responses. What do they reveal about the classroom and community you're helping to shape? What do they tell you about your role in sustaining connection?

Teachers are connection changemakers

As you've read this chapter, I hope two messages have stood out clearly. The first: connection is the answer to many of the persistent challenges faced by schools today. Perhaps not all of them, but a significant majority.

The second: teachers are the changemakers lying dormant in our schools. Every day, they execute their roles with dedication, guiding their students and navigating a complex profession they care deeply about. And yet, many remain quietly disheartened, longing for tools, strategies and opportunities to create the change they know is needed. This book isn't just a response to that longing – it's a *call to climb*.

> In *Becoming a Changemaker: Transform Your Career, Your Community, and the World*, author Alex Budak (2022) states the following:
>
> *"Change isn't reserved for a special few. In fact, change calls out for all of us to lead from wherever we might be and in whatever form is true to who we are."*

As Budak's (2022) words suggest, meaningful change isn't confined to those in formal leadership roles. It belongs to anyone willing to take initiative, work within their context and prioritise connection as the foundation for transformation. For teachers, this means recognising their unique power to influence and inspire, even amid the complexities of school systems that often resist change.

Start with small, purposeful actions, what Budak (2022) describes as "micro-leadership". These could be as simple as reaching out to a colleague to share an idea, fostering a deeper connection with a student by taking an interest in their passions or inviting families to participate more fully in school life. Each small action builds trust, strengthens relationships and contributes to a broader culture of connection within the school (Williams, 2023).

Connection, at its heart, isn't just a solution to the challenges faced by schools; it's the path forward. It enables teachers to transcend hierarchical barriers, empower their peers and model the values they wish to see in their communities. By prioritising authentic relationships and a shared sense of belonging, teachers become the changemakers their schools need, not by stepping outside their roles, but by leaning fully into them.

To all teachers reading this: you're already in the perfect position to lead. Your influence is felt every day in your classroom, among your colleagues and within your community. The challenges may be significant, but so too is your potential. The next chapter will explore how to transform this potential into actionable steps, building momentum for change and deepening connection within your school.

Will you answer the *call to connect*?

CHAPTER 2

Calling the explorer

The Connection Journey and the mountainous metaphor

Every explorer begins with a spark – an invitation to venture beyond the familiar. In this chapter, we rethink connection as a continuous journey rather than a fixed destination, using the metaphor of a mountain range to illustrate its evolving nature. Connection isn't built in a single moment but through a series of peaks and valleys. It is moments of deep relationships, belonging and meaning, as well as the inevitable challenges that test and shape us along the way.

This chapter details The Connection Journey, exploring how connection unfolds through the key landmarks of relationships, belonging and meaning, while recognising the role of mental, social and emotional development in shaping these experiences. Just as climbers prepare, adapt and push forward, educators and students navigate their own path of connection, tackling the mountainous metaphor, learning from each ascent and recalibrating after each setback. By embracing connection as a dynamic and evolving process, we can move beyond surface-level interactions and foster truly transformative learning experiences in our classrooms and communities.

Rethinking connection

Revisiting The Connection Journey

Connection is the essence of human experience, a core element that shapes our relationships, sense of belonging and the meaning we derive from life (Pitman, 2024). Connection underpins every interaction and defines the cultures we create in schools, workplaces and communities. For too long, connection has been misunderstood as a fixed outcome or a series of isolated efforts (Pitman, 2024). The Connection Journey challenges this perspective, offering not a rigid framework but a *new way of understanding connection*, one that is dynamic, holistic and deeply attuned to the realities of human development.

> Connection isn't a single destination but an *ongoing journey*.

The concept of The Connection Journey was first introduced in my earlier work, *The Connection Curriculum*, where it served as a framework for inspiring whole-school connection. While it's not necessary for readers of this book to have engaged with that earlier work, it's crucial to recognise that The Connection Journey still forms the foundation for how I want you to think about connection – not as a checklist or end point but as an evolving journey. This understanding is essential to engaging with the tools and strategies presented later in this book.

The landmarks of the journey

The Connection Journey invites us to view connection not as a series of outcomes but as a fluid, evolving process. This is essential knowledge and, as they say, knowledge is power. When paired with repetition, it becomes a force for tangible, long-term progress.

Let's explore the landmarks of relationships, belonging and meaning as touch-points to guide this journey and for understanding and nurturing connection in any context.

Relationships are foundational to the human experience. They're the starting point of connection, providing the trust, safety and care necessary for deeper interactions to flourish (Tschannen-Moran, 2014). Research highlights the transformative power of relationships in schools, linking them to higher academic performance, improved behaviour and increased happiness (Allen et al., 2018; Longobardi et al., 2021). However, not all relationships foster true connection. Authenticity, mutual respect and consistent effort are critical in building relationships that endure and inspire.

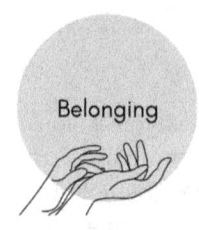

Belonging transcends individual relationships, encompassing the sense of being valued, accepted and included within a community (Allen et al., 2021). It represents the collective dimension of connection, where individuals see themselves as part of something larger. In educational settings, belonging is linked to increased engagement, resilience and wellbeing (Heinsch et al., 2020). Creating belonging requires more than occasional events or initiatives; it demands an environment where every voice is heard, and every individual feels safe and valued.

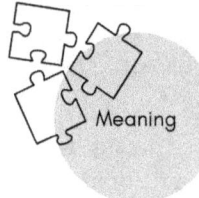

Meaning gives connection its depth. It's the understanding that our actions and experiences have significance, both for ourselves and others. In schools, meaning often becomes tangled with external goals like grades and future careers (Pitman, 2024). The Connection Journey challenges this view, urging us to focus on helping individuals find immediate relevance and purpose in their learning and interactions (Damon & Malin, 2020). By connecting to meaning, we foster intrinsic motivation and create a foundation for lifelong engagement.

These landmarks aren't static elements or sequential steps; they're interconnected and mutually reinforcing. Relationships lay the groundwork for belonging, while a sense of belonging enables individuals to explore and embrace meaning. Together, they create the conditions for connection to thrive.

The influence of mental, social and emotional development

To understand connection, we must see it as deeply human, rooted in how people grow, relate and make meaning over time. The journey of connection is shaped by the mental, social and emotional development of each individual. These developmental dimensions don't exist alongside connection; they're part of it.

Mental development: Cognitive growth influences how students understand and experience connection. Younger students often focus on concrete relationships, friendships, fairness and feeling included. As students grow, they become more capable of engaging with abstract ideas like belonging, purpose and identity (Siegel, 2020). Connection, therefore, must evolve with students. Schools play a vital role in making connection relevant at every developmental stage.

Social development: Connection doesn't happen in isolation; it relies on the social skills that allow people to interact meaningfully. Skills like empathy, communication and collaboration are developed through lived experience (Skaalvik & Skaalvik, 2021). Schools are one of the primary environments where these abilities are nurtured. The more intentional we are about fostering positive social interactions, the more we strengthen the social fabric that connection depends on.

Emotional development: Emotional resilience allows us to engage deeply, with ourselves and others. When students feel emotionally safe, they're better able to form healthy relationships and develop a sense of belonging (Siegel, 2020; Van Orden et al., 2021). Schools can either support or undermine this development especially during times of transition, adversity or growth. Meeting emotional needs isn't extra work; it's foundational to connection.

These aspects of development aren't separate from The Connection Journey. They shape how it unfolds and how lasting it becomes. When schools support students' mental, social and emotional growth, they create the conditions where connection can truly take root and flourish.

A dynamic and evolving understanding of connection

The Connection Journey challenges us to see connection as a living process. It's not an end point to be reached or a task to be completed, but a continuous cycle of growth and renewal. Individuals may revisit the landmarks of relationships, belonging and meaning multiple times, reflecting the fluid nature of connection. This isn't a failure but a natural part of the journey. Repetition is progress through small, consistent efforts that refine skills, correct mistakes and strengthen habits over time. By embracing this iterative process, we lay a steady path towards meaningful growth.

For example, a student who feels a strong sense of belonging at one moment may later need renewed support to re-establish that connection. Similarly, a teacher who has built meaningful relationships may find that new challenges require revisiting those foundations. The Connection Journey reminds us that connection isn't static; it evolves alongside the people and communities it encompasses.

Why does this understanding matter?

I believe that reframing connection as a journey opens new possibilities for educators and leaders. It emphasises the importance of ongoing reflection, adaptation and growth. By revisiting these ideas and practising intentional connection, we create the conditions for enduring impact in schools and beyond. By engaging with the landmarks as interconnected dimensions of human experience, we move beyond surface-level initiatives to create environments where connection can truly thrive.

This understanding isn't only central to this book but it's also a guiding principle for fostering sustainable connection in any context. The Connection Journey is a way of seeing connection as dynamic, holistic and essential to the work we do. By embracing this understanding, we lay the foundation for transformative change in schools and beyond.

A successful journey requires focus

In my first book, *The Connection Curriculum*, I focused on how whole schools can embed sustainable connection across their culture, structures and strategic plans. That book introduced six focus areas – core components that help build connection at scale. While this book shifts the focus specifically to the classroom, those six areas remain just as relevant. They're the foundation of sustainable connection, whether applied at an institutional level or by an individual teacher seeking to make a difference.

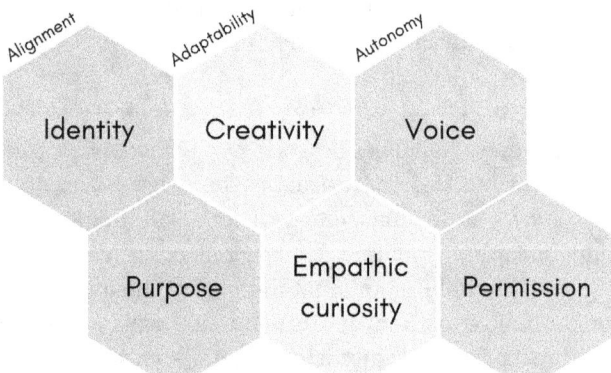

But this isn't the same book. My goal here isn't to replicate those discussions but to acknowledge the ongoing importance of these areas while giving you, the teacher, practical ways to initiate change within your own classroom. Whole-school approaches are powerful, but connection doesn't have to wait for system-wide buy-in. You can start in your classroom, and in doing so, influence the culture of your school from the ground up.

Here is how the six focus areas remain central to this work:

1. **Identity – know yourself, know your classroom:** Every classroom has an identity, intentional or not. What kind of culture are you creating? What do your students say about how it feels to be there? Identity isn't about mottos or posters. It's about creating a space where students feel they belong and where the values you live by are reflected in how people treat one another.
2. **Purpose – learning with meaning:** Students are more engaged when learning feels meaningful. Too often, purpose is positioned as something far off, linked to future careers or exams. But purpose matters now. Ask yourself: do students know *why* they're learning, or just *what* they need to do? When students can connect their learning to their values and interests, connection deepens.
3. **Creativity – a classroom of opportunity creators:** Creativity invites risk-taking, exploration and co-creation. It allows students to contribute, not just comply. A connected classroom isn't defined by rigid outcomes, but by the freedom to think differently and solve problems together. True creativity creates the conditions for shared meaning and that is where connection thrives.
4. **Empathic curiosity – the foundation of relationships:** Curiosity becomes connection when it's grounded in empathy. It's not just about asking questions, it's about wanting to understand. Do your students feel safe to wonder, to explore perspectives, to question ideas and each other? Empathic curiosity builds a climate of trust and openness.
5. **Voice – a seat at the classroom table:** Connection isn't just about being heard, it's about being included in decision-making. Do students feel their opinions matter? Do they help shape how learning unfolds? A connected classroom values all voices and creates space for contribution, not just compliance.
6. **Permission – a culture of trust:** Connection thrives where there is trust and trust shows up in what students are permitted to do. What if students didn't have to earn permission to create, express or explore? What if they already knew they had it? A culture of permission creates a classroom where students take ownership because they feel safe to do so.

Bringing the focus back to the classroom

These six focus areas were initially designed to help whole schools build sustainable connection, but they're just as critical in the microcosm of the classroom. The great news is they don't exist in isolation. These areas overlap, intersect and reinforce one another. The more you focus on one, the more the others naturally grow. A classroom that fosters creativity, for example, will inevitably give students more voice. A classroom built on empathic curiosity will naturally build a culture of permission.

Connection isn't a *new* responsibility for teachers; I'm just re-emphasising it as a core responsibility. You don't need to wait for a policy change or an official school-wide initiative.

The work starts with you, right where you are.

A mountain of a metaphor

Do we not have enough metaphors in education?

Education is rich with metaphors – gardens, puzzles, mazes, storms – all trying to articulate the complex and transformative nature of teaching and learning. In fact, it took quite a lot of effort not to align this book with a gardening metaphor. The growth, the cycles, the need for care and support, but ultimately, it wasn't the right fit. Let's face it, it's been done, and often, done very well.

What I knew I needed was a metaphor that reflected the process of building connection in classrooms with a sense of practicality, relevance and a touch of adventure. Something that resonated with the dynamic and demanding nature of teaching while inspiring a sense of possibility. In addressing these criteria, a mountain range metaphor, I decided, stands apart. It captures not only the challenges and effort required to build connection, but also the transformative potential of the journey itself, where every step forward is an act of exploration and discovery.

This metaphor provides a powerful lens through which to address the Connection Conundrum, while also noting that teaching is an ongoing adventure. It's unpredictable, full of twists and turns, moments of discovery, and sometimes, challenges that require us to dig deep. Teachers are explorers, preparing for the journeys ahead and tasked with supporting their students with what they will need to navigate the terrain. The metaphor connects with the everyday reality of teaching, but it also makes space for the joy, challenge and meaning that come from shared experiences and learning together.

Why a mountain range?

The mountain range metaphor is particularly fitting because it mirrors the ongoing nature of connection. Connection isn't the summit of one peak, it's many. Each step symbolises a milestone, whether it's establishing trust, fostering belonging or connecting learning to meaning, while the valleys represent the challenges and periods of recalibration that are essential to growth. Together, these peaks and valleys form a dynamic landscape, full of surprises, exploration and moments of triumph, that captures the rhythm of teaching and learning.

Climbing a mountain is an act of effort, persistence and resilience. Similarly, building connection in the classroom requires courage, patience and adaptability. Yet like any great adventure, it's not only about the effort; it's about the transformation that comes with it. Each summit changes the climber, offering a new perspective on the path travelled and a clearer vision of what lies ahead. Connection has the same transformative power. It not only enriches students' learning experiences but also reshapes how teachers see their role, their students and the possibilities within their classrooms.

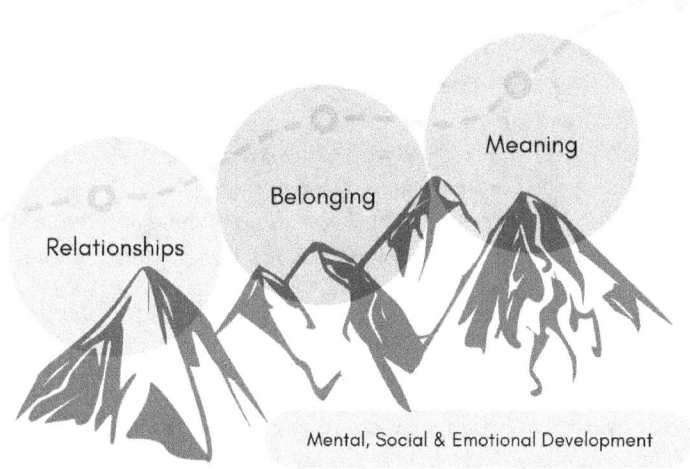

What sets this metaphor apart is its ability to capture incremental progress. In both climbing and teaching, small steps matter. Every act of kindness, every moment of inclusion, every opportunity to connect adds to the journey. The metaphor invites us to celebrate these moments, not just the big victories but the steady progress that builds something enduring.

Every small step matters

Ask yourself these quick questions:

1. What small steps in your classroom have helped build connection?
2. How can you celebrate those steps today?

But it's not all smooth ascent; valleys are an inevitable part of The Connection Journey. They represent the moments when challenges arise, such as disruptions in the classroom, resistance from students or colleagues, or external pressures that strain the learning environment. While these moments can feel like setbacks, they're also integral to the adventure. Like explorers navigating difficult terrain, they provide opportunities to reflect, adapt and build resilience.

Just as climbers use valleys to regroup and prepare for their next ascent, educators can view these moments as integral to the process. They teach us to navigate adversity, deepen our understanding of connection and develop the tools needed for future challenges. Valleys remind us that progress isn't always linear, and that meaningful growth often emerges from struggle.

> **Mapping your range**
> 1. Draw or outline your own 'connection journey'.
> 2. Label key moments where you've faced challenges (valleys) and successes (peaks).
> 3. How did you navigate the valleys? How/why?
> 4. How did you celebrate the peaks? How/why?
> 5. How did each experience help shape your teaching and the relationships in your classroom? Reflect on the lessons learned and how they might inform future climbs.

Climbing together

One of the most important aspects of the mountain range metaphor is its emphasis on collaboration. No climber ascends a mountain alone; they rely on guides, companions and the wisdom of those who have climbed before them. Similarly, connection in education isn't an individual pursuit. It's a shared adventure, one that thrives on trust, collaboration and mutual support.

In classrooms, the teacher may guide the way, but students are co-creators of the journey. Together, they form a learning community, supporting one another through the peaks and valleys. This collective effort also speaks to the broader educational environment. Connection isn't confined to a single classroom; it flows outward, creating a culture of belonging that transforms schools and communities.

Perspective and transformation

Reaching a summit offers more than a sense of accomplishment; it provides perspective. From the top, adventurers can look back on the terrain they have conquered and forward to the new challenges that lie ahead. In education, this perspective is transformative. It allows teachers to reflect on the progress they have made, celebrate their successes and gain clarity on the challenges ahead.

But perhaps, most importantly, it reveals how the process of connection has changed them.

The mountain range metaphor reminds us that connection isn't about reaching one final peak. It's about the continuous journey – each step forward, each relationship built, each moment of shared meaning. It's in this process that true transformation occurs, for teachers, students and communities alike.

A call to embrace connection

The mountain range metaphor is more than a conceptual tool; it's a call to action. It challenges you to prioritise connection as the foundation of your work. By framing connection as a journey, it encourages all educators to move beyond fragmented solutions and embrace the collective and ongoing process of building relationships, fostering belonging and creating meaning.

Like any great adventure, it invites educators to face the unknown with courage, knowing that every step forward brings the possibility of discovery and transformation. This metaphor also reminds us to value the journey itself. The summits matter, but so do the steps, the struggles and the shared effort that makes the climb possible.

Connection isn't easy, but it's profoundly worth it for the transformation it brings, the communities it creates and the enduring impact it leaves.

CHAPTER 3
Charting the first route
The 4Cs and how to leverage them for sustainable connection

No climber embarks on a journey without a map. In the same way, building meaningful connection in the classroom requires a framework to guide the way. This chapter introduces the 4Cs of connection: *culture, communication, collaboration* and *curiosity* – a modified version of Das' 4C Model, tailored for education. These four elements provide a practical approach to fostering relationships, creating inclusive environments and deepening engagement in learning.

Das' original model, which focused on organisational effectiveness, inspires the creation of our adapted version, which prioritises connection over competency. Through this lens, we will examine how a strong classroom culture fosters belonging, how clear and empathetic communication strengthens trust, how collaboration moves beyond mere cooperation to shared ownership, and how curiosity fuels engagement and growth. These principles won't only shape this chapter but will also serve as a guide throughout the book, offering a simple yet powerful direction towards creating classrooms where connection thrives.

The 4Cs of connection
Reinventing Das' 4C Model

The 4C Model, developed by Debabrata Das (2011), represents a conceptual framework designed to assess and enhance organisational effectiveness. Das identified four critical principles, *competency, communication, cooperation* and *collaboration* as universal drivers of success across organisational contexts. But what happens when connection is the missing piece?

While the original 4C Model provides a robust framework, this chapter proposes a modified version tailored to the purpose of building connection in educational settings that aligns with The Connection Journey and the six focus areas discussed in the previous chapter.

A revised model consisting of *culture, communication, collaboration* and *curiosity* shifts the focus from individual competencies to collective connection and growth. This adaptation is grounded in the belief that fostering relationships, inclusivity, belonging and shared exploration are paramount for creating meaningful learning environments.

Culture

Culture (formerly competency)

The first principle, culture, replaces competency to prioritise inclusivity, shared values and belonging over individual performance. Culture reflects the social and emotional fabric of the classroom, shaping how students interact, collaborate and learn. Schein's (2004) work on organisational culture is particularly relevant here, as he argued that culture defines "how things are done" within a group. In classrooms, culture manifests in norms, rituals and expectations that foster a sense of safety and inclusion (Hattie & Yates, 2013).

Shifting from competency to culture aligns with the growing emphasis on social-emotional learning (SEL) in education. Research demonstrates that classrooms with strong, positive cultures promote higher engagement, reduced behavioural issues and improved academic outcomes (Collaborative for Academic, Social, and Emotional Learning [CASEL], n.d.). Teachers play a pivotal role in cultivating culture by modelling trust and psychological safety, establishing inclusive norms and celebrating diversity.

> **Ask yourself these quick questions:**
> 1. How does the culture in your classroom support inclusivity and belonging?
> 2. Are there areas where it could grow?

Communication

Communication

The second principle, communication, remains unchanged in name but is reframed to emphasise its role in fostering connection. Clear and empathetic communication enables students to feel heard, valued and understood. Research highlights the link between teacher-student communication and student outcomes, showing that positive interactions build trust and enhance motivation (Robinson, 2022; Xie & Derakhshan, 2021). While the original model emphasised clear communication for information exchange, in pursuing connection we need to also focus on the human impacts.

Effective communication in classrooms involves both verbal and non-verbal elements, including active listening, feedback and tone (Wahyuni, 2018). Teachers must also facilitate communication among students, encouraging dialogue that respects diverse perspectives, empathy and promotes understanding. Circle time, peer feedback sessions and collaborative discussions are examples of practices that foster meaningful communication in classrooms.

Ask yourself these quick questions:
1. Do you create opportunities for students to feel heard and understood?
2. In what ways could your classroom communication practices be more inclusive or relationship-focused?

Collaboration (formerly cooperation)

Collaboration
Collaboration replaces cooperation to reflect the deeper integration required for building connection. Where the original model had both surface and deeper principles of cooperative and collaborative work, we need to accept that surface-level work is already occurring in schools and as such, focuses solely on increasing the depth and meaning that comes with authentic collaboration.

Collaboration is authentic when it emphasises collective ownership, mutual trust and joint problem-solving, which aligns with Vygotsky's (1978) (infamous) theory of social constructivism. Vygotsky argued that learning is inherently social, and collaboration enables students to construct knowledge through shared experiences.

In practice, fostering collaboration involves the teacher intentionally designing learning experiences that promote shared responsibility and meaningful outcomes. This can be achieved through approaches like project-based learning

(PBL), where the teacher facilitates opportunities for students to engage with real-world problems or create purposeful products (Rohm et al., 2021). By guiding collaborative activities, the teacher helps students draw on individual strengths while contributing to a common goal, building a sense of connection, purpose and interdependence (Sharratt & Planche, 2016). When implemented thoughtfully, this supports differentiation, inclusion and engagement, while also reducing behavioural challenges.

Ask yourself these quick questions:
1. Are your students engaging in meaningful, interdependent work or simply working side by side?
2. What changes could you make to deepen collaboration and promote shared ownership of learning?

Curiosity

Curiosity (formerly collaboration)

The final principle in the 4C Model, curiosity, introduces a reflective and forward-looking dimension to classroom connection. While the earlier principles focus on building trust, understanding and shared action, Curiosity sustains and deepens those connections by fostering reflection, inspiration and ongoing growth.

Because authentic learning cannot exist without curiosity, it will appear throughout this book, often woven into other areas of practice. However, within the 4C Model, curiosity takes on a distinct role. Drawing on Berlyne's (1960) foundational work, this component highlights two key expressions of curiosity: *diversive curiosity*, which drives engagement and creativity by prompting us to seek out new ideas, perspectives and challenges; and *epistemic curiosity*, which deepens learning by motivating us to ask thoughtful questions and explore complex concepts.

You will also encounter *empathic curiosity* earlier in the communication component, where it supports understanding others' perspectives. Together, these forms of curiosity not only enrich the relational work of teaching but also sustain meaningful learning and forward momentum. In this way, curiosity completes the 4Cs of connection by inviting both teachers and students to remain open, reflective and future-focused.

Ask yourself these quick questions:
1. How do you currently foster curiosity in your teaching?
2. How could this component be expanded to build deeper connection?

Charting the first route 33

How to begin with the modified 4Cs

The modified 4C Model is both a practical framework and a lens for understanding connection in education. While this book will use the 4Cs to structure its exploration of diverse topics, you can also begin to incorporate its principles directly into your teaching practice. Starting small and focusing on intentional actions is the most effective way to introduce the 4Cs into your classroom without feeling overwhelmed.

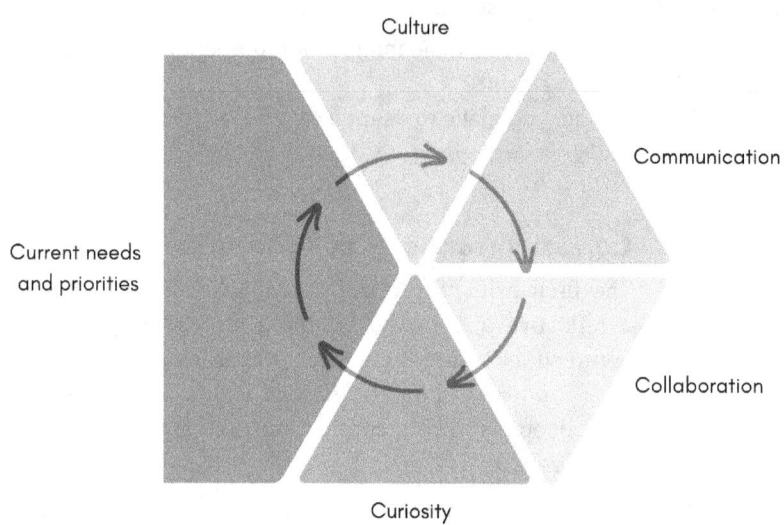

The best way to start is by reflecting on your classroom's current needs and your teaching priorities. Think about which of the four components feels most relevant. For example, if your students need a greater sense of belonging, you might start with culture by working with them to create shared norms or by fostering routines that celebrate diversity. Alternatively, if clear communication feels like an area for growth, you might focus on practices that encourage listening and respectful dialogue. Starting with one component allows you to experiment with focused changes that feel achievable, building confidence and momentum as you go.

The beauty of the 4C Model lies in its flexibility. There is no single way to apply its principles; instead, it encourages experimentation and adaptation to fit your unique context. Small, thoughtful actions, like adjusting how you facilitate group discussions or creating opportunities for student input, can have an outsized impact. Take time to reflect on how these changes influence your classroom dynamic. What seems to be working? What might need tweaking? Simple journalling or sharing insights with colleagues can help you refine your approach and inspire new ideas.

Engaging your students is another powerful way to begin working with the 4Cs. Involving them in decisions about culture, communication, collaboration or curiosity not only gives them ownership but also strengthens their connection to the classroom community. Ask for their input on what makes a good classroom culture or let them co-create processes for group work. By involving students, you reinforce the model's principles while also fostering trust and mutual respect.

The 4Cs are designed to work together, and as you grow more comfortable with one component, you will likely notice how it naturally supports the others. For example, building a strong culture of belonging lays the groundwork for better communication, which in turn supports effective collaboration. Curiosity thrives in an environment where students feel safe, valued and empowered to explore. These connections will emerge organically as you incorporate more elements of the model into your teaching.

Beginning with the 4Cs isn't about overhauling everything at once; it's about taking small, deliberate steps towards fostering greater connection in your classroom. Each step helps build a foundation for lasting change, making your classroom a place where students feel supported, relationships flourish and learning becomes a shared journey. As this book continues, the 4Cs will provide the structure for exploring key aspects of connective teaching, offering practical strategies and insights to help you deepen connection and engagement – that being said, don't wait, start experimenting now!

Ask yourself these quick questions:
1. Which of the 4Cs do you feel most confident using? Which do you feel could use more focus in your teaching?
2. How might embedding the principles of the modified 4C Model change the way your students experience learning?

4Cs action planning
Take a moment to brainstorm one actionable step you can take for each of the 4Cs (culture, communication, collaboration, curiosity) in your classroom. You could use a table like the one below:

4Cs of connection	Action to take
Culture	
Communication	
Collaboration	
Curiosity	

Using the 4Cs to address The Connection Conundrum

The modified 4Cs serve as a guiding structure for this book. Each chapter explores a distinct area of teaching and learning, a component of the climb, but the principles of the 4Cs provide the lens through which these topics are examined. While the components may not always be discussed explicitly, they underpin the strategies, ideas and practices presented throughout the book.

Our journey starts at base camp, where the focus is on culture and establishing the foundations, whether that be trust, safety and a sense of community, this first 'C' is crucial preparation that will determine the success of the climb ahead. The second is communication and is characterised by the first steps on the journey along the trailhead. Our success at the start of this movement will be dictated by how well we collectively understand the humans on our journey with us, their strengths, areas to improve and how effectively we engage with them.

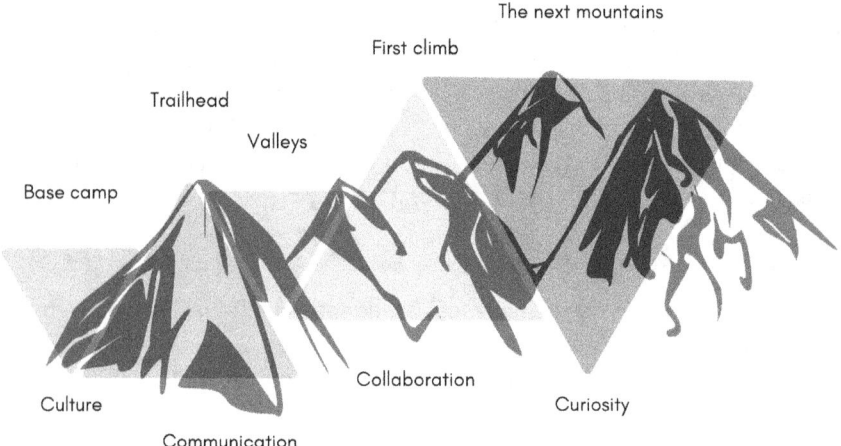

As the terrain becomes more challenging, we move on to the first climbs and the need for collaboration. Shared purpose and clarity of meaning is essential here as we traverse the initial inclines and address the challenges of the valleys we inevitably will meet. Finally, we celebrate success but always maintain a high level of curiosity and a view towards the next mountains and inspiring more climbers to join the next leg.

As you continue reading, keep the modified 4C Model in mind as a tool for framing your reflections and strategies. While the details may vary from one chapter to the next, the 4Cs remain a steady guide for understanding how culture, communication, collaboration and curiosity can transform your teaching practice and your classroom environment.

Where to from here?

From preparation to base camp

The chapters in Part 2 through Part 6 follow a consistent structure designed to guide you through key questions, unpack the evidence and provide practical strategies to help you foster meaningful, sustainable connection in your classroom. At its core, this book is about empowering *you*, the teacher, as the changemaker in creating environments where connection thrives. The chapter structure is designed to support that journey, blending theory with action in a way that is both practical and impactful.

Each chapter begins with *The big two* – two major questions that frame the discussion. These aren't abstract concepts; they're the big, guiding questions that shape how we think about connection and teaching. Through evidence, debate and exploration, we dig into what makes these questions so important and what the research and experience tell us about them.

From there, we move into *Unpack your journey*, where we break down the key learning of the chapter. This is the heart of the discussion, making clear links between the big ideas and what they mean for your day-to-day practice.

Next, we shift into action. *What to do?* lays out specific strategies, tools and initiatives that directly address the chapter's key questions – practical, tangible steps you can take in your classroom linked to the relevant 4C principle. This is followed by *Why do it?* which connects these strategies to their deeper benefits, particularly how they strengthen connection between students, teachers and the learning process itself.

Of course, knowing *what* to do isn't enough, you also need to know the direction you're heading in. In *Where to next?* I offer key questions, tips and ideas to help you refine, adapt and extend your practice as you build confidence and start seeing the impact of these approaches.

Finally, each chapter wraps up with *TL;DR* (short for *Too Long; Didn't Read* – a common internet term for a condensed version of something lengthy). This section isn't designed as a shortcut to skip the chapter, but as a quick reference when you need to revisit key points.

This structure ensures that each chapter isn't just informative, but is immediately useful in supporting you to act, make meaningful changes and ultimately build a classroom where connection isn't just an idea, but a daily reality.

Pack your bag, put your 4C lenses on and let's continue the journey!

Culture

Connection begins with culture.

When students feel safe, seen and valued, learning comes alive.

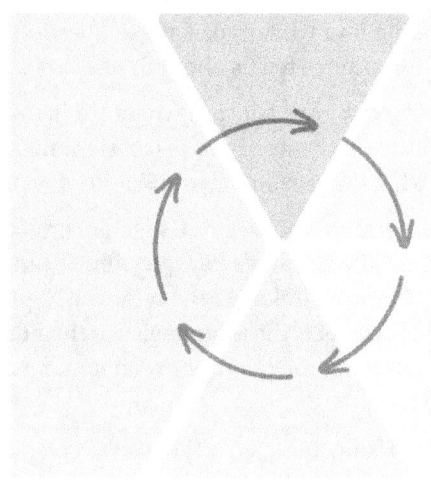

Connection pause

Take 60 seconds to jot down three small ways your classroom shows students they belong – a poster, a routine, a phrase you use.

Then ask: *What's one more small thing I could add tomorrow?*

PART 2
BASE CAMP
Building the foundations for connection

"The best preparation for tomorrow is doing your best today"

– H. JACKSON BROWN JR.

Base camp is a paradox; it's where the real adventure begins, but it's also a place of stillness. For climbers, it's a temporary home filled with tension and anticipation – a space to gather supplies, study the terrain and wait for the right moment. The summit may be the goal, but base camp is where the true work begins. The air is thinner here, but the vision becomes clearer. Before anyone climbs, they must prepare, mentally, physically and emotionally. Because no one reaches the peak without first learning how to stay grounded.

In education, base camp isn't a place, but a mindset – a commitment to build the right conditions before the ascent begins. Part 2 is about this preparation: laying the foundations of trust, safety and direction that make sustained connection possible. We begin in *Chapter 4: Packing the essentials*, where we explore the twin supports of psychological safety and trust. These are the emotional gear students need to navigate the often-unpredictable landscape of learning. Next, in *Chapter 5: Mapping the journey*, we shift our focus from culture to individual clarity. Through goal setting and motivation, we look at how to help students take ownership of their learning and develop the agency needed to move with confidence and intention. Just as a climber must understand the route ahead, students need to see where they're going and why it matters, if they're to persist through challenges.

Preparation isn't passive. It's active, intentional and deeply human. The choices we make at base camp will determine the strength of the steps to come on The Connection Journey.

The mountain waits. But first, we prepare.

CHAPTER 4
Packing the essentials
Building trust and safety

Before the climb begins, every adventurer must prepare. Long before content or curriculum comes into play, students must feel safe: emotionally, socially and intellectually. This chapter focuses on two of the most critical foundations for connection: trust and psychological safety. These aren't just abstract ideals; they're tangible, observable conditions that shape how students engage, interact and take risks in their learning.

When students feel secure and respected, they're more likely to participate, persist and grow. In this chapter you will find practical, research-informed strategies to help build a classroom culture where students feel they belong, where mistakes are part of the process and where relationships underpin everything. Because just like on any great expedition, the quality of the journey depends on what you take with you, and trust and safety are non-negotiables on your journey to be sustainably connected.

The big two

Creating a safe space for learning and building trust

Ask teachers, students or families about key components of a great school, and safety will undoubtedly appear. A trusting classroom environment is the absolute starting point for this to become reality, but it's not just about setting rules; it's about creating a culture where students feel respected, valued and encouraged to take risks. This concept is better known as *psychological safety*.

> Psychological safety is defined by Dr Amy Edmondson (1999), Novartis professor of leadership and management at the Harvard Business School, as:
>
> *"The belief that one won't be punished or humiliated for speaking up with ideas, questions, concerns, or mistakes, and the team is safe for interpersonal risk taking."*

Psychological safety plays a crucial role in student engagement and success (Edmondson & Bransby, 2023) because being open to learning new things is a vulnerable state to be in. This is why, when students feel safe, they participate more actively, take academic risks and persist through challenges (Edmondson, 2018). They feel safe to open themselves into that vulnerable space.

Unsurprisingly, this isn't just true of students. When any human experiences uncertainty, fear or exclusion, their cognitive energy is diverted towards self-preservation rather than learning as their natural defences kick into action (Picione & Lozzi, 2021).

To build a classroom environment in which *everyone feels they can learn, share and experience in safety*, we must address two fundamental questions at this earliest stage of our journey:

1. What makes a classroom feel like a safe space for learning?
2. How does trust between students and teachers shape engagement?

These big questions help us start our examination of how the emotional and relational climate of a classroom impacts connection across multiple factors, including learning, motivation and overall wellbeing. Unpacking the answers to these questions will also provide us with a direction towards making connection a consistent reality every single day.

1. What makes a classroom feel like a safe space for learning?

A classroom that fosters psychological safety is one where students feel free to express themselves without fear of embarrassment or retribution. If we are to establish environments that embrace not only an understanding of, but a shared belief that anyone in the classroom (and hopefully the wider school community) can voice their thoughts without negative consequences (Edmondson, 2018), we need to actively create and sustain a sense of security around each individual and their needs.

This sense of security is essential for encouraging:

- **Active participation** – students are more likely to engage in discussions and contribute ideas.
- **Collaboration** – learning becomes a shared experience rather than an isolated task.
- **Intellectual risk-taking** – students feel comfortable making mistakes and challenging assumptions.

To approach from a slightly different and perhaps more familiar perspective, Maslow's Hierarchy of Needs (1943), a teaching staple, reinforces this idea by emphasising that before students can engage in critical thinking and problem-solving, they must first feel secure in their environment.

Which tool will your students need in your classroom?

Zaretta Hammond's *Culturally Responsive Teaching and the Brain* (2015) further supports this, highlighting that a strong sense of belonging reduces cognitive stress, allowing students to access the prefrontal cortex, the part of the brain responsible for critical thinking and problem-solving. On the other hand, when students feel anxious or unsafe, the amygdala is triggered, initiating a stress response that hinders learning.

> Think about a conversation with a disengaged or frustrated student. They likely saw the classroom as:
>
> - *Unpredictable* – inconsistent rules and expectations: *"Others are doing it!"*
> - *Exclusionary* – some voices prioritised over others: *"You only listen to them."*

- *Punitive* – mistakes met with punishment, not learning: *"I'm always the one in trouble."*

Feeling unsafe, their focus shifts from learning to self-protection (Hammond, 2015).

By understanding what influences a student's sense of safety, we gain insight into why some students engage freely, while others remain silent, withdrawn or disengaged.

2. How does trust between students and teachers shape engagement?

'Trust' is a dangerous term as it consistently sits on the edge of completely overused and undeniably effective. Trust is a key feature of most effective classrooms, but it's not just a positive classroom dynamic, it's a core factor influencing student engagement, participation and achievement.

Visible Learning Meta^x (2024) has consistently highlighted the importance of teacher-student relationships, which have a current effect size of 0.57 (the 'hinge point' is 0.40, meaning anything higher is positively impacting learning), making them a powerful contributor towards student success.

But knowing trust is important isn't enough in our pursuit of a connected classroom. What does trust actually look like?

Research suggests students are more likely to trust teachers who are:
- Genuinely invested in their success
- Fair and consistent in expectations and actions
- Open to student perspectives

When students trust their teacher, they tend to:
- Engage more in discussions
- Take academic risks without fear
- Own their learning more fully

Without trust, students may:
- Withdraw out of fear of criticism
- Disengage from learning
- See authority as adversarial

(Holzer & Daumiller, 2025; Khatter et al., 2024)

This raises critical questions about what builds (or erodes) trust in a classroom:
- How do students determine whether a teacher is trustworthy?

- What past experiences shape a student's willingness to engage and take risks?
- How does a teacher's response to mistakes and challenges influence student confidence?

These further questions emphasise that trust isn't built through authority alone, it's cultivated through consistent actions, respect and relational investment. By shifting the conversation from compliance to connection, we can build classrooms where students aren't just physically present but fully engaged in their own learning.

Unpack your journey

The pillars of trust and safety

As you read this chapter, it should be becoming clear now, that a safe and trusting classroom doesn't happen by accident, it's cultivated with intention. While it's essential that every teacher brings their unique style and personality to the learning space, I've found that a classroom that fosters psychological safety, trust and ultimately, connection, consistently rests on four key pillars (Brown & Bartlett, 2024; De Neve et al., 2023). These pillars create the conditions in which students feel secure, valued and empowered to engage fully in their learning. The four pillars are:

1. Predictability
2. Fairness and equity
3. Emotional regulation
4. Mutual respect

Let's unpack each of these pillars and discuss the research that will help you make them a *reality* in your classroom and set your group on its connection journey.

Predictability

Predictability is the foundation of emotional security in the classroom. When students know what to expect, including things like how the day will flow, how the teacher will respond to challenges and how interactions will unfold, they feel more in control and can manage the normal, small changes that come with working in a group more effectively (Brown & Bartlett, 2024; Meyer et al., 2021).

This sense of structure reduces anxiety and allows students to focus on learning rather than the unknown (Brown & Bartlett, 2024). Seminal research in child development highlights the importance of consistency, with Bronfenbrenner (1981) emphasising how stable, predictable environments help students regulate emotions and behaviours. Predictability also fosters academic risk-taking as when students trust that their environment won't shift unexpectedly, they're more willing to participate, make mistakes and engage in problem-solving (Meyer et al., 2021).

In practical terms, predictability isn't about rigid adherence to routines but about creating a sense of stability. It's not about clearing the path of all obstructions but approaching each one with a known and accepted methodology.

Fairness and equity

Students are acutely aware of fairness – just ask them!

There is no bigger barrier to creating a culture of connection within a classroom than inconsistent behaviours from the adult in the room. Students notice when expectations seem variable. A classroom built on trust requires teachers to ensure that every student is treated with respect, fairness and impartiality (Kaufman & Killen, 2022).

To be clear, fairness doesn't mean treating every student the same. Treating every student the same ignores the diverse backgrounds, learning needs and lived experiences that shape their ability to engage in the classroom (Tomlinson & Imbeau, 2023).

Teachers must be willing to examine their own biases, notice patterns in their interactions, and actively create an environment where every student feels seen and supported (Brown & Bartlett, 2024; Kaufman & Killen, 2022). The goal is to establish a learning space where fairness isn't just about rule enforcement but about recognising and responding to students' individual needs in a way that upholds their dignity and self-worth.

Emotional regulation

After a few years in the profession, I'd like to think that we all know that the energy we carry in the classroom door is what frames the nature of the class you're about to teach. When a teacher models calmness, patience and composure, students are more likely to mirror that stability (De Neve et al., 2023). Equally, when teachers respond with frustration, unpredictability or harshness, students may experience heightened stress, making engagement and learning more difficult (De Neve et al., 2023).

Significant neuroscientific research supports this. Siegel (2011) highlights the concept of 'co-regulation' – the idea that students, particularly younger ones, take emotional cues from adults. Similarly, Porges' (2011) Polyvagal Theory (see Figure 5) explains how students' nervous systems react to perceived threats, including unpredictable or emotionally charged responses from authority figures. A dysregulated teacher can unintentionally create a climate of stress rather than safety (De Neve et al., 2023).

Emotional regulation isn't about suppressing feelings; it's about modelling healthy ways to manage them (De Neve et al., 2023). Demonstrating how to handle stress, disappointment and conflict in constructive ways teaches students essential life skills (Valente et al., 2022). It reassures them that their classroom isn't a place of emotional volatility but one where they can rely on stability, even in moments of difficulty.

Figure 5: Polyvagal Theory

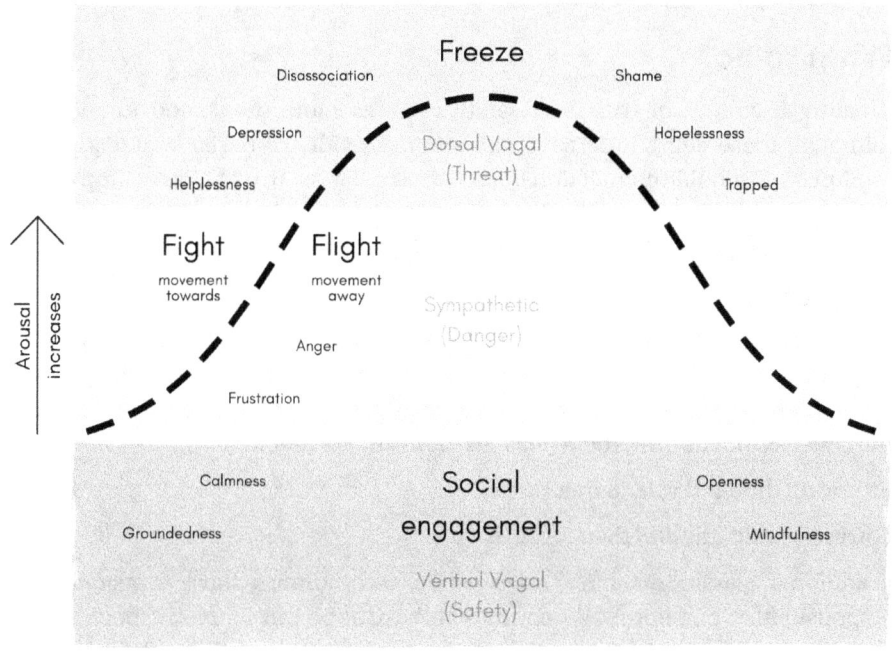

(ADAPTED FROM PORGES, 2011)

Mutual respect

Trust thrives in environments where students feel that their autonomy is acknowledged and their voices are valued (Han, 2021; Schaefer et al., 2024). Traditional, compliance-driven classrooms often rely on rigid rules and top-down control, leaving little room for student agency. In contrast, trust-centred classrooms cultivate a culture where students are active participants in shaping their learning experiences (Holzer & Daumiller, 2025; Schaefer et al., 2024).

This aligns with Social Cognitive Theory, as developed by Bandura (1986), which emphasises the role of observational learning, self-efficacy and reciprocal interactions in shaping behaviour. When respect is consistently demonstrated, students are given choices, involved in decision-making and encouraged to express their perspectives. They internalise these behaviours and become more engaged, responsible learners (Brown & Bartlett, 2024).

A culture of mutual respect doesn't mean relinquishing authority but rather creating an environment where power is shared appropriately (García-Moya, 2020). When students feel heard and valued, they're more likely to invest in their learning, collaborate with their peers and uphold classroom agreements (Brown & Bartlett, 2024). They're more likely to do this, not because they fear consequences, but because they see themselves as integral members of the classroom community and are, therefore, responsible for the culture within it.

What to do?

Creating a culture of trust and safety requires more than good intentions (although these help); it demands intentional, evidence-based strategies that reinforce sustainable connection *daily*. This is what the work at base camp is all about, preparation that positively supports the journey. Here are four strategies to start making this shift *before* we start to climb.

1. Agree to agree

Instead of imposing a list of rules, even a set of classroom rules collaborated on by your students, I'd encourage you to invite your students to define the *norms* of their learning space. This isn't just different language – we're trying to shift the collective focus from the typical 'us versus them' mentality.

From *I* do this, and *you* do that.

Towards *we* do this *and* that, *together*.

Traditional classrooms have rules, while communities have expectations, responsibilities and *norms*. When students have a voice in shaping expectations and responsibilities and creating what's 'normal' for them collectively, they feel a greater sense of ownership and accountability for upholding them (Schaefer et al., 2024; Thibodeaux et al., 2019).

Rules tell students what *not* to do. Norms guide them towards what *should* be done. A classroom built on norms positively supports students to make choices based on the potential positive impacts rather than the negative ones, creating a learning environment based on trust, not control.

> **Implementing a Respect Agreement**
>
> A 'Respect Agreement' is a powerful alternative to a traditional rules list and is based on this idea of collating norms. Rather than dictating what students *cannot* do, it establishes what the classroom community collectively values.
>
> Try these strategies when creating your agreement:
> - Facilitate discussions: *"What do we need to feel safe? How should we handle disagreements?"*

- Visibly record and group responses (for example, respect, kindness).
- Draft and regularly revisit a positively framed Respect Agreement (*"We listen respectfully"* rather than *"No interrupting"*).

2. Establish belief in effort

Over the years, I've noticed a shift from lively class discussions that flowed naturally to students becoming more hesitant to speak up. These days, drawing out student voice often takes more effort, but it's effort that matters deeply.

Students will do almost anything to avoid embarrassment. The fear of getting it wrong in front of their peers can shut them down before they begin (Archbell & Coplan, 2022; Maeda, 2017). Yet research shows that students thrive when their questions are answered, their opinions are valued and their successes are recognised (Amerstorfer & von Münster-Kistner, 2021). Creating a classroom where this feels possible means creating psychological safety and that starts with belief. Students need to believe they *can* succeed.

This kind of belief doesn't come easily, and I'll not pretend it does. But it's possible and powerful. When we model vulnerability, speak to effort and consistently show belief in our students, we create a shift: from *"I cannot"* to *"Maybe I can"*.

Dweck (2006) found that when students believe ability can grow through effort, they're more likely to embrace challenges. Psychological safety supports this by helping students feel safe to try, fail and grow (Edmondson, 2018). And that is where real learning begins.

Get them growing!

Create a classroom culture that is informed by a growth mindset and supported with psychological safety by implementing the following:

- Use low-stakes participation (Think-Pair-Share, anonymous polls).
- Privately redirect mistakes rather than publicly correcting them.
- Normalise mistakes ('fail forward') and celebrate effort.
- Foster student-led problem-solving through guided questioning rather than immediate answers.

3. Ritualise connection

Trust isn't built in a single conversation, it grows over time through consistent, everyday interactions. In schools, where change and challenge are part of the rhythm, the strength of our connections with students depends on how reliable those interactions are (AERO, 2023b).

Consistency doesn't mean repetition. It means students can expect a familiar structure in how we engage with them both spoken and unspoken. That predictability creates safety, and safety builds trust. If we want students to feel they belong, we need to create patterns they can rely on (AERO, 2023b).

Connection: free with entry

Classroom rituals are a powerful way to do this. Simple routines – how we start and end lessons, how we check in, how we acknowledge effort – become signals that say:

You matter here. You're safe to be yourself. You can take risks.

The surprises in your classroom should come from the learning, not the environment.

Building trust doesn't require big gestures. It's the small, consistent things that lower barriers, even for the most hesitant students. Research supports this: when routines are explicitly taught and consistently applied, classrooms become calmer, safer and more conducive to learning (Lester et al., 2017).

Connection-building rituals

Use small, consistent actions to show students they matter, without overhauling your routines.

Try these low-effort, high-impact strategies:
- Greet students personally at the door each day.
- Hold regular class check-ins or reflection circles to share challenges and wins.
- Set aside time weekly for students to recognise each other's strengths.
- Use quick, daily emotional check-ins (for example, thumbs up/down, one-word moods).

These rituals reinforce belonging, build trust and create a more connected classroom.

4. Open up!

Trust in the classroom grows through openness, honesty and vulnerability. When teachers model these qualities, they create a space where students feel safe to take risks, make mistakes and engage authentically. Research professor and author Brené Brown, known for her work on courage and connection, reminds us that vulnerability isn't weakness, it's the birthplace of trust and meaningful learning (Brown, 2018).

> In *Dare to Lead: Brave Work. Tough Conversations. Whole Hearts.* Brené Brown (2018) declares:
>> "The courage to be vulnerable is not about winning or losing, it's about the courage to show up when you can't predict or control the outcome."
>
> Students need to see that mistakes are normal, not shameful. That starts with us.

Owning a forgotten deadline or a wrong answer doesn't diminish our authority, it models accountability and resilience. Sharing personal struggles or learning journeys reminds students that growth is messy, and that is OK.

Early in my career, I was encouraged to say, *"I don't know, but let's find out."* That simple phrase invited curiosity and reminded students we were learning together. It's a small moment but a powerful one. We would do well to bring it back.

When we show up with honesty and vulnerability, we invite our students to do the same. They're more likely to speak up, take risks and stay engaged, not just in school, but in life. And that is the foundation of real connection.

> **Try this…**
> When a student asks a question that you don't know the answer to, respond with:
>> *"That is a great question – I don't know, but let's find out together."*
>
> This simple response builds trust, models curiosity and shows students that learning is a shared journey, not something only the teacher controls.

Why do it?

Trust and safety are foundational

A connected classroom isn't just a place where students learn; it's a space where they feel they have no doubt that they're able to do so. They need to feel supported, trusted and safe. Everything we've explored so far – psychological safety, trust, predictability, fairness – exists for one reason: to strengthen the connection that makes meaningful learning possible.

This needs to be central to our thoughts at base camp and prior to setting out on our journey because without connection, learning is fragile. When students feel they need to consciously protect or defend themselves, they become isolated, feel unheard and are unable to engage (Holzer & Daumiller, 2025). But if we can establish the foundational relationships and create the space for the development of a sense of belonging, students are likely to be more willing to participate in challenges, take risks by asking questions, and persist through the natural ebbs and flows of learning.

At base camp, we need to ensure that everything we do in the earliest stages of establishing our classrooms is based on the understanding that connection creates the conditions for learning to become a shared journey rather than an individual task.

Emotional availability

Building trust and safety isn't just about creating a 'nice' environment, it's about ensuring that students are emotionally available for learning.

Research consistently shows that when students experience strong relationships in the classroom:

1. They engage more deeply (Roorda et al., 2017).
2. They build resilience (Dweck, 2006; Edmondson, 2018).
3. They comfortably take academic risks (Cornelius-White, 2007).
4. They regulate their behaviour better (Wachtel, 2016).

Connection isn't simply relationships, and relationships aren't just a tool to be used to improve classroom conditions for teaching. We cannot continue to treat both as so. Connection makes learning a shared journey rather than an isolated task. To truly improve learning outcomes, we must consistently prioritise deep, sustainable connections within our classrooms.

Turning understanding into action

This chapter has hopefully reinforced that connection is the goal, and for our preparations at base camp, trust and safety are the means. We need to make all members of our community feel psychologically safe and aligned with the thinking that trust shapes engagement. This is how to make connection a daily reality.

Creating a culture of trust and safety requires more than understanding, it demands intentional, evidence-based action. A great teacher consistently questions their practice and in doing so, will ensure that specific strategies to ensure that students experience connection every single day are commonplace. Trust and safety aren't control or compliance; they're about empowerment. By embedding these types of approaches into practice, we move beyond theory and into the heart of what truly makes schools a place of connection.

Where to next?

The journey towards a truly connected learning environment involves continual self-awareness and responsiveness to students' needs. It's my hope that where to next isn't just the title of this section, but the natural question weighing on your mind. To embed connection as a core practice, you must regularly reflect on the interactions, classroom culture and student engagement seen in your classroom.

The following reflective prompts can help guide this process and prepare your thinking for the journey ahead.

1. Are some students hesitant to participate? Why?

Engagement is a key indicator of psychological safety. If certain students remain silent, avoid asking questions or disengage from learning activities, it may signal underlying trust concerns. Consider:

- Is the classroom dynamic unintentionally discouraging participation? Some students may fear being wrong, worry about peer judgement or struggle with confidence.
- Have I built strong enough relationships with every student? Sometimes, quieter students need more one-on-one interactions to feel comfortable engaging in the larger group.
- Are my participation strategies inclusive? Using Think-Pair-Share, anonymous responses or group discussions before individual answers can ease participation anxiety.

2. Do my verbal and non-verbal signals build or break trust?

Students are highly attuned to both what we say and how we say it. Our tone, body language and facial expressions all contribute to the sense of trust in the room. Consider:

- Do I communicate encouragement and openness? Maintaining warm eye contact, using a calm tone and offering validating responses (for example, *"That is an interesting perspective"*) reinforce trust.

- Do I unintentionally shut down student contributions? Reacting with visible frustration, dismissiveness or sarcasm, especially in moments of student struggle, can undermine safety.
- How do I handle mistakes, both mine and students'? Modelling a growth mindset by embracing errors as learning opportunities encourages students to do the same.

3. Do classroom expectations reinforce connection or compliance?

Norms and expectations shape classroom culture. When designed with connection in mind, they foster responsibility and belonging. When overly rigid, they can prioritise compliance over meaningful engagement. Consider:

- Are classroom agreements co-created and student-centred? If expectations are imposed without student input, they may feel like restrictions rather than shared commitments.
- Do I prioritise relationships in behaviour management? Restorative approaches (for example, conflict-resolution conversations) build trust more effectively than punitive measures.
- Are my expectations culturally responsive and inclusive? Acknowledging students' diverse backgrounds, communication styles and learning needs strengthens connection.

4. Embedding connection into daily practice

Trust and safety are a foundation for deep engagement and meaningful progress. We must keep this at the heart of daily teaching practice to build sustainable connection. Consider:

- Starting each day with intention: setting a personal goal (for example, *"Today, I'll check in with three students I haven't spoken to much this week"*) ensures connection remains a priority.
- Seeking student feedback: asking students what helps them feel safe and supported can provide valuable insights into classroom culture.
- Continuing to learn: exploring research on relationships, engagement and emotional safety keeps teaching practice evolving.

By consistently questioning, reflecting and refining these practices, teachers can sustain a classroom environment where students feel safe, trusted and connected, and therefore, ready to learn.

There is no better preparation at base camp than this.

Onward!

TL;DR

Key takeaways

1. **Psychological safety is a foundation of learning**
   Students cannot engage meaningfully in learning unless they feel emotionally, socially and intellectually safe. A classroom that values voice, risk-taking and mistakes as part of the process creates space for true participation and growth.

2. **Trust transforms engagement**
   Trust between teacher and student isn't just a nice-to-have, it's a proven driver of academic achievement and wellbeing. When students feel seen, heard and respected, they show up, speak up and step up.

3. **Connective trust is built on four pillars**
   A connected classroom rests on predictability, fairness and equity, emotional regulation and mutual respect. These pillars shape a culture where students feel they belong – and belonging powers learning.

4. **Consistent actions build culture**
   Big change doesn't come from grand gestures but from small, consistent practices. Greeting students, modelling vulnerability, following through on promises and co-creating norms all send the message: *"You matter here."*

5. **Connection is the core, not a bonus**
   Without connection, even the best strategies fall flat. Building safety and trust isn't just about better behaviour or smoother lessons, it's about making learning possible, every single day.

CHAPTER 5
Mapping the journey
Setting goals and inspiring motivation

At base camp, climbers do more than rest, they orient themselves. They lay out the route, align their vision and prepare for what's ahead. In our classrooms, this moment reflects the shift from building shared norms to guiding students in setting individual goals. While trust and safety connect the group, clarity and motivation help each learner navigate their own ascent. Without clear direction, even the most connected student can feel lost. Emotional safety matters, but without purpose, progress stalls.

This chapter explores two powerful drivers of individual connection: goal setting and motivation. These practices aren't just academic, they're identity-shaping. When students are supported to set meaningful goals and understand the value of their efforts, they begin to take ownership of their learning. We've established a vision, now it's time to focus on the individual. Because connection isn't just something we give to students, it's something they must begin to carry for themselves.

The big two

How clarity shapes the journey

A classroom without clear goals, both individual and shared, creates a chasm for learner motivation and breeds disconnection. It would be like leaving base camp and setting off on the journey with no map. Without this sense of specific direction, without the clarity to support each step of the journey, students may feel lost, disengaged or anxious about what they're doing and to be honest, I can relate.

When a teacher can provide clarity around mastery goals and provide a sense of motivation to achieve them, they establish a foundation for deep learning and sustainable connection (Korpershoek et al., 2020). This clarity fosters an environment where students feel confident that they know what's expected of them, both academically and behaviourally (Hattie & Zierer, 2019; Wisniewski et al., 2020).

You may be thinking, *"I thought expectations were discussed in the previous chapter."* You would be correct. Like a great scaffolded lesson, our preparation at base camp must also be scaffolded too. Now that we have collective trust and safety and a shared understanding of what we're expected to do as a community, it's time to focus on the individuals in the classroom.

However, as you probably are aware, simply setting goals and expecting students to be motivated to reach them isn't enough. The way students engage with their goals needs to be coached, guided and nurtured (Wolff et al., 2020). It's a skill, and one they may not have in their toolkit yet. It's essential work of the connected teacher, because whether your students passively comply or actively participate within the classroom is determined by their level of motivation and connection to the learning process itself (Ryan & Deci, 2020).

To explore this further, we must consider two essential questions:

1. How do clear goals and learning targets support connection?
2. What role do students play in shaping their learning journey?

These questions help us examine how structured guidance and student agency work together to create an engaging, high-performing classroom environment. One that is grounded in a strong foundation of connection.

1. How do clear goals and learning targets support connection?

Clear direction should always be a key component of your classroom. Well-defined goals play a crucial role in fostering a sense of connection within the learning process, to both internal connection to progress and relational connection to the broader learning environment (Wolff et al., 2020).

Clarity in goals directly supports a student's belief in their ability to achieve success (Korpershoek et al., 2020). Building a student's ability to see the path you're asking them to take is no small task, but it most certainly can be done. Albert Bandura's (1977) theory of Self-Efficacy highlights that when people have a clear understanding of what's expected of them, they're more likely to feel confident about their ability to meet those expectations.

And is that not a hard-hitting truth?

Think about your own experience as a teacher and I'm sure you could find an example that relates. We're all better when we have a clear goal in mind.

> Bandura, a psychologist and professor of social science at Stanford University, was quoted as saying:
>
> *"The stronger the perceived self-efficacy, the higher the goal challenges people set for themselves and the firmer their commitment to them."* (2002, p. 3)
>
> In our classrooms, goal setting isn't just for students who already have self-belief, but a powerful catalyst for developing self-efficacy, as achieving goals can lead to increased confidence and belief in their own abilities.

Whether it's a staff member or a student, clarity is essential, because it acts as a bridge, helping connect *their* efforts to *our* outcomes in a tangible way. In other words, they make it *real*. The benefits of this are cyclical, too. The clearer the learning targets, the more students can envision themselves succeeding, which in turn strengthens their motivation to engage with the material and persevere through challenges (Bălănescu, 2024).

As students experience small successes along the way, these incremental achievements further build their confidence and reinforce their belief that they're capable learners (O'Keefe et al., 2021). In turn, they begin to feel more connected not just to the content, but to the process of learning itself – an emotional and cognitive investment that is crucial for sustained engagement (Steinmayr et al., 2019).

2. What role do students play in shaping their learning journey?

Students should never feel like they're on someone else's journey, especially while being told otherwise. This is one of the greatest disconnectors in our schools today. Learning is a deeply personal experience, and one of the most common misconceptions is that the teacher is, or needs to be, the chief influence upon this learning.

The learner has that power, they have the greatest influence on *their* learning.

This is a necessary shift in thinking grounded in Expectancy-Value Theory. Developed (and consistently refined) by Wigfield and Eccles (2000), expectancy-value suggests students determine the value they attach to their learning experiences, which in turn shapes how they engage with and navigate those tasks and their overall learning journey itself.

This thinking emphasises that motivation isn't just about how capable students feel, but also about how much value they place on the task at hand. Students then shape their learning journey by deciding what tasks to engage with and how much effort to invest based on this perceived value.

Consider your classroom for a moment. Does this ring true?

> **We must give them a reason to invest!**
>
> Student engagement is often a reflection of connection. They're constantly assessing how learning fits with their identity, interests and future goals.
>
> For example:
>
> - A student may invest more in a task that aligns with their passions or aspirations.
> - They may also value a task as a step towards a bigger goal.
>
> These internal judgements shape how students focus, use resources and prioritise. Our job isn't to convince them something matters, it's to support their evaluation by making the value clear and the cost manageable.
>
> When students understand the 'why' behind learning and see its relevance, they're far more likely to lean in and do the work.

With our support, a student may alter their approach based on whether they perceive the task as worthwhile and achievable. In this way, their ongoing reflection and self-regulation are acts of maintaining or reestablishing connection to the learning, to their goals and to their evolving sense of self. By actively shaping what learning looks like for them, students develop a sense of ownership, purpose and meaning in their educational experiences.

Unpack your journey

Building early

Connection can be built and sustained no matter what time of the year you're in. There is no perfect entry point, especially if you're working from zero or a deficit. My advice would be to go for it wherever and whenever you find yourself ready. There are obvious benefits to starting your preparations at the beginning of the school year (or school term), as these moments often allow scheduled time for the work required. Starting with this work is a great way to build connective momentum, too.

> Monday: CONNECTION
> Tuesday: CONNECTION
> Wednesday: CONNECTION
> Thursday: CONNECTION
> Friday: CONNECTION
> Saturday: CONNECTION
> Sunday: CONNECTION
>
> Clear my calendar...
> (Personal connections on the weekends, though!)

At these natural entry points, students are still forming habits, developing relationships and orienting themselves to the rhythm of a new learning environment. It's in this period that the powerful benefits of goal setting are obvious, in both establishing a sense of direction and a sense of engagement.

When we guide our students to set goals, both personal and collective, they begin to feel the first instances of personal investment in their learning (Steinmayr et al., 2019). These goals, therefore, provide much more than focus, activation and a sense of progress, they give the classroom and the people within it the essential early energy it needs to breed intrinsic desire to know more (Hattie & Zierer, 2019).

If the earliest stages of these efforts are characterised by ambiguity, the results can be long lasting and difficult to overcome. Once the journey has been marked by hesitation or disengagement, the steps required to reorientate to the path of connection become not impossible, but larger in number.

As discussed in Chapter 4, students often look for structure to help them feel safe and oriented for learning. Clear, achievable goals reduce uncertainty and give students a better understanding of what to focus on, which increases their ability to participate meaningfully in learning activities (Hattie & Zierer, 2019; Wisniewski et al., 2020).

According to Marzano et al. (2003), when expectations and goals are explicitly communicated, students are more likely to meet them because they understand what success looks like. Clear goals reduce cognitive load by helping students prioritise their efforts, which allows more mental energy to be directed towards learning (Swain, 2024).

High standards, early wins

There isn't anything more powerful than allowing students to be involved. Motivation drastically increases when students are involved in the process of setting their own goals. It doesn't mean it's easy; but rather than being passive recipients of teacher-defined expectations, students who engage in goal setting take on a more active role in shaping their learning experience (Chiu, 2022).

Even small acts of student input, such as setting weekly learning targets or agreeing on group goals for a collaborative task, can make a significant difference in how motivated and responsible students feel (Chiu, 2022). It's essential that they're guided towards creating suitably challenging goals, and this is where the teacher's expertise and knowledge are key.

Setting high, yet achievable goals early in the school year, term, unit or subject can be a powerful way to build momentum. The Pygmalion Effect (see Figure 6), as demonstrated by Rosenthal and Jacobson (1968), shows that students often perform in line with the expectations set for them.

Figure 6: The Pygmalion Effect

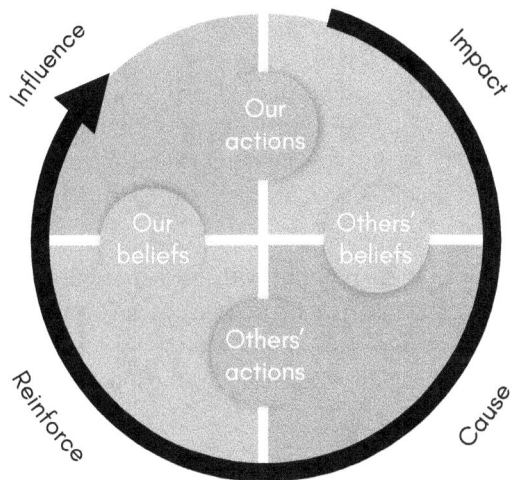

(ADAPTED FROM ROSENTHAL & JACOBSEN, 1968)

When educators set ambitious goals and support students in reaching them, students rise to meet the challenge. Critical to this is scaffolding, to reduce overload and to allow the greatest space for early successes (Puntambekar, 2022). Achieving short-term goals builds confidence and reinforces the belief that effort leads to progress – an essential motivator, especially at the start of the learning journey (Bandura, 1977; Patrick & Kaplan, 2022).

Momentum that is shared

While individual goal setting is powerful, collaborative classroom goals also play an important role in building early momentum. Creating shared objectives helps establish a sense of community and common direction, which can energise the group and reinforce collective responsibility (Dörnyei & Muir, 2019; Schunk & Zimmerman, 2023a). This doesn't require full consensus on every detail; even simple acts like identifying what the group wants to achieve in the first month can be powerful. It helps students feel that they're part of something larger, and that their contributions matter.

The key to all this work is ensuring that, no matter where your entry point, the work at base camp is treated as more than just a planning tool. It's a motivational strategy that creates energy, direction and investment. By involving students in identifying *their* goals, clarifying what success looks like *for them* and celebrating early progress *together*, teachers can build energy that carries students into deeper learning and connection.

These early steps lay the groundwork for greater autonomy, persistence and engagement throughout the journey to come.

What to do?

Creating a motivated, engaged classroom is every teacher's dream, but it's not always easy. Students of all ages can make this challenging. Sometimes it's anxiety, past experiences or just skipping breakfast. Still, one thing they all have in common is: a need for direction, structure and belonging, whether they're ready to admit it or not.

Teachers can harness that energy, not with pressure, but with purpose. Goal setting can be more than a tool of measurement; it can be a driver of connection and motivation. The four approaches below support students in owning their learning and building confidence, essential for the journey ahead.

1. Go for goals

When students have a voice in what they want to achieve, they're more likely to engage, commit and persist, three traits often said to be missing in classrooms today. But maybe what's missing isn't student willpower, it's the right approach.

Ask yourself: *Are your goals about assessment or aspiration?*

> **Let them dream**
>
> Simple prompts like *"What do you want to achieve this term?"* or *"What would progress look like for you?"* invite students to think intentionally about learning and take ownership.

That is where frameworks help.

You likely know SMART goals (Specific, Measurable, Achievable, Relevant, Time-bound). Originally introduced by George Doran (1981), they're great for individual academic goals: focused, structured and ideal for tracking short-term progress.

Less familiar, but just as powerful, are FAST goals (Frequently discussed, Ambitious, Specific, Transparent). These foster ongoing dialogue and shared accountability, making them perfect for group projects or collaborative learning (Sull & Sull, 2018).

SMART supports personal growth. FAST nurtures collective motivation and adaptability. Together, they balance clarity with creativity, developing qualities like perseverance, reflection and ownership.

SMART or FAST?

SMART goal – individual focus (Year 8 English)

"By semester's end, I'll raise my reading comprehension from 70% to 85% by doing weekly quizzes and attending two after-school sessions monthly."

Why it works:
- Specific – improve comprehension score.
- Measurable – from 70% to 85%.
- Achievable – with support.
- Relevant – aligned to curriculum.
- Time-bound – by semester's end.

FAST goal – group project focus (Secondary STEM)

"Our group will design and present a water filter prototype that meets community needs. We'll post weekly updates, share challenges and aim for a creative, high-impact solution."

Why it works:
- Frequently discussed – weekly updates and discussions.
- Ambitious – beyond basic criteria.
- Specific – functional prototype.
- Transparent – shared with the class.

2. Let them hear it

Too often, I've seen strong goal setting followed by weak follow-through. Students and adults need support in turning goals into action. It's risky to assume that once a goal is set, the path to it is understood.

Motivation grows when students hear goals regularly echoed in classroom life (Patrick & Kaplan, 2022). And this starts with *you*.

Ensure you model goal-directed behaviour: share your own learning goals, think aloud while planning, acknowledge when a goal shifts. Show students that goals are *living*, not one and done.

Always use consistent language and embed goals into your conversations:

> *"Let's revisit your goal from last week."*
> *"How does this task move you closer to your writing target?"*

Over time, these phrases help turn goal setting into culture, not just a moment. Students begin to link intention with action. Motivation becomes part of how your classroom breathes.

3. Seeing is believing

To keep motivation alive, students need to *see* their progress (Hattie & Zierer, 2019; Schunk & Zimmerman, 2023a). Learning becomes real when students track their growth over time (Gan et al., 2021). This doesn't require complex systems, just intentional visibility. Try:

- A classroom goal-tracking wall
- Periodic self-assessment rubrics
- Learning journals with regular reflection

Celebrate small milestones. Completing a tough task, improving a skill or supporting a peer can be just as powerful as the result. According to Hattie and Timperley (2007), recognition and feedback are key drivers of motivation while also teaching students *how* they learn. When they can see what's working, they start to own their strategies and their confidence grows.

4. Feedback, feednow, feedforward

Even in the most supportive classrooms, setbacks happen. Missed deadlines, low marks, challenging tasks. These aren't failures; they're part of the process.

You already know this. But are we really acting like we believe it?

> **Build me up**
>
> Think of *scaffolding*.
>
> Teachers love it, especially when planning units. It helps align goals with standards, layer by layer. But remember that scaffolding is support, not the structure itself. We don't live in scaffolding; we use it temporarily. Yet sometimes, we teach like it's permanent.

When a build hits a snag, the scaffold holds things up until the issue is addressed.

Do you stop to reflect, discuss and plan at the point of struggle before moving a student forward?

Are we truly scaffolding, or just pushing ahead?

The only way to make these moments learning opportunities is to provide comprehensive feedback (Gan et al., 2021). According to Hattie and Timperley (2007), feedback is most powerful when it's timely, specific *and* focused on what students can do next.

The key here is '*and*'.

If we only focus on the right side of the 'and' we can highlight important feedback, *feedforward* feedback, which helps students see a path ahead and keeps them engaged in the learning process (Wisniewski et al., 2020). However, this doesn't explicitly connect them to the work they have done, not in the moment. Timely and specific feedback also needs a deliberate pause, to not only look backward to move forward, but to look backward to understand where they are now as a result (Gan et al., 2021).

Scaffolding and feedback are connective processes that have been hijacked as administrative ones. Ensure your feedback considers:

- Where the student has been
- Where they are now
- Where they can go next

Why do it?

Building initial connection

In the early stages of any group formation or in response to change, building motivation through goal setting isn't just a matter of improving individual outcomes – it plays a powerful role in creating classroom connection. When students feel connected to their learning, their teacher and their peers, they're more likely to engage meaningfully, creating the foundation for the positive learning environment we all dream of. Goal setting and motivation are deeply relational practices that help foster a culture of partnership, shared investment and self-regulation (Schunk & Zimmerman, 2023a).

One reason this approach is so effective is that it raises student expectations for themselves and for each other (Wisniewski et al., 2020). Although it may not always feel true, students look to us as influential figures and will internalise the beliefs and attitudes they perceive their teachers to have (Rosenthal & Jacobson, 1968).

We need to expand our motivational toolkit

When teachers involve students in setting goals and express belief in their capacity to achieve them, students begin to raise their own expectations of success (Schunk & Zimmerman, 2023a). This contributes to a classroom environment where effort is normalised and success is seen as achievable by all, not just a few. Over time, students begin to mirror these positive expectations in their interactions with one another, building a sense of collective efficacy and support (Schunk & Zimmerman, 2023a; Schunk & Zimmerman, 2023b).

Goal setting also allows students to see, with clarity, evidence of their own abilities (Schunk & Zimmerman, 2023a). This sense of mastery boosts confidence and motivation, even in the face of challenges (Schunk & Zimmerman, 2023b). As Bandura (1977) explains, self-efficacy develops not just from success, but from seeing growth through effort and strategy. When students feel capable, they're more likely to engage fully, ask for help when needed and support others who are working through similar struggles.

These practices also make the learning environment more connected. As students share goals, reflect on progress and celebrate small successes, they begin to see themselves as part of a community of learners. Teachers who consistently reference student goals, acknowledge effort and provide feedback aligned with student aspirations show that they know and care about each learner's journey. This builds stronger relationships, increases student engagement and develops a sense of belonging (Bryk & Schneider, 2002).

Importantly, connection through goal setting helps students reframe setbacks. When challenges arise, students with high self-efficacy and supportive classroom relationships are more likely to persevere, drawing on strategies and encouragement from both their teacher and peers. Instead of viewing difficulty as failure, they see it as part of the process – something that is often spoken about in professional learning but not engaged enough in practice (Bandura, 1977; Schunk & Zimmerman, 2023b). We need to ensure our students consistently have something to reflect on and, therefore, connection to grow from.

This mindset not only deepens motivation but strengthens the social fabric of the classroom. In essence, goal setting and motivation aren't isolated strategies. When thoughtfully implemented, they lay the groundwork for connected classrooms – places where students feel known, capable and supported by those around them. This connection is what helps learning communities thrive, especially in the critical early phases of the school year.

Setting high aspirations is an act of connection – it says *I believe in you, I'm here for you, and we will grow together.*

Where to next?

Creating initial momentum through student goal setting is a powerful first step, but sustaining that energy over time requires continued reflection, intentional practice and community. It's not just about setting goals once but embedding them into the rhythm of learning so that motivation remains active and visible.

The following prompts and strategies will help you reflect on your current practices and continue building a classroom culture where student motivation grows and evolves throughout the journey.

1. Do my practices promote student agency and ownership?

Motivation thrives when students feel ownership over their learning. Goal setting can easily become a teacher-driven task if we're not careful, something done *to* students rather than *with* them. Consider:

- Do students help define their own learning goals, or are these mostly teacher-prescribed?
- Are students encouraged to revisit, revise or abandon goals when needed?
- Am I making space for students to talk about what motivates them and why their goals matter to them?

2. Are students tracking their own progress in meaningful ways?

Goal setting has little impact if students don't know whether they're making progress. To sustain motivation, students need regular, visible evidence of growth, and they need to be the ones interpreting it. Consider:

- Do students use learning journals, progress trackers or self-assessment tools to reflect on their goals?
- Am I helping students build the habit of noticing and naming their own progress?
- Are progress check-ins student-led, or am I the one always driving them?

3. Is goal setting embedded into the flow of classroom life?

If goal setting is a one-off event, its impact fades quickly. To build long-term motivation, goals must be part of how the class talks, learns and reflects together. Consider:

- Do students revisit their goals regularly? Weekly, monthly or after major tasks?
- Do classroom routines include time for students to reflect on what's working and what they want to improve?
- Am I modelling goal setting and reflection in my own practice to show that it matters?

4. Am I supporting motivation across the full school year?

The early energy of a new term can be powerful, but it fades unless it's renewed. Sustaining student motivation requires both structure and flexibility over time. Consider:

- Do I build in mid-term and end-of-term reflection points to refresh and revise goals?
- Do students see goal setting as a skill they're developing, not just a classroom activity?
- Am I offering enough encouragement, feedback and celebration to keep motivation alive?

5. Am I extending the conversation beyond the classroom?

Motivation deepens when students feel their learning goals matter in the wider world. When families and the broader school community engage with student goals, it sends a powerful message: *this learning is real, and it matters*. Consider:

- Have I shared our class's approach to goal setting with families so they can support it at home?
- Do I collaborate with other teachers to reinforce a consistent message about student agency and effort?
- Have I created opportunities for students to share their goals and successes publicly, with peers, families or the school community?

Teacher self-check

Use the following tool to reflect on how your current practices support student motivation through goal setting. You might revisit it at the start, middle and end of term to help you stay responsive and intentional.

Question	Reflection notes
Do my practices support student ownership of goals?	
Are students tracking their own progress or waiting for my feedback?	
How do I keep motivation alive when energy dips mid-term?	
Do classroom routines regularly include time for goal reflection?	
Am I connecting students' goals with life beyond the classroom?	

If we intentionally build consistent reflection and adaptation through the expansion of goal setting in our classrooms, we can strengthen the conditions in which motivation and connection can flourish, not just for now, but for the entire journey ahead.

It's time to take this learning from base camp to the first leg of the journey.

TL;DR

Key takeaways

1. **Clarity connects the classroom**
   Clear, well-communicated learning goals give students a sense of direction and purpose. When students understand what's expected, they feel more confident, motivated and connected to the learning process.

2. **Students shape their own learning journey**
   Motivation thrives when students see value in what they're learning. Involving them in goal setting helps them take ownership, build agency and connect learning to their personal interests and future aspirations.

3. **Early wins build lasting momentum**
   Setting high (but achievable) goals early in the year fosters motivation, confidence and a positive classroom culture. Both individual and collective goals create energy and investment that sustain engagement over time.

4. **Goal setting is a strategy, not a task**
   Embedding goal setting into daily practice through visible tracking, regular reflection and ongoing dialogue helps students stay focused, resilient and self-aware. It must be coached and supported, not left to chance.

5. **Connection grows when students feel seen and supported**
   Authentic feedback, celebration of progress and a consistent focus on growth help students feel known, capable and part of a learning community. These conditions foster long-term motivation and a deeper sense of belonging.

Communication

Speak to be heard.

Listen to understand.

Connection grows when every voice matters.

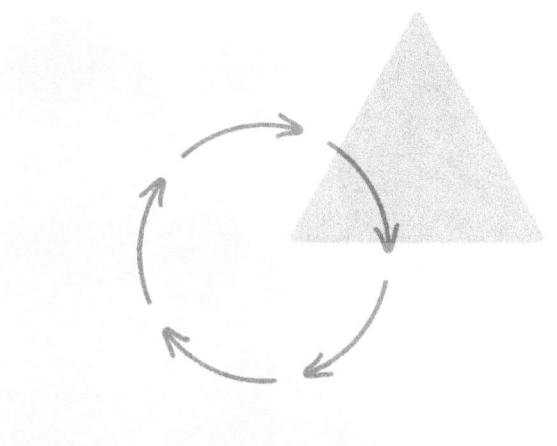

Connection pause

Think of a recent student interaction. Replay it in your mind and imagine responding with even more curiosity or empathy.

What might you have said differently?

PART 3
TRAILHEAD
Beginning the Journey of Connection

"When we seek to discover the best in others, we somehow bring out the best in ourselves"

– WILLIAM ARTHUR WARD

The trailhead is where footsteps meet earth, where dreams shift from the abstract to the tangible. Legendary Italian climber Reinhold Messner, the first person to summit Everest without supplemental oxygen, spoke of this moment as a transition from planning to action. The trailhead represents commitment – the decision to leave the comfort of the known and venture into terrain that promises both challenge and transformation. At the trailhead, you realise the climb is no longer a distant idea. It's happening.

In education, the trailhead isn't just a moment, but a commitment – a set of conscious steps towards building something with others. Part 3 is about this movement: how we begin walking together. It marks the shift from preparing the ground for connection to stepping into it with intention – side by side, student and teacher, peer to peer.

We begin in *Chapter 6: Exploring new horizons*, where we explore the powerful foundations of empathic curiosity and inclusivity. These aren't just dispositions – they're practices that invite every student into the learning space with dignity and value. Without these twin guides, connection remains surface-level. With them, it deepens into something real and lasting. In *Chapter 7: Navigating together*, we turn our attention to classroom community – what it means to move forward not just as individuals, but as a collective. This is where belonging becomes lived experience, where students shift from occupying the same space to building a shared one. Community, when nurtured with care and consistency, transforms learning from an isolated act into a cooperative journey.

Together, these chapters mark a turning point in The Connection Journey. Because once you step onto the trail, everything changes. The path is no longer imagined – it's underfoot. The real work begins not in the safety of theory, but in the slow, steady rhythm of movement.

The summit's far off. But the journey has begun.

CHAPTER 6
Exploring new horizons
Fostering empathic curiosity and inclusivity

At the trailhead, climbers do more than begin, they attune themselves to the journey ahead. They check their gear, adjust to the conditions and prepare to move with awareness. In our classrooms, this moment reflects the shift from creating a welcoming environment to cultivating deeper understanding. It's where inclusion becomes lived, not just planned. Empathic curiosity encourages students to look beyond assumptions. Inclusivity ensures that every learner feels seen, valued and invited to contribute. Without both, connection remains shallow. A student may feel safe, but not significant. Present, but not included.

This is why inclusion cannot be passive; it must be intentional. This chapter explores two powerful drivers of connection: empathic curiosity and inclusivity. These aren't just practices; they're ways of being. When students are encouraged to care about others' experiences and see value in every voice, connection grows stronger. Because belonging isn't something we do to students, it's something they build with us.

The big two

The power of being curious and inclusive

A thriving classroom is one where students feel both intellectually engaged and socially connected (Frey et al., 2019). Learning isn't just about acquiring knowledge, it's about developing the ability to explore new ideas, engage with diverse perspectives and foster a sense of belonging.

Have we drifted too far from this in reality?

Curiosity (notably *empathic curiosity*) and inclusivity are two essential elements of a connected learning environment in which all students can thrive. Empathic curiosity fuels inquiry, deepens understanding and strengthens connections between students and staff (Han et al., 2025; Pitman, 2024). It encourages them to move beyond surface-level interactions and engage genuinely with one another's thoughts, experiences and perspectives.

Meanwhile, inclusivity ensures that every student not only feels, but *is* valued, seen and empowered to contribute. A truly inclusive classroom is one where diverse voices aren't only present but actively celebrated, and where students feel a sense of shared ownership over the learning experience.

Without empathic curiosity, students may hesitate to challenge their assumptions. Without inclusivity, students may struggle to see themselves as important members of the learning community.

To explore how these elements shape the classroom experience, we must consider two essential questions:

1. How can empathic curiosity help students authentically connect with each other?
2. What does it mean to create a truly inclusive learning space?

These questions serve as the foundation for fostering deep learning, strong peer relationships, and an environment where all students feel a sense of belonging and connection.

1. How can empathic curiosity help students authentically connect with each other?

Curiosity is often seen as a tool for intellectual growth, but it's equally important in shaping social connections (Frey et al., 2019; Schoem et al., 2023). When students are encouraged to be curious about each other's ideas, experiences and backgrounds, they develop:

- **Empathy** – the ability to understand and appreciate different perspectives
- **Openness** – a willingness to explore unfamiliar ideas

- **A stronger sense of collaboration** – the recognition that learning is enhanced through shared exploration (Han et al., 2025)

In a connected classroom, it's the empathy that needs to be focused on first. People should be inherently curious about those around them. Empathic curiosity is a gateway to being more authentically curious about the world in which we all live, but one we often don't take because it's not explicitly in the syllabus.

If we want to encourage our students (and staff) to engage in deeper learning, that actively pursues questions, explores the answers and retains the knowledge gained (Kashdan et al., 2013), and critical thinking, that encourages students to challenge assumptions, seek evidence and consider multiple viewpoints, we must embrace empathic curiosity as we take the first steps on our connection journey.

A classroom rich in empathic curiosity allows students to see one another not as competitors, but as partners in exploration (Pitman, 2024). Instead of merely absorbing information, they engage actively with peers, asking not just about the subject matter, but about each other's experiences of the subject matter (Han et al., 2025). In this way, empathic curiosity transforms the classroom into a space of authentic, shared discovery rather than isolated learning.

However, we shouldn't assume that curiosity always emerges naturally. Some students may hesitate to ask questions out of fear of judgement or failure. Others may struggle with curiosity because they haven't been encouraged to see learning as an open-ended process rather than a set of predetermined answers.

In our pursuit of connection, we must ask ourselves about the conditions, the culture and the barriers we may face when attempting to establish a community of shared curiosity. To do so, we must let go of curiosity as a skill and see it for what it truly is: a human *need*.

By accepting this truth, we can start to better understand why empathic curiosity isn't just about engagement in the classroom, but a key driver of meaningful learning and human connection.

2. What does it mean to create a truly inclusive learning space?

Inclusivity goes beyond diversity in representation, it's about creating a learning environment where every student feels safe, valued and empowered to participate.

A truly inclusive classroom ensures that:
- Students see themselves reflected in the learning experience.
- Differences aren't just tolerated but embraced as valuable contributions.
- Every student feels that their voice matters in discussions, activities and decision-making.

Contact Theory (Allport, 1954) suggests that when individuals engage with diverse perspectives under conditions of cooperation and equal status, bias is reduced and understanding is strengthened. This is particularly important in education, where classrooms are often the first place students encounter ideas, identities and lived experiences different from their own.

Yet, like curiosity, inclusivity isn't automatic, it's shaped by the structures, interactions and expectations within a learning space. A student may be physically present in a classroom but still feel disconnected if they don't see their identity, background or perspective valued in the learning process (Clark et al., 2018).

This should raise important questions for your own self-reflection. I haven't met an educator in my time who didn't believe that education should be inclusive, but do you really, despite all intentions, have that kind of environment? An environment that makes a student feel truly included beyond just being present, that has equity in value and breaks all barriers, spoken and unspoken?

These are difficult considerations, but in simply thinking on their potential answers, we move beyond the conceptualisation of surface-level inclusivity (Clark, 2018; Tomlinson & Murphy, 2018) and begin to understand what it truly means to create a classroom culture and what that kind of connected environment may take to bring to life.

Unpack your journey

Why so curious?

Is anything more powerful than curiosity in the classroom?

In the pursuit of deep, connected learning, *empathic curiosity* acts as a catalyst, fostering strong relationships, a sense of belonging and meaningful inquiry. When students are encouraged to be empathically curious, they become more open to diverse perspectives, more willing to engage with unfamiliar ideas and more connected to their peers (Tomlinson & Murphy, 2018). In a world increasingly shaped by technology, this type of connection is vital.

At its core, curiosity invites exploration. It pushes learners beyond surface-level understanding and towards deeper questions:

- *Why does this happen?*
- *What if things were different?*
- *How does this relate to me and others?*

When students learn to question not just content but also the people and contexts around them, they develop stronger critical thinking skills and greater empathy (Engel, 2015). Research shows this kind of questioning supports *cognitive flexibility* – the ability to adapt thinking when faced with new evidence (Kashdan et al., 2013). This flexibility helps prevent rigid thinking and fosters understanding rather than judgement (Tomlinson & Murphy, 2018).

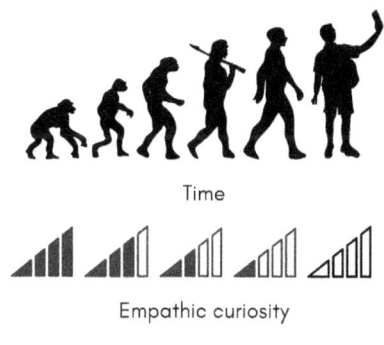

Time

Empathic curiosity

Don't let this be the human story

Think globally!

The United Nations Educational, Scientific and Cultural Organisation (UNESCO) (2015) embraces empathic curiosity as a key component of its Global Citizenship Education movement, stating that through this curiosity:

> "Learners experience a sense of belonging to a common humanity, sharing values and responsibilities, based on human rights. Learners develop attitudes of empathy, solidarity, and respect for differences and diversity." (p. 22)

This kind of curiosity moves beyond *"What's this person experiencing?"* to *"Why?"* and *"How can I connect meaningfully with that?"*

Empathically curious learners aren't only more aware of global issues; they're driven by compassion to engage with them (UNESCO, 2015). They grow into citizens who don't just tolerate difference, they're drawn to it, eager to understand perspectives unlike their own.

In this way, empathic curiosity becomes essential to global citizenship, linking knowledge with human connection, and nurturing both the head and the heart.

Dig a little deeper

Rather than memorising facts, students encouraged to be empathically curious are driven by authentic questions that matter to them (Paul & Elder, 2019). This fosters deeper engagement and stronger retention.

This requires shifting our focus, from abstract content to human stories, from isolated facts to real-world connections. Ask not just *what* happened, but *who* was involved, *why* it mattered and *how* it relates to students' lives today. We must make learning personal and locally relevant (Barr, 2024).

Multiple experts show that when students feel connected to what they're learning, they're more motivated, engaged and willing to take intellectual risks (Baehr, 2022; Hammond, 2015; Naz et al., 2023). These risks involve questioning, challenging assumptions and offering new viewpoints, strengthening learning communities rooted in empathy and respect (Cai et al., 2023; Naz et al., 2023; Ryan & Deci, 2020).

Increase exposure

Empathic curiosity thrives in classrooms that embrace diversity. When students explore different cultures, histories and lived experiences, they develop a broader, more inclusive worldview (Naz et al., 2023).

Allport's (1954) Contact Theory (see Figure 7) suggests that meaningful interactions across diverse populations reduce prejudice. Research supports this: engaging with diverse perspectives lowers reliance on stereotypes and increases empathy (Khattak et al., 2025). In contrast, lack of exposure can lead to unconscious biases.

Teachers can nurture curiosity about others by creating space for students to ask questions about each other's experiences, beliefs and cultures. Activities like storytelling, role-playing and structured debates help students step into others' shoes. When these practices are embedded into classroom routines, students learn not only to understand but to celebrate difference (Khattak et al., 2025).

Figure 7: Contact Theory

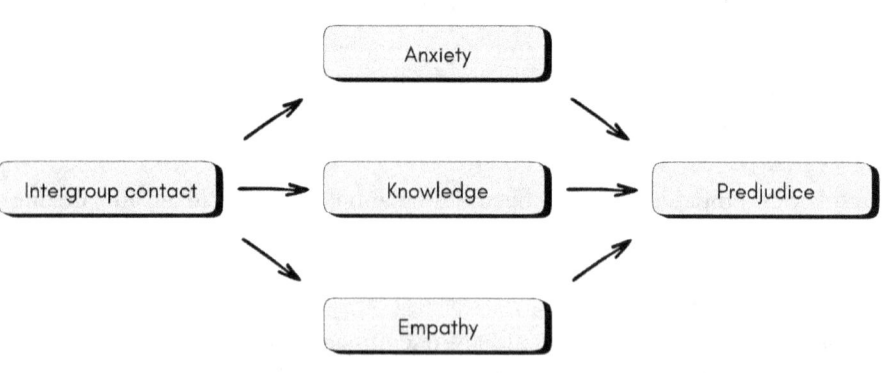

(ADAPTED FROM ZUMA, 2014)

By reframing curiosity and inclusivity as core cultural practices, not just instructional strategies, we can create classrooms where students feel seen, valued and connected to each other and their own potential.

What to do?

Empowering students to develop empathic curiosity and embrace inclusivity requires intentional strategies that are embedded in daily classroom practice. The three strategies presented below do just this. They guide your work at the beginning of our mountainous undertaking.

By cultivating a culture of inquiry, integrating diverse perspectives and encouraging perspective-taking activities, teachers can create an environment where students not only connect with knowledge but also with each other.

1. Think about thinking

Curiosity flourishes in classrooms where questioning is encouraged and inquiry is seen as a natural part of learning. When students are invited to ask deep questions and challenge assumptions, they develop a mindset that values exploration over certainty. Research suggests that inquiry-driven learning improves engagement and helps students develop *metacognition* – the ability to think about their own thinking (Barr, 2024; Hastuti et al., 2020).

Developing a culture of inquiry seems like an easy hill to climb. It's been popularised in recent years and certainly has a large following online. But what is it actually?

> Edgar Schein, Professor Emeritus at MIT Sloan and a pioneer of inquiry thinking, believed that questions should take centre stage in learning. In *Humble Inquiry: The Gentle Art of Asking Instead of Telling* (2018), he wrote:
>
>> "Questions are taken for granted rather than given a starring role in the human drama. Yet all my teaching and consulting experience has taught me that what builds a relationship, what solves problems, what moves things forward is asking the right questions."
>
> Schein argued that questions shouldn't come after the learning, they should *start* it. Inquiry-based learning gives students ownership of their thinking, encouraging them to ask meaningful questions that lead to deeper understanding, stronger relationships and real problem-solving.

We can embrace Schein's ideology in several different ways, but chief among them is to actively model curiosity each day. Teachers can play a crucial role in shaping how students approach questioning, especially in how questions are asked and responded to respectfully (Yi et al., 2023).

Start with the types of questions being asked. Instead of asking students what they think, ask them *why they think that way*. This small change models intellectual humility and encourages students to seek knowledge collaboratively (Krumrei-Mancuso et al., 2020). By incorporating the use of *"I wonder" statements*, such as *"I wonder why this happened…"* or *"I wonder what would change if…"* students can engage with a higher level of critical thought and explore alternative possibilities beyond the first that come to mind.

Research on curiosity-driven learning suggests that framing content in the form of intriguing questions increases students' intrinsic motivation to engage (Engel, 2015; Paul & Elder, 2019). This is where *Socratic questioning* can be invaluable.

Be like Socrates

Inspired by the methods of Socrates, *Socratic questioning* encourages students to move beyond surface-level answers and think more deeply about their reasoning (Paul & Elder, 2019).

Rather than asking, *"What's the main idea?"*, teachers can prompt richer reflection with questions like:

> *"What assumptions are we making?"* or
> *"How does this connect to real life?"*

In practice, this might look like:

- Instead of: *"What causes climate change?"*
  Ask: *"What evidence shows that climate change is happening?"*
- Instead of: *"Is this source reliable?"*
  Ask: *"Why do you think this source is reliable?"*
- Instead of: *"What's the answer?"*
  Ask: *"Could there be another explanation for this data?"*

These kinds of questions help students develop critical thinking, explore multiple perspectives and engage more deeply with content.

2. Represent!

Inclusivity is supported by more than a set of policies; it must be a practice that shapes the way students engage with content and each other, becoming part of the classroom culture. True inclusivity ensures that every student sees themselves reflected in the curriculum and feels that their perspectives are valued (Akintayo et al., 2024; Kunwar & Adhikari, 2023). By starting strong in your classroom, you can not only create engaging lessons that connect students to their learning but model a school that is connected to its community.

Diversity is one of the most valuable components of our modern schools. But how do we align with the diverse cultures, varied abilities and unique thinking each individual can bring to our classes? Representation in a connected school matters.

If students only encounter dominant narratives, including those from neurotypical individuals, they may internalise the idea that other perspectives, such as theirs, are less important (Botha & Cage, 2022). When considering this in your context, throw a wide net, including literature, historical accounts and case studies from diverse backgrounds as a start. Each step you take helps broaden students' understanding of the world and how they fit within it (Tikkanen et al., 2022).

Building from this, create opportunities where student-led discussions highlight the value of different perspectives by structuring discussion. *Philosophical Chairs* or *Harkness Circles* ensure that multiple viewpoints are explored and debated in a respectful way. Research shows that when students actively engage in perspective-sharing, they become more empathetic and less likely to hold biases (Parker-Shandal, 2023).

Chairs and circles

These two methods are summarised below. Read here and I then recommend you do some research online.

Philosophical Chairs – A structured, debate-style strategy that encourages students to engage in critical thinking and respectful discourse. The teacher presents a thought-provoking statement, and students physically position themselves in the room according to whether they agree, disagree or are undecided. One speaker talks at a time, responding to others' ideas rather than attacking individuals. Students are encouraged to listen actively and may switch sides if their perspective changes. This method promotes openmindedness, logical reasoning and the courage to reconsider one's views (Fletcher, 2019).

Harkness Circles – Focuses on student-led discussion rather than debate. Students sit in a circle and collaboratively explore a text, topic or question. The teacher takes a backseat role, facilitating only when needed, while students take responsibility for maintaining and deepening the conversation. The method encourages equal participation, active listening and thoughtful questioning (Frommert, 2024).

3. Give a thought, take a thought

Perspective-taking is one of the most powerful ways to build empathy and strengthen student connection. When students are encouraged to consider experiences beyond their own, they develop a deeper understanding of the world and greater acceptance of difference (Dweck, 2017).

If we want connection to be central in our classrooms, we need to make perspective-taking part of everyday learning. In fact, this goes beyond connection, it's foundational to the future of education.

Creating a welcoming, empathically curious classroom takes time and practice. One powerful strategy is *empathy interviewing*, which works at any point in the year but is especially valuable early on. Pair students up and have them interview each other about their experiences, challenges and viewpoints, focusing on understanding, not judgement. Afterwards, students reflect on what they learned and how their perspective shifted. Research shows that active listening like this boosts emotional intelligence and strengthens classroom cohesion (Brooks & John, 2018).

Structured peer dialogue also helps. Techniques like *Think-Pair-Share* give students the chance to explore different viewpoints in a supportive, low-pressure way. Through this kind of reflection, students learn that differing ideas aren't threats, they're opportunities to grow.

To ensure all voices are heard, introduce the *step up, step back* protocol. We've all seen discussions dominated by a few voices while others stay silent. This strategy invites frequent speakers to pause and listen, while encouraging quieter students to share. It's a simple but effective way to create more equitable, inclusive conversations (Hammond, 2015).

When we embed these strategies into our classrooms, we create spaces that aren't only intellectually challenging but also emotionally connected, where students learn to think critically and care deeply.

Why do it?

Fostering both empathic curiosity and inclusivity in the classroom isn't simply about creating an engaging learning environment, there are many other factors that contribute to this space. But what this focus does create at the trailhead of our journey is a profound impact on student development, academic achievement and social-emotional wellbeing (Van Pham, 2024).

When curiosity is combined with empathy for the world students live in, and inclusivity is embedded in learning every day, students develop stronger cognitive skills, form deeper connections with peers and become more engaged, enlightened and motivated learners.

In a connected classroom and indeed, a connected world, empathic curiosity and inclusivity are the drivers of positive change. Research shows their impact on reducing bias, promoting open-mindedness and on the importance of asking questions not only about things, but about people (Dolbier et al., 2025). This then opens conversation to the exploration of new perspectives.

Opening this part of the journey develops students' ability to think not only in problems or about the future (components we spend far too much time on in schools currently), but on becoming flexible in their thinking and less likely to rely on stereotypes (Dweck, 2017).

A flexible thinker is a *connected learner.* Connected learners are preparing for today, not tomorrow. We cannot delay by continuing to be engrossed in the preparation for a future that doesn't exist yet.

To develop this flexibility, students need to understand that working with people is the key to effective learning today. Building connection between children of all ages requires teachers to explicitly discuss, embed and model equal status, cooperative learning and shared understanding. These elements must be embedded in classroom discussions and collaborative activities (Cai et al., 2023).

This not only enhances classroom relationships but also prepares students for today's world where cultural competency and empathy are essential. Early sharing of voices, identities and lived experiences create not only feelings of acceptance but recognition that people are stronger together.

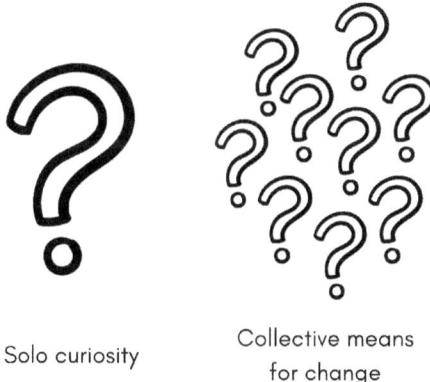

Solo curiosity

Collective means for change

By shifting the focus at the trailhead, teachers have the power to generate young citizens who, in alignment with constructivist theories of education, actively question their world rather than just accept it as delivered (Vygotsky, 1978). When students are taught to question in this way, practise evaluating evidence and engage in deep discussions often, they develop higher-order thinking skills that extend beyond the classroom.

Skills the world needs *now*.

The ability to think critically, embrace diverse perspectives and engage in meaningful discussions are essential skills not in the future, but in the interconnected world we live in presently. When curiosity and inclusivity become core elements of education, students are better equipped to navigate complex social issues, build meaningful relationships and contribute positively to society.

By focusing on connecting students to each other, teachers aren't just improving student learning outcomes, they're shaping future citizens who are open-minded, empathetic and capable of engaging with the world in thoughtful and meaningful ways.

Where to next?

Your approach to fostering both empathic curiosity and inclusivity must evolve with each class, lesson and student interaction. As educators, our role is to continuously reflect on these practices, seek new ways to create inclusive learning experiences and adapt our approaches based on the needs of our students. Framing our work around connection helps us to make this a part of our culture, not just our routine.

The following questions and strategies can support you in reflecting on your current approach and continuing to grow a learning environment where every student feels seen, heard and valued.

1. Are students curious about each other's perspectives?

When students are genuinely interested in one another's experiences, cultures and ideas, it creates space for empathy and deeper learning. Curiosity cannot be forced, but it can be modelled, nurtured and celebrated. Consider:

- Do students ask thoughtful questions about their peers' ideas and experiences?
- Are classroom discussions structured in ways that invite multiple viewpoints and challenge assumptions?
- How do I respond when students express unfamiliar or conflicting perspectives?

2. Is every student's identity represented and respected?

Representation matters. Students are more likely to engage when they see their backgrounds, languages and experiences reflected in the curriculum and when they're invited to explore and share them authentically. Consider:

- Does my curriculum reflect a wide range of voices, cultures and identities?
- Am I actively including narratives that challenge dominant viewpoints?
- Do students have opportunities to share their own stories in meaningful, affirming ways?

3. Do students feel safe to speak, listen and take intellectual risks?

An inclusive classroom isn't just diverse – it's emotionally safe. Students need to know that their contributions will be met with respect, and that mistakes are part of learning. Consider:

- Are quieter students offered different ways to participate (for example, writing, small groups)?
- Do I model and reinforce active listening and empathy in discussions?
- Am I creating space for students to explore uncertainty and disagreement without fear?

4. Am I continuing to grow my own inclusive practice?

Inclusivity isn't static, it grows with ongoing reflection, learning and collaboration. Our own curiosity as educators fuels the kind of classroom culture we hope to create. Consider:

- Am I regularly engaging with research, PD or colleagues to expand my understanding?
- Do I gather student feedback to learn what's working and what's not?
- Am I willing to try new strategies and adjust based on student needs and responses?

5. Am I building a culture where connection drives learning?

When students feel connected to each other, to their learning and to the classroom community, motivation and empathy flourish. This isn't about reaching a finish line, it's about building a culture that grows over time. Consider:

- Do students feel a sense of belonging in the classroom every day? How do I know?
- Are we celebrating progress in how we treat and learn from one another, not just academic growth?
- Do I make time to pause, reflect and appreciate moments of authentic connection?

TL;DR

Key takeaways

1. **Empathic curiosity opens the door for connection**
   When students are encouraged to be curious about each other, not just the content, they develop empathy, deeper understanding and stronger collaboration. It's not just about asking questions but about asking the *right* ones with genuine interest in others.

2. **Inclusivity is more than presence – it's participation with purpose**
   A truly inclusive classroom actively reflects, values and elevates diverse voices. It's a space where every student feels empowered to contribute, and where differences are embraced as essential to the learning journey.

3. **Psychological safety unlocks critical thinking**
   For students to think critically and take intellectual risks, they must first feel safe to speak, wonder and be wrong. Curiosity and inclusivity flourish in classrooms grounded in respect, active listening and trust.

4. **Representation drives relevance and engagement**
   Students engage more deeply when they see themselves in what they learn and when they're invited to connect that learning to their identities, experiences and communities. Representation isn't an add-on, it's foundational.

5. **Connection is a culture, not a one-off strategy**
   Building a connected classroom takes daily practice. When curiosity and inclusivity are embedded in routines, modelled by educators and nurtured through intentional structures, students grow into compassionate, open-minded learners who are ready for today's world – not just tomorrow's.

CHAPTER 7

Navigating together
Building classroom community

At the trailhead, climbers recognise unity as essential to the journey ahead. They align expectations, affirm mutual support and understand that individual success depends on collective strength. This is more than a moment of readiness, it's a commitment to community. Building classroom community moves us from merely gathering students together to cultivating an environment where every learner feels actively included, valued and essential. Without genuine community, students may share space without sharing purpose, present but not truly belonging.

This chapter explores why community matters profoundly to learning, and how to foster a sense of belonging that endures beyond initial connections. Strong classroom communities are intentional; they grow from daily, meaningful interactions and collective responsibility. Because, ultimately, a connected classroom doesn't just facilitate learning, it transforms it.

The big two

Learning is belonging, belonging is community

A classroom should be more than just a physical space where students gather for instruction, it should be considered dynamic, evolving, interwoven – a *community.*

Would you consider your classroom to align with these adjectives?

I believe each classroom *is* a community and the strength of that community determines whether students are able and willing to engage in meaningful learning.

When students experience a deep sense of belonging along The Connection Journey, they're more likely to be an active partner within that community. Equally, when classroom cohesion is weak, students may withdraw, disengage or feel isolated, significantly impacting both their learning and overall wellbeing (Allen & Boyle, 2022).

A robust body of research supports the importance of classroom community in shaping both academic and social outcomes, research you've likely heard of but perhaps not engaged with (Korpershoek et al., 2020; St-Amand et al., 2017). Lev Vygotsky (1978) emphasised that learning is fundamentally a social process, developed through interaction with others. His Sociocultural Theory (see Figure 8) highlights that students don't learn in isolation but through collaboration with peers and teachers.

Figure 8: Vygotsky's Sociocultural Theory of Cognitive Development

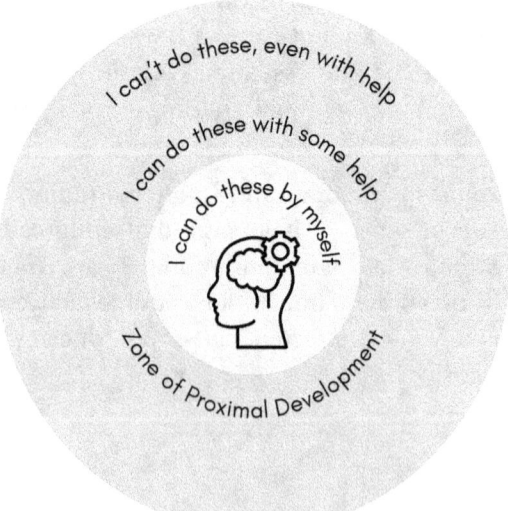

(ADAPTED FROM VYGOTSKY, 1978)

Similarly, Visible Learning Meta^X (2024) has found that classroom cohesion has an effect size of 0.66, meaning it has a substantial impact on student achievement, up there with instructional quality, which seems to be one of the big 'fixes' for education at the moment.

To understand how to take your current classroom community and build and sustain a stronger one supported by connection, we must explore two essential questions:
1. How does a strong sense of community (*actually*) impact learning?
2. What factors contribute to sustainable classroom belonging?

These questions will help us examine the ways in which connection enhances academic performance and how a sense of community transforms the learning experience.

1. How does a strong sense of community (*actually*) impact learning?

A well-connected classroom provides the foundation for student success (Darling-Hammond & Cook-Harvey, 2018). As discussed earlier in this book, support creates the conditions for safety, but to take that initial safety beyond base camp and onto the trailhead, we need to look at sustaining the work we've already done and build as we take each step of the journey.

If the goal is for our students to develop a sense of belonging, they need to feel a sense of psychological safety early, so they are therefore more likely to engage more deeply, act on challenges with confidence and persist through difficulties (Edmondson, 2018). We need to build on our work completed in the previous chapters of this book.

In *The Fearless Organization: Creating Psychological Safety in the Workplace for Learning, Innovation, and Growth*, Dr Amy Edmondson (2018), Novartis professor of leadership and management at the Harvard Business School, states:

> "Creating psychological safety is a constant process of smaller and larger corrections that add up to forward progress. Like tacking upwind, you must zig right and then zag left and then right again, never able to head exactly where you want to go and never quite knowing when the wind will change."

Sounds a lot like a statement drawn from all the 'future of work' reports I've read lately!

The Belonging Hypothesis (Baumeister & Leary, 1995) reinforces this idea, arguing that the human need for belonging is as fundamental as the need for

food and shelter. They state that when students feel disconnected from their peers or the classroom environment, they may experience:
- Anxiety about participation
- Reduced motivation to engage with learning
- Disengagement from academic tasks

Feeling familiar?

Beyond individual benefits, a strong classroom community fosters collective responsibility – the idea that students feel accountable not just for their own learning but for the success of their peers. Quickly skim any curriculum or learning standards anywhere in the world and I guarantee this type of collaborative learning is a valuable and (a likely) mandated component.

Why then, not a focus on connection?

When students build and then can take ownership of their classroom community, they're more likely to:
- Develop a sense of shared purpose in learning
- Build mutual respect and trust among their peers
- Recognise that collaboration enhances academic and social growth (St-Amand et al., 2017)

In other words, they become authentically connected, improving academic achievement, self-esteem and social health and wellbeing (Pitman, 2024). A cooperative, in its truest sense.

The role of community in learning isn't just about making students feel cosy, it's a fundamental component of motivation, engagement and success (Allen et al., 2021). When students experience a sense of belonging, community and connection, learning becomes more than an individual task, it becomes the shared journey we're seeking.

2. What factors contribute to sustainable classroom belonging?

Building a sense of belonging takes time.

Let's get that out on the table immediately.

There are ways you can build belonging and comfort just through osmosis, hoping that it builds itself through good intentions. I've seen it. But to truly embrace a focus on connection is going to require some consistent time and effort to evolve relationships, experiences and expectations into something that dramatically shapes the learning environment for the better.

This type of environment requires nurturing. Moving from relationships to belonging requires more than a nicely decorated classroom or a welcome sign, it needs those things to represent something, a feeling, rather than just covering up the graffiti or the '80s paint job on the wall.

It grows through attention, patience and the willingness to show up, day after day, with intention. It's not loud or performative. More often, it's quiet. It lives in the way we listen. The way we make space. The way we adapt when something isn't working.

Belonging is nurtured when students feel safe enough to bring their full selves into the room (Allen et al., 2021). When connection is prioritised in this way, not just to an academic end but as an essential part of the learning experience itself, identity isn't just tolerated but affirmed (Pendergast et al., 2018).

And it's nurtured in community. Belonging doesn't fall solely on the teacher's shoulders. It's built when every member of the classroom sees themselves as responsible for the wellbeing of others (Ibarra, 2022). That kind of culture doesn't emerge overnight, but it can be built along the journey – if we're willing to give it time each day to do it.

So, answering this question is about asking: are we serious about creating spaces where belonging isn't only felt but sustained?

If so, we must treat it like something that has a heartbeat. Something that needs our ongoing attention. Because what we nurture now will give us the direction for the mountains and possibilities ahead.

Unpack your journey

Why community matters

Up until this point in the book, I believe I've made a fairly strong argument for community and connection. The importance of community in education is well-established across multiple fields, from psychology to educational research. Building a strong classroom community isn't just for the website or the school tour, it's a fundamental part of ensuring that students thrive academically, socially and emotionally (Deng, 2024; Pendergast et al., 2018).

Beyond all this evidence, however, community is simply a need that is felt. A great, left-of-field example is the online gaming community.

There are a lot of video games available and not all of them require or are designed to be played cooperatively or online in large groups, but the ones that do offer this are incredibly popular, especially with teenagers.

We could sit and discuss the concerns with some of the communication, the interactions and the addictive or non-addictive components of on and offline video games, but the fact is, they're thriving communities of young (and older) people from around the world, sharing common interests and one of the most valuable assets we have: our *time*.

The aspect I want to focus on here is *membership*. Communities require people to actively commit to them, otherwise they don't grow or, frankly, exist at all.

Common interests in gaming, music, sports and arts, among many others, draw people together and create sustainable communities while doing so. In the case of video gaming, like all communities, not all the aspects are positive, but a gigantic number of them are. These are authentic communities because they're based on choice, supported by commitment and in many cases, reinforcing and connection-building (Sofoluke, 2024).

They create a space, albeit virtually, where people of all ages feel they belong.

Your classroom and your school should offer the same feeling – now imagine saying that to a teenager!

LIVE: A teenager's reaction to that last thought

In a connected classroom we ideally want this feeling of community to build from day one. The threads of collective engagement, persistence and responsibility should permeate the entire environment and everything it encompasses (Allen et al., 2021). We need to actively reframe connection from a tool in the kit to a need that must be addressed not for the sake of the class, but the sake of the humans within it.

Belonging as the motivator

This reframing is why I like Baumeister and Leary's (1995) work on the belonging hypothesis, stating that the need to belong is a powerful, fundamental and extremely pervasive motivation. Their research suggests that when individuals experience consistent, positive interactions within a stable environment, they feel a sense of security and wellbeing that nourishes, not simply satisfies, a deep and innate human need.

> **In a classroom setting, students who feel they belong are more likely to:**
> - Have higher self-esteem and academic motivation
> - Demonstrate lower levels of anxiety and stress

- Engage in prosocial behaviours, such as helping peers and participating in group activities
  (Allen et al., 2021; Deng, 2024; Pendergast et al., 2018; St-Amand et al., 2017)

This need is based in a history of collective responsibility. We, once upon a time, needed to work together to survive, now we need to work together to *thrive* (St-Amand et al., 2017).

The bottom line: a connected classroom isn't teacher-centred but *community-centred*.

I've worked with teenagers predominantly, and through this work I know from first-hand experience, when students feel they belong to their learning environment, they're more likely to engage meaningfully, help peers and demonstrate resilience when faced with challenges.

I also know the same is true of primary-aged students and, let's be honest, many adults I know also. Again, we're human, we need this.

Signs of a strong classroom community

A well-connected classroom doesn't happen by accident; it's built intentionally over time (Greenwood & Kelly, 2019). I know I've mentioned this many times, but it cannot be stressed enough!

At this stage it's important to take a step back and examine your existing community, whether that be micro or macro, classroom or school.

What kind of community do you have?

Important to note: you will have one; no school has zero community, but what are its characteristics?

Some key indicators that a strong sense of community exists include:
- *Students support each other academically and emotionally* – they celebrate each other's successes and provide encouragement during struggles.
- *Classroom discussions feel inclusive and respectful* – all students feel their voice matters, and differences in perspective are valued rather than dismissed.
- *A culture of shared ownership is present* – students contribute to class traditions, help manage the environment and take pride in their learning space.

  (Deng, 2024; Lubicz-Nawrocka & Bao, 2025)

Creating this kind of culture is tough, which is why it's at the trailhead of our journey, but the rewards are immense. A strong classroom community leads to greater engagement, stronger relationships, a sense of belonging and higher academic achievement, all vital 'must-haves' not just for The Connection Journey, but a future of learning and personal growth.

What to do?

The key to creating a thriving classroom community is to embed connection into the daily routines and interactions of the class so that students experience a sense of belonging not just occasionally, but every day. We seek this intention into action here because the start of any journey, the first steps and challenges of the trailhead, are where connection is tested.

Below are four practical and research-backed strategies to build a strong classroom community. Each is designed to strengthen the ties between the humans in your classrooms to prepare them for the connective challenges ahead.

1. Think co-op, not collab (yet)

We focus a lot on collaboration in schools these days, or to be perhaps more accurate, we talk (a lot!) about collaboration in schools these days, but again, talk is cheap.

True collaboration comes with time and requires connection to have formed to be effective (Deng, 2024). At the trailhead we should, therefore, focus on cooperation rather than collaboration, to introduce shared contribution, as the community within our classroom starts to form.

Cooperative learning strategies are essential for building this connection. When structured well, they ensure all students have a role, a voice and an opportunity to contribute, both building and strengthening the community they're members of (Deng, 2024).

> **Strategic cooperation**
>
> I'm a fan of the classics. These three remain favourites because they work. What's different here is the lens of connection through which we apply them:
>
> - *Jigsaw Method* – each student becomes an 'expert' on part of a topic and teaches it to peers. This boosts academic understanding and nurtures peer trust, respect and interdependence.
> - *Peer Coaching* – when students support each other's learning via peer feedback, paired problem-solving or study buddies, they build stronger relationships and accountability.

- *Think-Pair-Share* – a simple, low-risk way to get all students engaging in discussion. It ensures everyone is heard and reduces anxiety.

2. Give thanks

One of the most powerful and simple ways to build classroom community is through appreciation. In the last chapter, we explored empathic curiosity. Here, we apply it.

Schools are marketed as champions of young people, but who are we really championing? Often, it's programs or achievements, not the students themselves. While awards for academics, sport, science and increasingly the arts are important (though humanities still need more love), they don't always build connection.

Genuine recognition should go beyond marks and certificates. When students notice and acknowledge each other's efforts, kindness and growth, peer relationships and classroom morale improve. This is essential work early on The Connection Journey.

Start with your own class. Yes, it might feel awkward at first, but stick with it. Make appreciation a regular part of classroom culture and watch it spread.

Promote gratitude, recognise people

Try these approaches:

- *Shout-Out Board* – a space, physical or digital, where students can post appreciations, named or anonymous. It encourages students to notice kindness and effort.
- *"What I appreciate about you" circles* – at the end of a week, month or term, structured peer appreciation improves wellbeing and strengthens relationships.
- *Positive feedback prompts* – encourage students to say things like *"I liked what [classmate] said because…"* to build respectful dialogue.

3. Squad up

Schools constantly offer chances to form and re-form groups. While the first few weeks of school set the tone, connection evolves throughout the year. That means your approach to building it should be dynamic, too.

When asked, *"When is the best time to start working on connection?"* my answer is always: *"Right now."*

Yes, the beginning of the year offers formal activities to build rapport, but that isn't the only opportunity. Connection doesn't need to follow the school calendar. Use every chance to create peer relationships and a sense of belonging. Every time you connect a student to someone or something in your class, you increase engagement, motivation, support and meaning (Deng, 2024).

The key to great team building? *Purpose.* If you want to avoid the dreaded 'icebreaker' eyeroll, remember: your aim isn't just for students to meet, but to see each other as allies.

> **Be effective. Be, be effective**
>
> Try these purposeful activities:
>
> - *Icebreakers with purpose* – avoid surface-level questions. Instead, use activities that help students share strengths, values and interests.
> - *"Find someone who…"* – students search for peers with shared experiences.
> - *Personalised intros* – have students introduce themselves with three words that represent them.
> - *Collaborative problem-solving* – Escape Room challenges, marshmallow towers, puzzles! These tasks build teamwork and a shared sense of achievement.

4. Pivot. Pivot. Pivot!

Leadership is a set of skills that all teachers hope to instil in their students, but it requires a little more than hope.

A thriving and connected classroom community is one where students feel a sense of responsibility, not just for their own learning but for the success of the entire group. One way to embed this principle is through rotating leadership roles, which empowers students and creates a sense of collective ownership over the learning environment, providing an opportunity for students to step outside of their social role (Deng, 2024).

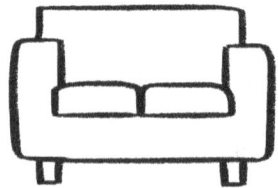

Rotating leadership roles is not too difficult
(Unlike moving a couch upstairs)

Creating and consistently rotating through roles, from primary to secondary school, works well because it leverages skills and knowledge that aren't assessed (Khatter et al., 2024). When a student engages in a task they have never attempted before, it creates an opportunity for deep learning. When paired with the removal of constant measurement, it can also reduce stress and anxiety. They learn new skills and see the impact it has immediately on their classroom community.

These types of roles:

- Increase student engagement – when students have specific responsibilities, they invest more deeply in classroom life (Ryan & Deci, 2000).
- Encourage peer accountability – when students take turns leading discussions or managing tasks, they develop a sense of responsibility for the group's success, rather than just their own individual performance.
- Develop leadership and communication skills – regular exposure to leadership builds confidence, communication skills and problem-solving abilities (Dwivedi & Srivastava, 2021).

> **Roles to play**
>
> If you're not sure where to start, try these:
>
> - *Discussion Leaders* – students facilitate conversations using inclusive prompts.
> - *Classroom Ambassadors* – they welcome new students, assist visitors or introduce class events.
> - *Learning Captains* – weekly roles like tech support or materials manager build collective responsibility.
> - *Peer Mentors* – pair older students with younger ones to create cross-year connections and mutual support.

Why do it?

Community is essential to connection. We address it here early on in our journey not because it's insignificant, but because it provides incredible support for the ascent to come. I hope to have compiled a compelling argument in this chapter so far, but in fairness, you may be asking: *Why? When? Are you serious?*

- *Why* – as in, why focus on this when my classes seem to do quite well without changes?
- *When* – as in, when am I going to find time to make this a priority?
- *Are you serious* – as in, well perhaps that makes sense on its own.

Let's address these three in reverse. Firstly, I'm *incredibly serious*. Classrooms with a strong sense of connection function more effectively because students feel invested, accountable and supported (Korpershoek et al., 2020).

Taking this journey and engaging with the initial challenges of the trailhead are necessary. I know these types of endeavours require effort, but that effort will reap incredible benefits for your students and your future practice. I'm confident that if you commit, you won't go back to teaching without connection being front of mind.

Community is an essential human need and one that has been stripped from the educational experience at all levels in favour of testing, measurement and academic bureaucracy (Pitman, 2024). We owe it to our students, current and future, to focus on connection and to gradually distance ourselves from any model of teaching that serves a historical purpose no longer relevant.

The real question is: *Are you serious?*

Second question. *When?* This in my mind is an easier question to answer than you may think. All that is required is some modification to the language being used. This isn't a question of *when*, it's a question of *how*. I've had the discussion of time on many occasions, and I always come back to this simple realisation about myself:

> *If I had more time, I'd just fill it up with something else.*

Perhaps that speaks volumes about me and less about education, but there is no more time, so as teachers we cannot wait on initiatives that will provide benefits to our community (Pitman, 2024). That time isn't coming. So, it's not that we *shouldn't* ask *"when"*, it's that we *cannot* ask *"when"*.

The real question is: *how will I* introduce this? With extra emphasis on the *will*. It's happening. To be perfectly honest, if you're still thinking *"when"*, you're probably actually thinking, *"No, I'm not going to do this."*

The last one, *why*, I hope has in some ways been answered. There are decades of research highlighting the benefits of a connected classroom community from the Visible Learning work (Hattie, 2009; 2023) back to Vygotsky's (1978) Sociocultural Theory. While your classes may currently perform well, intentionally fostering a sense of community and connection is critical to preparing students for the uncertain and rapidly changing future they will face.

More recent research emphasises that community-oriented classrooms equip students with essential skills such as adaptability, resilience, collaboration and emotional intelligence – competencies increasingly necessary in navigating complexities and uncertainties ahead (Hammack et al., 2020).

A strong classroom community not only enhances academic outcomes but also nurtures students' capacity to confidently engage with the unpredictable social, economic and technological landscapes they will inevitably encounter (OECD, 2019).

Community is a *human need*.

Where to next?

Building a connected classroom is an ongoing journey, evolving through consistent reflection, adaptation and meaningful student involvement. Just as a climber pauses to assess progress and recalibrate the route, educators must regularly pause, reflect and adapt their approaches to maintain a thriving community. Connection deepens over time, especially when educators remain intentional about nurturing a classroom culture of belonging, collaboration and shared ownership.

The following questions and strategies can support your continued reflection and help you foster a classroom where connection consistently strengthens and evolves over time.

1. Are all students actively participating in the community?

Participation doesn't always look the same for every student, but all should feel invited, comfortable and willing to engage. Thoughtful reflection can uncover barriers and opportunities to engage all learners. Consider:

- Are there students who consistently remain on the fringes of discussions, group activities or class projects?
- How might I create lower-risk opportunities for these students to participate meaningfully?
- Have I individually checked in with quieter or less engaged students to understand their perspective?

2. Do students naturally support one another beyond structured activities?

An authentically connected classroom extends beyond teacher-led activities into organic interactions. When students begin supporting one another naturally, a deeper sense of community emerges. Consider:

- Do students offer help and support to peers without teacher prompting, or does collaboration only occur during assigned activities?
- Are students recognising and appreciating each other's efforts, achievements and contributions?
- Is there a positive culture of peer accountability, where students encourage and influence each other constructively?

3. Are classroom traditions and rituals still meaningful?

Traditions and rituals are powerful tools for building connection, but their effectiveness can change as student interests and dynamics evolve. Consider:

- Do the established class rituals and routines continue to resonate meaningfully with students?
- How might rituals or traditions need to adapt as group dynamics shift over time?
- Can students propose new traditions or rituals to better reflect their current interests and relationships?

4. Am I regularly seeking and incorporating student input?

True community-building thrives when students feel their voices matter. Incorporating student perspectives creates a stronger sense of ownership and engagement in classroom culture. Consider:

- Am I regularly asking students how they feel about our classroom culture and what they would like to change or improve?
- How am I gathering student feedback (for example, informal conversations, quick surveys, end-of-term reflections)?
- Do students see their input visibly reflected in our classroom decisions and agreements?

5. Are we actively celebrating our growth and progress as a community?

Recognising and celebrating growth motivates students to continue investing in connection, especially when the journey is highlighted as clearly as the achievements. Consider:

- Do students regularly hear and celebrate the progress they have made together as a community?
- Am I acknowledging specific moments where students overcame challenges, showed kindness or significantly contributed to the community?
- How can we more intentionally mark these milestones to sustain momentum?

TL;DR

Key takeaways

1. **Belonging transforms learning into a communal experience**
   Learning thrives within strong classroom communities. When students feel they truly belong, they engage more deeply, take intellectual risks and persist through challenges. Belonging isn't a passive experience; it's actively nurtured through everyday interactions and shared responsibilities.

2. **Community is a fundamental human need driving student engagement**
   The Belonging Hypothesis emphasises that students have a deep, intrinsic need to feel connected and accepted. When this need is met through a supportive classroom community, students experience increased motivation, higher self-esteem, reduced anxiety and greater academic engagement.

3. **Community-building is intentional, ongoing and reflective**
   A robust classroom community doesn't form by accident, it requires consistent effort, intentional practices and ongoing reflection. Teachers and students alike must continuously nurture connection through deliberate, daily routines and actions.

4. **Collective responsibility cultivates motivation and resilience**
   When students share responsibility for their learning environment, they become more invested, motivated and resilient. Cooperative strategies like peer coaching, structured appreciation and rotating leadership roles create a culture of shared ownership and mutual accountability.

5. **Connection is a human need, not an educational luxury**
   Community and connection are essential, foundational human needs. Prioritising genuine connection in classrooms not only boosts academic success, but also equips students with essential skills, like adaptability, collaboration and emotional intelligence, that they need for an increasingly complex and uncertain future.

Collaboration

True collaboration is more than working together.
It's building together, with trust, purpose and shared ownership.

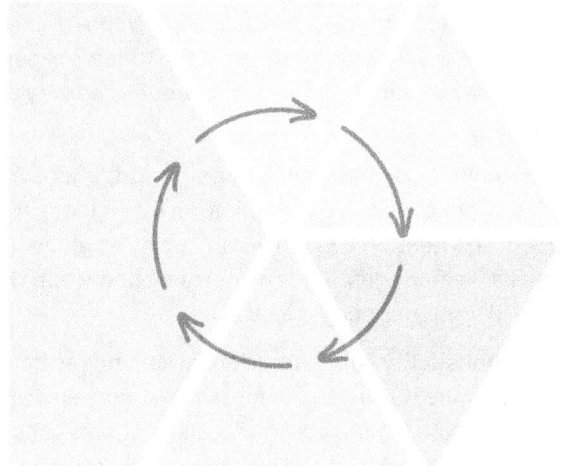

Connection pause

List the last group task your students did.

Now rate it (1-5) on: shared ownership, student voice and depth of engagement.

What could you tweak to deepen the experience?

PART 4
THE FIRST CLIMB

Cultivating an environment for connection

> "The strength of the team is each individual member. The strength of each member is the team"
>
> – PHIL JACKSON

The first climb is rarely the hardest, but it's often the most revealing. It's where the rhythm of the mountain starts to speak to you. Junko Tabei, a Japanese mountaineer who became the first woman to summit Everest in 1975, described the early stages of her climbs as a chance to test her mettle and adjust her focus. The mountain isn't conquered here, but respect is earned. The first climb shows you what you're up against – and what you're capable of.

Here, we begin the climb purposeful, tested and ready to respond to the challenge. Part 4 is about *why* we climb and *how* we sustain the movement forward. It explores what gives learning its meaning and momentum. We're no longer simply walking together; we're climbing with intention. And intention, without purpose and adaptability, won't carry us far. We begin in *Chapter 8: Guiding the way*, where we look at the role of purpose in learning. Purpose isn't a luxury, it's a compass. It gives direction when the path narrows and resolve when the gradient steepens. This chapter explores what it means to connect learning to something that matters now, not someday. From here we move to *Chapter 9: Finding your rhythm*, where we unpack the challenge of differentiation. Differentiation isn't about simplifying the climb; it's about recognising different approaches to the same summit. When learning is designed to meet students where they are, it builds trust, motivation and momentum.

Together, these chapters reflect the work of the connected classroom in motion. The journey is no longer hypothetical. It's happening in real time, with real students, in all their complexity. We're no longer preparing for connection; we're doing the work that sustains it. The trail still rises ahead, and there will be harder climbs. But for now, we've found our rhythm, anchored in purpose, and ready to rise.

Let's keep going.

CHAPTER 8
Guiding the way
Connecting learning to purpose

As climbers ascend, they need more than strength, they need direction. Without a clear sense of purpose, even the most determined steps can lead to nowhere. Purpose not only offers clarity but fuels the drive to keep going when the trail steepens. In classrooms, it's no different. Connecting learning to purpose transforms education from a set of disconnected tasks into a meaningful, personal journey.

This chapter explores how purpose deepens motivation and connects students to their learning in powerful ways. When students understand why their learning matters now, not just in some distant future, engagement becomes more than participation; it becomes passion. Purposeful classrooms foster curiosity, creativity and connection, giving students tools that aren't just useful, but usable. Because when learners see the point, they start to see their place – not just in the lesson, but in the world beyond it.

The big two

There is no spoon

If schools were cutlery drawers, they would be full of spoons. Maybe the odd fork or knife for a few keen students to tackle a real challenge, but mostly, schools are built for regurgitation, and you get further with a nice big spoon.

> "Spoon feeding in the long run teaches us nothing but the shape of the spoon" – E.M. Forster

A little dramatic perhaps, but I think this holds true.

As I write these very words an article has just appeared on my social media feeds with the title 'Why NAPLAN alone won't future-proof students'* and I'm dumbfounded.

Are we really to the point where we're expecting standardised assessment to drive learning?

There is a beautiful, natural curiosity in small children. I'm fortunate to see this every day as a father. My daughter runs around moving from picnics to colouring and even to supermarkets where the automated register breaks down mid-scan of a plastic tomato. It's brilliant to see her mind free and exploring.

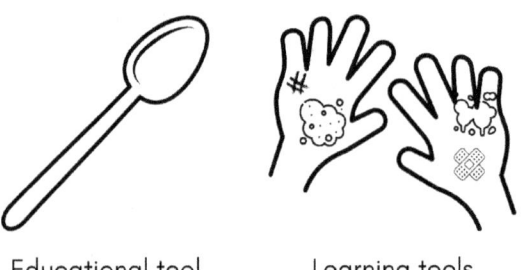

Educational tool   Learning tools

Our students, even the most resistant, are also curious, but schooling often dulls that curiosity by treating learning as a checklist rather than an exploration (Post & van der Molen, 2018; Singh & Manjaly, 2022).

Earlier, we explored empathic curiosity. Now, with a heart more open to community, we need to consider the purpose of learning. For me, that purpose is curiosity, creativity and connection.

---

* For those outside of Australia, NAPLAN is an annual assessment for students in Years 3, 5, 7 and 9. NAPLAN results don't measure overall school quality, yet results are often used to this effect much more than they're utilised to inform student progress.

Too often, students ask, *"Why are we learning this?"* or *"When will I use this?"* and if left unanswered, those questions breed disengagement. I wonder: why are we not answering them? I've heard teachers claim, *"They never ask any questions"* even when I've heard students asking these very things.

Could it be that we're unsure ourselves? Do we avoid answering because we're not confident we know?

We need clarity on the purpose of what's explored in our classrooms. This clarity empowers students to engage creatively, connect learning to their lives and tackle challenges with curiosity (Adeoye et al., 2024; Madison, 2023). Purpose-driven learning ditches the spoon in favour of whatever tool will help students connect and progress. When they understand why they're learning, they're more likely to:

- Take ownership
- Develop intrinsic motivation
- Retain knowledge because it's meaningful

A strong sense of purpose transforms learning from something students must do into something they want to do. To understand how this transformation occurs, we must explore two key questions:

1. How does purpose-driven learning boost engagement?
2. How can we support students to see the value in their learning?

These questions highlight the psychological and practical foundations of purposeful learning and explore how educators can design experiences that ignite curiosity, increase motivation and sustain meaningful engagement.

1. How does purpose-driven learning boost engagement?

You'll see throughout this chapter, there is a lot of research demonstrating that motivation thrives when learning is meaningful (Reeve, 2024). Similarly, there is a lot of research that focuses on strategies for increased engagement, particularly of late, as the media has begun a nationwide focus on disengagement since the COVID-19 pandemic (Burger et al., 2024; Fayed & Cummings, 2021; Oranga & Matere, 2022). These two components aren't isolated in make, model or causation, so it serves no purpose to separate them in our discussion.

Purpose boosts motivation, which leads to increased engagement (Kong, 2021). Before we look at any evidence of this fact, you must know it to be true. As adults, in the classroom and outside, when we feel the work is purposeful and has meaning, we're more likely to do it and, therefore, learn from it (Malin, 2021).

If we know this about ourselves, why is it so hard to transfer to our students?

Self-Determination Theory (SDT) (Ryan & Deci, 2020) is a theory I often return to when unpacking motivation, as it explains, in relatively simple terms, that individuals are most motivated when they experience:

- **Autonomy** – a sense of control over their learning.
- **Competence** – the belief that they can succeed and improve.
- **Relatedness** – a connection to others and a sense of belonging.

To put it in plain English: students will engage with your lesson if they know why they're doing it and that 'why' makes them feel it will be worth it.

Theories like SDT gives us a recipe; we just need to start following it.

2. How can we support students to see the value in their learning?

Teachers, I must be clear, myself included, have a real habit of limiting the *value* conversation with students to several less than useful statements, including:

- You will need it for the exam
- Some things we just need to cover, I have no choice
- I'm not sure why, but let's get through it

These are useless distractions and, despite some honesty and good intentions, they're harmful to our students. A student should never feel as though their concentration, input and time aren't valuable (Willingham, 2021).

> **Value (*noun*) is defined as:**
> *the regard that something is held to deserve; the importance, worth, or usefulness of something* (from the Oxford English Dictionary).
>
> Do any of those previous statements, or the many more like them, align with this definition?

If we want students to feel genuinely invested in their learning, connected to the skills and knowledge, and feel as though it's valuable, we need to move beyond surface-level relevance and embed purpose at the heart of our classrooms.

This means designing lessons that:

- Allow students to see *current* real-world applications of what they're learning
- Connect learning to their personal interests and goals
- Engage students in projects that extend beyond the classroom

Authentic and valuable learning is linked to the world, both micro and macro. It's full of opportunities to draw on personal skills and interests and governed by choice, creation and challenge (Darling-Hammond et al., 2020). Our schools already do many of these things in isolation, but when they do, it's not through the eyes of our current generation of students, it's through the eyes of my great-grandparents.

It's not hard to see why that doesn't seem very valuable to our students.

Unpack your journey

Why are we doing this?

A purposeful education is one where students see their learning as meaningful, relevant and connected to their own lives (Malin, 2021). When students understand *why* they're learning something and how it applies beyond the classroom, they're far more likely to engage, persist and take ownership of their learning journey (Malone & Lepper, 2021).

Providing students with a clear purpose is, therefore, a key driver of intrinsic motivation as we head into the first climb of our journey. When students can see how their learning relates to their personal experiences, goals or future aspirations, they become more engaged and self-motivated (Barr, 2024). Instead of relying on external incentives like grades or praise, they find satisfaction in the learning process itself (Ryan & Deci, 2020).

Working towards purpose is ingrained in our psyche; our brains are wired to pay attention when we believe something is important (Damon & Malin, 2020) – 'believe' being the key term here. We cannot be told something is important; we must *know* it to be true ourselves.

Once, perhaps, these types of tasks linked to our survival, through provision of food, shelter or water; now, we're trying to pigeonhole them into a single teaching period and are frustrated at the results. It doesn't really make sense.

Put your thinking hat on

Cognitive engagement, defined as the psychological investment a student puts into the learning process (i.e. value), deepens when learning is connected to a student's life (Hattie, 2023). When students see and understand these connections between classroom content and their own experiences, they move beyond rote memorisation to deeper understanding. This engagement leads to greater curiosity, more meaningful discussions and a willingness to persist with the work at hand (Swain, 2024).

While much of our current model of education relies on memorisation, we need to ensure the connections are even more pronounced. Brown et al. (2014) found that students retain information better when it's tied to not only meaningful experiences but reflection on those experiences.

Memorisation without context often leads to rapid forgetting, whereas knowledge connected to real-world applications is more likely to stick (Brown et al., 2014). While I'd never advocate blindly for all aspects of the education system as it currently stands, we're building connection in our schools now, not in a rosy vision of the future.

Choose your hat

Ultimately, if we can connect our students to their learning through purpose, value and intrinsic motivation, we will be working within the box, but not in the way it's been prescribed to us.

Finding our drive

In *Drive: The Surprising Truth About What Motivates Us*, Daniel Pink (2009) expands on SDT and building intrinsic motivation, emphasising that motivation is strongest when driven by:

- **Autonomy** – the freedom to explore and make choices in learning
- **Mastery** – the desire to improve and develop new skills
- **Purpose** – a meaningful reason to engage with the material

Pink explains that without purpose, learning becomes an exercise in hoop-jumping (Pink, 2009). In our classrooms, this equates to students completing tasks simply to meet external expectations (such as ours) rather than because they see value in them. This leads to the rote memorisation, disengagement and a lack of meaningful learning experiences that are characterising the school experience at present.

I'm certainly not an advocate for clearing the path on our climb for our students and not removing them from accountability either. However, if an explicit focus on purposeful learning leads to students who are more likely to persevere and critically think through challenges, emotionally connect to what they're learning and retain more information from each learning experience, we have no other choice.

A functional classroom is great. But a purposeful classroom doesn't just address content, it inspires students to connect their learning to their lives and aspirations.

This is the goal as we begin our *ascent*.

What to do?

Bringing purpose into learning doesn't require a complete transformation overnight. Instead, small but intentional changes can shift students' perceptions of their education from something abstract to something personally meaningful.

The following strategies provide actionable ways to connect learning to students' lives, their futures and the world around them.

1. Is this real life?

Students engage more when they can see how classroom learning applies to their everyday experiences (Malin, 2021). So much of our current approach to education is about pathways and preparation for the future, but learning is so much more than this.

Learning is for *now*.

Students should attend school and feel, each day, like they're taking something meaningful home with them. Something applicable to the person they currently are, not the future version we keep trying to convince them they're working for.

When students attend and lessons feel disconnected from reality, despite best efforts and the most incredible teachers, they become mere exercises in memorisation rather than meaningful explorations of knowledge (Brown et al., 2014). By anchoring content in students' lived experiences, teachers can bridge this gap.

Start with small changes like using student choice to allow students to explore personal passions within subject areas or integrating personal reflections by asking students, *"How does this apply to my life?"* after key lessons. These changes encourage students to see learning as relevant rather than isolated from their experiences.

> **Focus on projects and inquiry**
>
> Implementing project-based learning (PBL) or inquiry-based learning (Larmer & Mergendoller, 2015) to tackle real-world challenges has several benefits over traditional 'chalk and talk'-type lessons.
>
> PBL not only boosts engagement but also strengthens problem-solving and collaboration skills, shifts ownership and requires students to link their learning to purpose.

Benefits of PBL include:
- *It encourages students to solve authentic problems* – engaging with real-world challenges fosters critical thinking and intrinsic motivation.
- *It allows students to create something meaningful* – instead of completing worksheets, students can write proposals, conduct experiments or build prototypes that have real-world impact.

2. Look to the future, focus on the now

For many students, school feels disconnected from their aspirations.

The research suggests when they can see a direct link between their education and their future goals, motivation increases (Albrecht & Karabenick, 2018). Therefore, it seems obvious that connecting lessons to careers, industries and real-world applications would give students a sense of direction, however, think about your classes quickly – would most students be intrinsically motivated by focusing just on working towards where they want to be, not where they are right now?

To effectively link learning to a pathway, teachers, wherever possible, need to provide opportunities for students to engage with meaningful work that serves an aspirational purpose, but isn't just in service of it. To be clear, what I mean is, most students won't be able to fuel their work now, by just knowing that it will be useful later. Feed that aspiration by providing relevant and progressive work that not only links to, but provides for, both now and that desired future.

When the numbers became letters

At school I generally struggled with mathematics. My brain preferred English classes, social studies and physical education. When algebra came along, and the numbers started partnering with letters, I remember vividly thinking:

> "*When will I ever use this?*"

Students today are still asking the same question. Several professions use algebra, both obviously and less obviously, such as engineers, architects, video-game developers, medical professionals, scientists and bakers (think ratios and proportions).

The key to making this pathway specific, purpose-friendly and, of course, valuable now, is in the framing. Here are some ways to make algebra feel (more) useful now:

- *Link to technology they use* – your phone's face ID? It's built on algebra – mapping points, analysing data.

- *Gamify it* – turn equations into power-ups or levels. Build a character who gets stronger by solving problems.
- *Real money, real maths* – saving $10 a week for sneakers? That's a linear equation in action.
- *Use data from their lives* – graph real stuff: sleep versus grades, height versus shoe size – algebra shows patterns.
- *Algebra in pop culture* – use clips from *Hidden Figures*, *Moneyball* or *Iron Man* to show maths in action.
- *Let them build something* – make a mini catapult, code a bouncing ball – each uses algebraic thinking.

3. Socially network

In my experience, all young people want to feel valued. In our classrooms we can harness this by creating opportunities for students to see their learning making a tangible impact.

Purpose is amplified when knowledge is used; a funny sentence to write, but honestly, is an exam using knowledge in a meaningful way? How often do students actually *use* the information they gain in their lessons? On a day-to-day basis, how much of the 'learning' can be applied immediately at home for the benefit of others?

I personally find these questions as concerning as I do fascinating.

In any case, we can increase the amplification of purpose by allowing our students to address real-world challenges, contribute to their communities or improve the lives of others (Reimers, 2020). There are problems to solve and community-based organisations that are desperate for assistance in almost every corner of the globe.

With a little planning, communication and collaboration, we can create not only meaningful and purposeful experiences for our students, but memorable and impactful ones (Reimers, 2020).

Experience an experience

How to do it:

- Design community-based projects where students apply what they've learned to solve local problems.
- Encourage mentorship and peer teaching, as teaching others strengthens both knowledge and a sense of responsibility.
- Integrate service learning, where academic content is connected to meaningful social action.

Why do it?

The first climb presents the first real challenge for teachers in building a connected classroom. Every single lesson should have some meaning for students; this will, in reality, be to varying degrees, but when students see their learning as meaningful, everything you do changes.

As we've unpacked, students become more engaged, motivated and willing to persist through challenges when driven by purpose, but more importantly, it makes learning in school more enjoyable, which leads to increased student achievement, knowledge retention and long-term motivation to learn more (Pink, 2009).

Increasing connection in any capacity requires us to start with why; student classwork is no different. When we sit our students down and set them a task, we need them to be invested in completing that work, it needs to matter to them. This is core to the connected teacher's role.

Ryan and Deci (2020), through their work on developing SDT, know the incredible value of students' intrinsic motivation and "regulation through identification" (p. 72). In our classrooms this identification represents how strongly a student links the work to be completed towards their own purpose.

In *Drive: The Surprising Truth About What Motivates Us*, Daniel Pink (2009) speaks on connection through purpose, stating:

> "*What you decide not to do is probably more important than what you decide to do.*"

As we start this first climb on our journey to be more connected, perhaps we need to listen to our students more intently. Not only their voices and the calls of *"Why are we doing this?"* but pay attention to the truth informing their actions. What work are they not doing and why might they not be doing it?

> **Starting with why**
>
> Simon Sinek (2009) explores the concept of purpose in his first book, *Start With Why: How Great Leaders Inspire Everyone to Take Action* and two specific quotes stand out:
>
>> "Working hard for something we don't care about is called stress, working hard for something we love is called passion."
>
>> "There are only two ways to influence human behaviour: you can manipulate it or you can inspire it."
>
> Both quotes are powerful reflections on the current state of our classrooms. While not specifically aimed at schools, Sinek's words align deeply with our discussion of purpose.

Your classroom should be more passion than stress, inspiration over manipulation.

That is connection at work.

In older students especially, the choice behind what work they're willing to complete and what work they aren't is all about the pursuit of independence and ownership. Allowing a shift in ownership, not through extrinsic means but through carefully explored purpose, means the decision to complete the work is theirs. This is essential to the connected classroom.

Why does this matter?

Because purpose leads to value, value leads to:

- **Compliance moving to engagement** – *"I have to do this"* to genuine interest, *"I want to learn more"*
- **Students developing resilience** – when learning has meaning, they're more likely to persist through challenges
- **Teachers no longer have to 'force' participation** – when students see value in learning, engagement happens naturally

Students retain information better when it's connected to not only real-world applications but their world. Abstract concepts are easily forgotten, but when knowledge is applied in meaningful ways, it becomes embedded in long-term memory (Hultberg et al., 2018).

If we want our students to feel connected in our classrooms and our schools, we need to *start with why*.

So, let them ask and *always be ready with an answer*.

Where to next?

Bringing purpose into learning is an essential contributor to our continued ascent, much like the journey of a climber pressing on after the terrain starts to incline. The view may change, but the need to pause, reassess and adjust remains constant. In the same way, educators must regularly reflect on whether students see meaning in their learning and consider how to deepen that sense of purpose. Purpose isn't a fixed point, it's something that grows through curiosity, relevance and shared commitment.

The following questions and strategies can support your ongoing reflection and help you sustain a learning environment where purpose continues to guide, motivate and inspire.

1. Do students see the relevance of their learning?

When students recognise how their learning connects to their lives, passions and futures, they're more likely to engage meaningfully. Relevance isn't just a bonus; it's a driving force that helps students invest in the journey. Consider:

- Are students able to explain how today's learning relates to their world outside the classroom?
- Have I created regular opportunities for students to reflect on the real-world relevance of what they're learning?
- Do students feel their learning connects to their identities, goals or interests?

2. Are students engaged beyond just completing tasks?

Purpose-driven learning moves students from compliance to curiosity. When learning feels meaningful, students move beyond surface-level engagement and start to climb with intention, not just direction. Consider:

- Do students show interest and initiative during lessons, or are they just 'going through the motions'?
- Are my tasks designed to challenge and inspire, or simply to be completed?
- Do I notice students asking thoughtful questions or exploring ideas further on their own?

3. How often do I incorporate authentic learning experiences?

The most rewarding stretches of the climb often mirror real conditions – unpredictable, dynamic and deeply engaging. Likewise, learning becomes more purposeful when it mirrors the complexity and relevance of the world beyond the classroom. Consider:

- Am I offering learning experiences that reflect real-world contexts, challenges or audiences?
- Have I provided opportunities for students to pursue projects or inquiries that matter to them?
- Could I partner with community members or organisations to enrich student learning?

4. Am I using student voice to shape learning experiences?

Just as climbers rely on one another for perspective and insight, students' voices offer valuable guidance. When students help shape the learning path, their sense of ownership, and purpose, naturally grows. Consider:

- Do I regularly seek feedback from students about their learning experiences?
- Are there spaces in my planning for students to make choices, share ideas or lead elements of the learning process?
- Do students see their suggestions and perspectives reflected in the learning environment?

5. Are we recognising and celebrating meaningful learning moments?

Milestones matter, whether on a mountain or in a classroom. Acknowledging purposeful learning moments reinforces the value of the climb and helps students see how far they've come. Consider:

- Do I take time to highlight and celebrate when students make meaningful connections in their learning?
- Are students given opportunities to share their learning with authentic audiences such as peers, families or the wider community?
- How might we collectively reflect on and honour moments of growth, impact and insight?

TL;DR

Key takeaways

1. **Purpose is a powerful driver of student motivation and engagement**
   When learning feels purposeful, students are more likely to engage deeply and take ownership of their education. Purpose gives meaning to learning, shifting students from compliance to genuine investment.

2. **Real-world relevance transforms learning into a meaningful experience**
   Project-based learning shows that when learning is tied to real-world issues, students are more engaged and retain knowledge more effectively. Designing authentic tasks and projects allows students to see the value and application of what they're learning beyond the classroom.

3. **Inquiry and student choice cultivate ownership and curiosity**
   Purposeful learning flourishes when students are empowered to ask questions, explore interests and take the lead in their learning. Approaches like inquiry-based learning and student-driven projects invite students to engage creatively and critically, resulting in more meaningful and memorable learning experiences.

4. **Small, intentional shifts in teaching can create big impacts**
   Purpose-driven learning doesn't require a complete overhaul, it's built through everyday decisions that prioritise relevance, curiosity and student voice. Strategies like open-ended questions, real-world connections and offering choice in assessments can dramatically increase engagement and motivation.

5. **Purpose connects education to identity, motivation and future goals**
   When students see how learning connects to who they are and who they want to become, they're more likely to persist, take initiative and find joy in the process. A classroom rooted in purpose cultivates not just academic success, but lifelong learners who see education as a meaningful part of their lives.

CHAPTER 9
Finding your rhythm
Differentiating for meaningful learning

As climbers push forward, they don't all take the same steps at the same speed. Some pause to catch their breath; others surge ahead. Each responds to the slope in their own way. Progress isn't uniform and neither is learning. In the classroom, just like on the trail, learners find their rhythm not through conformity, but through connection. Differentiation recognises that students travel different paths, shaped by their strengths, challenges, interests and readiness. It's not about making things easier or harder. It's about making them *accessible*, *meaningful* and *authentic*. When students feel that learning is designed with them in mind, it fuels confidence and momentum.

This chapter explores how differentiation ensures that every learner is both supported and stretched – not in spite of their uniqueness, but because of it. When learning is matched to a student's point on the journey, connection deepens. Not just to the content, but to the process, the community and, most importantly, to themselves. Because when learners are met where they are, they start to believe they can go further than they ever thought possible.

The big two

The role of differentiation in connected learning

A classroom is made up of students who bring unique experiences, strengths and challenges to the learning process. No two students are identical in their background knowledge, learning pace or engagement preference.

As educators, this presents a fundamental challenge: how do we ensure that *every* student feels both capable and connected in their learning journey?

Traditional approaches to teaching often assume that all students can progress at the same pace with the same level of support. However, this one-size-fits-all model fails to recognise the diversity of learners, leading to boredom for some and frustration for others (Tomlinson, 2022; Tomlinson & Imbeau, 2023).

We know this doesn't work, *yet here we are*. This is why we desperately need to address this part of the journey.

Differentiation provides a way to bridge the gaps, whether they're pedagogical, school-wide or system-wide, ensuring that learning is both accessible and appropriately challenging for every student (Porta, 2024).

> In her influential book, *How to Differentiate Instruction in Academically Diverse Classrooms*, Carol Ann Tomlinson (2017), a leading authority in the field of differentiated instruction, writes:
>
> > "Acknowledging that students learn on different timetables, and that they differ widely in their ability to think abstractly or understand complex ideas, is no different than acknowledging that students at any given age aren't all the same height. It is not a statement of worth but of reality." (p. xii)

But are we clear on what authentic differentiation is? I'm not so sure. This is why we find it here as we continue the challenging first climb. I believe we all think we know what the aims of the climb are, but I'm not so sure we're all working from the same base knowledge.

This chapter explores the art of effective differentiation in a connected classroom, and at its core lie two essential questions:

1. How does differentiation create more connected learning?
2. What are practical ways to meet students where they are?

These questions guide us towards understanding why differentiation is critical for both student engagement and classroom culture. Before we explore how to implement it, however, we must first understand why it matters.

1. How does differentiation create more connected learning?

Learning is most effective when it exists in the 'just right' zone – not too easy, not too difficult. I'd argue that connection could exist on a similar scale. Natural processes, like learning, connection, growth in general, all align with this type of modelling.

We don't grow without challenges, but too much creates unwanted stress, and too little doesn't light a big enough fire. Authentic differentiation, then, is finding the right balance for everyone so that they may find the right amount of challenge to stimulate growth and connect with what they're learning (Gheyssens et al., 2022; Porta, 2024).

In the zone

Lev Vygotsky's (1978) Zone of Proximal Development (refer back to Figure 8 in Chapter 7) explains that optimal learning occurs just beyond what a student can do independently, requiring appropriate guidance and support. The key thinking is:

- When learning is too easy, students lose motivation because they feel *unchallenged.*
- When learning is too difficult, frustration builds and students begin to *disengage.*
- When learning is *appropriately tailored*, students remain engaged, challenged and confident in their ability to grow.

When we consider differentiation in this way, we're moving beyond impacts solely on academic success and recognising another component that directly shapes a student's sense of belonging and meaning – their *connection.*

When students experience learning that aligns with their needs, we start to see the links between the challenge of the first climb and the steps of the journey already behind us. They're more likely to:

- Develop a growth mindset, believing they can succeed with effort and support
- See themselves as active participants in their learning rather than passive recipients
- Form deeper connections with their teacher and peers, knowing their abilities and interests are valued

    (Gheyssens et al., 2022; Van Geel et al., 2019)

As discussed in Chapter 6, inclusivity is essential to a classroom that communicates connection; as the journey becomes potentially more challenging on our climb, this previous work is further progressed and shaped by differentiation.

When students recognise that everyone learns at different paces and will be at different stages, it fosters an environment of mutual respect, collaboration and inclusivity (Porta, 2024). Rather than seeing differences in ability as deficits, students begin to understand that variation in learning is *natural, expected* and, most importantly, *accepted* (Tomlinson, 2022).

This thinking is very important to the rest of the chapter to come. Because we need to be clear here, differentiation isn't just about adjusting instruction – it's about creating a classroom where every student feels seen, challenged and connected to the learning process (Sobel & Alston, 2021).

2. What are practical ways to meet students where they are?

If differentiation is key to engagement and classroom connection, the real challenge becomes:

> *How do we make it work in practice?*

Before we discuss strategies, it's important to highlight that differentiation isn't about creating separate pathways for every student, it's about thoughtfully responding to students' diverse learning needs in a way that is both effective and manageable (Tomlinson & Imbeau, 2023).

This is why I believe differentiation is often misunderstood as an excessive burden rather than a natural part of effective teaching. When done well, it's not a rigid framework but a fluid, responsive approach that allows students to engage with learning in ways that make sense for them (Tomlinson & Jarvis, 2023).

I'll be the first to highlight that I don't always get this right myself. I don't write this book in the mindset of the most incredible educator on the planet. But I do actively try to, each day, reflect on those efforts, and attempt to be better at the next opportunity.

Because meeting students where they are should be a given. We do it pretty much right up until formal schooling starts with our children and then, we don't.

This is where the need for differentiation raises some deeper questions about equity in education:

- Are all students given the opportunity to succeed, or only those who fit a traditional mould of learning?
- Do students feel ownership over their progress, or do they feel trapped by a system that moves at a predetermined pace?
- How can we challenge every student appropriately without making them feel isolated or overwhelmed?

These questions matter because they highlight the core purpose of differentiation: ensuring that no student feels left behind or held back. By meeting students where they are, we create an environment where learning isn't about competition, but about continuous growth (Porta, 2024; Tomlinson & Jarvis, 2023).

I'm desperately trying not to answer questions with more questions throughout this book, but these are important reflections before we start thinking practically.

Differentiation has become, in many ways, an instructional approach (Van Geel et al., 2019). In others, I'd argue, it's become a regulatory checkbox.

This is unacceptable.

The first step to understanding the practical ways to effectively differentiate is to understand true differentiation is a philosophy that recognises each student's potential and need for connection in their learning (Gheyssens et al., 2022; Porta, 2024).

When applied effectively, differentiation doesn't just support individual learners – it transforms the entire classroom.

Unpack your journey

Why differentiation matters

To understand why differentiation is essential, we need to go back to university level and examine the cognitive and pedagogical principles that underpin effective teaching.

Differentiation isn't just about making learning 'easier', in fact, it's not about that at all. It's about ensuring every student is challenged at the right level, supported appropriately and engaged in a way that fosters growth (Tomlinson, 2023; Porta, 2024).

Three key frameworks help us understand why differentiation is a foundation of meaningful learning:

- Cognitive Load Theory (CLT)
- Universal Design for Learning (UDL)
- Tomlinson's elements of differentiation

Filling our cognitive bucket

John Sweller's Cognitive Load Theory (CLT) (1988) highlights the importance of structuring learning to prevent cognitive overload. CLT explains that working memory has limited capacity, and when students are presented with too much new information at once, they struggle to process and retain it (Sweller, 1988).

This aligns with Atkinson and Shiffrin's (1968) model of memory (see Figure 9 overleaf), which explains how information flows through three stages of memory: sensory, short-term and long-term memory.

Figure 9: Atkinson & Shiffrin's model of memory

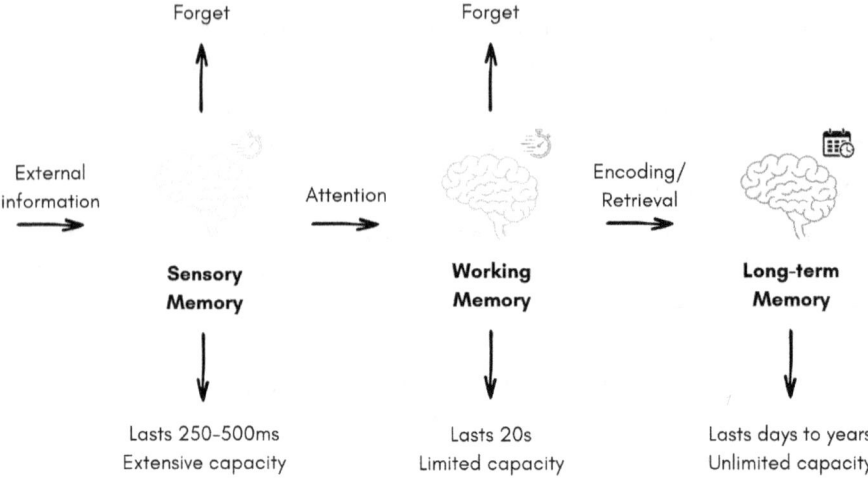

(ADAPTED FROM CENTURY, 2022)

First, we take in information through our senses, but it only stays in sensory memory for a very short time, milliseconds in fact. If we pay attention to it, the information moves into short-term memory, where it can be held for a little longer, usually around 15 to 30 seconds. If we rehearse or practise it enough, the information can be stored in long-term memory, where it can stay for a much longer time, even for life (Atkinson & Shiffrin, 1968).

Using this understanding, CLT breaks cognitive load into three types: intrinsic, extraneous and germane.

1. **Intrinsic load** refers to the inherent complexity of the material being learned – some content is naturally more difficult due to the number of elements and how they interact. While we cannot change this, we can manage it by sequencing material appropriately and providing scaffolding.
2. **Extraneous load** comes from poor instructional design – anything that distracts or confuses learners, like unclear instructions, unnecessary information or split attention between multiple sources. This type of load should be minimised.
3. **Germane load** is the desirable effort learners invest in making sense of the content, building connections and developing plans. Effective teaching aims to maximise this.

(Klepsch & Seufert, 2020)

By differentiating content, process and output, teachers can create learning experiences that are both rigorous and accessible while also not overloading their memory.

Learning by design

Universal Design for Learning (UDL) is a framework designed to make learning accessible to all students by providing multiple means of engagement, representation and action/expression (see Figure 10) (Meyer et al., 2014).

Figure 10: Universal Design for Learning framework

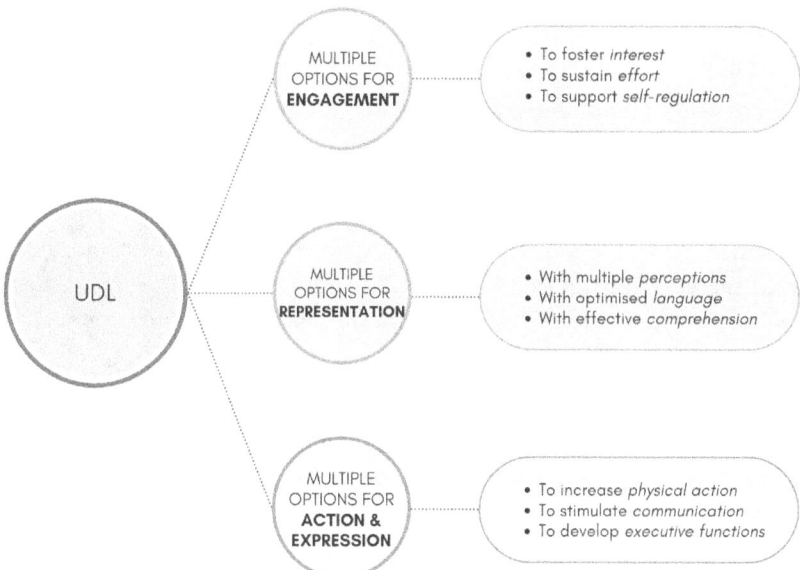

(ADAPTED FROM CAST, 2018)

UDL requires a mindset shift in which the role of the teacher is reimagined from the traditional deliverer of content to a *learning architect* (Griful-Freixenet et al., 2020). It challenges the assumption of a 'typical' learner and instead acknowledges that variability is the norm in every classroom.

UDL is built on the understanding that students differ not only in what they learn, but in how they learn and why they engage (Griful-Freixenet et al., 2020). These differences are shaped by a complex interplay of cognitive, emotional, cultural and experiential factors. UDL asks educators to proactively design learning environments that remove barriers, rather than retrofitting them after challenges arise (Mackey et al., 2023).

It emphasises the importance of anticipating diversity, embedding flexibility into the learning process, and fostering a sense of belonging and autonomy (Saborío-Taylor & Rojas-Ramírez, 2024). By rooting practice in UDL principles, teachers move towards a more equitable and responsive approach to education; an approach that recognises and values each student's unique pathway to understanding.

Be proactive!

Carol Ann Tomlinson, a leading authority on differentiation, describes it as "proactively modifying instruction to meet diverse needs" (Tomlinson, 2017). Differentiation isn't about waiting for students to fail before offering support, it's about anticipating different learning needs and planning accordingly.

Tomlinson (2017) identifies four key elements that teachers can differentiate:

1. **Content** – what students learn (for example, offering different reading levels, scaffolded texts).
2. **Process** – how students engage with learning (for example, using small-group instruction, peer mentoring or independent study).
3. **Product** – how students demonstrate learning (for example, essays, videos, presentations, models).
4. **Learning environment** – the classroom set-up, routines and support systems that foster inclusivity.

By proactively addressing these areas, differentiation becomes an intentional and embedded part of teaching, rather than an add-on or afterthought. As we continue to climb on our connection journey, we must make differentiation much, much more than just a conversation regarding some students.

All students deserve differentiation. All deserve connection.

What to do?

Differentiation is only effective when it moves from theory to practice (Coffey, 2023; Porta, 2024).

While the principles of differentiation make intuitive sense, the challenge, of course, lies in implementation. How do we design lessons that meet diverse needs without creating an overwhelming (or even a feeling of an overwhelming) workload for teachers?

As we continue to climb, we're going to keep our focus simple in the hope that this simplicity will allow it a greater chance of becoming an ingrained part of our practice. By doing so, I hope it is less likely to fall away in times of scheduled chaos (think report-writing time!).

Inspired by CLT, UDL and Tomlinson, we will focus on three core aspects of differentiation:

1. **Content** – what students learn
2. **Process** – how students engage with learning
3. **Output** – how students demonstrate understanding

Each of these elements can be tailored to create more accessible, engaging and meaningful learning experiences, but more importantly, keep things nice and focused.

1. Differentiate content

When considering differentiation of content, we need to ensure that we understand what this means. I've seen many an experienced (and respected) teacher remove content from assessments, sections of rubrics and whole tasks from units in the name of differentiation and, in doing so, they have removed the key learning also.

When you set a learning intention and success criteria for a task, lesson or unit, every student should be working towards that learning intention and demonstrating that criteria (Tomlinson & Imbeau, 2023). That is the content. If this is the knowledge that has been deemed the learning, every student should have the opportunity to learn it, demonstrate that learning and use it as the foundation for the next part of their learning journey (Tomlinson, 2022).

Content differentiation ensures that all students work towards the same essential learning goals, but *engage* with material in ways that match their readiness, interests and learning preferences (Tomlinson & Jarvis, 2023). Importantly, differentiation doesn't mean simplifying tasks or lowering expectations; it means providing the right scaffolding so that all students can engage successfully with the core learning objective (Tomlinson & Imbeau, 2023).

When you remove the 'hard parts' from a task, rather than modifying or scaffolding, you're removing the actual challenge from the learning. You're robbing that student of the opportunity to show you what they know.

Same, same but different

Try these simple strategies to differentiate content:

- *Tiered activities* – instead of providing different students with entirely different tasks (which can create inequity and limit growth), tiered activities adjust the level of support, complexity or approach while maintaining the same learning outcome.
- *Learning menus* – a learning menu provides students with options on how to engage with content while ensuring that all choices align

with the learning goal. For example, a maths problem-solving menu may include a video tutorial, a hands-on manipulative option or a collaborative discussion group, all leading to the same conceptual understanding.
- *Multiple entry points* – students have different strengths; some prefer information through visuals, others through discussion and others through hands-on exploration. Offering multiple ways to access the same core content ensures equity without compromising rigor.

2. Differentiate process

When we're considering the way in which students work through the learning, we need to ensure that we're always differentiating the process and not changing the content completely (Tomlinson & Imbeau, 2023). Differentiating the learning process means offering varied ways *for all students* to engage with material and develop understanding (Roberts & Inman, 2023).

Again, we're not explicitly changing or removing what we want to be learned, just differentiating *how* it will be learned. All students can benefit from this approach as this ensures they're supported at their challenge level while fostering deeper engagement. It sets them up for visible success.

Differentiation: as told by apples
(The what? Eat apple. The how? Have it your way!)

This visibility is so important to connect a student's thoughts, actions and results to their effort. Differentiation of processes allows students to not only have success but understand how they had it and what they need to do next to achieve more (Van Geel et al., 2019). That is what a connected classroom is all about. That is the real learning.

Great success!

Try incorporating these strategies to differentiate process for greater success:

- *Flexible grouping* – organise students into dynamic groups based on skill level, learning preferences or interests. Groups should be fluid, changing as students progress.
- *Choice-based learning stations* – set up different learning stations where students work on different aspects of a concept. One station might involve teacher-led instruction, another might include collaborative work and a third might be an independent challenge.
- *Varied levels of scaffolding* – some students may need guided instruction with worked examples, while others benefit from open-ended inquiry tasks.

3. Differentiate output

Finally, we come to the end point and, arguably in our current climate, the most measurable component: the output. Once we understand (and accept) that students can, will and prefer to demonstrate learning in different ways, we're not actually adding a tremendous amount to our workload. Differentiation of output isn't about the teacher at all. It's about the student.

While some students will have natural inclinations and talents for excelling at written tasks, others express their understanding more effectively through presentations, artistic representations or practical demonstrations.

At its most simplistic, differentiating output provides students with meaningful ways to *show what they know*. At its most complex, it provides opportunities for new knowledge to be retained through the development of new neural pathways and the encoding of information into the long-term memory (Haelermans, 2022).

The car that taught me to test

Think about a project from your own school days. I still remember one vividly from primary school, though the exact year escapes me.

Our task was to design something that would roll down a ramp, testing how far it could go. Our teacher supported us all through the learning about gravity, friction and the mechanics of wheels and axles. Then, we were given the freedom to design our own devices. I chose to build a NASCAR-style car.

I spent a weekend at my grandparents' house working on it. The car was a block of wood with axles held by pins, a cardboard frame and proudly decorated with paint and stickers. I was excited about what we had created.

On the testing day, there were other car-like designs, some with many wheels, some with one. I remember vaguely something that reminded me of what I could only call a 'Barbie party boat'. My car worked but veered off the track because of a loose pin. It didn't win for distance, but my peers voted it best design – a proud moment for me.

This project left a lasting lesson: always test, revise and check your work before finalising it. It's something I still apply today, even as I write and revise this book.

The key takeaway for teachers is that our teacher gave us the support to learn the key concepts first, then the freedom to show our understanding in different ways. We had the same goal and assessment criteria, but room to experiment and create.

While my car is a specific example, consider including these strategies in your classroom:

- *Choice of demonstration* – let students choose how they show their understanding: essay, video, infographic, role play or model.
- *Rubric-based assessment* – use rubrics that focus on skills and understanding, not just a specific task format.
- *Creative applications* – encourage creative approaches, like making a documentary instead of a traditional report.

We have to get this right!

Differentiation is just one part of building strong connections in your classroom. I don't want to go on about it too long, but I want to make sure you have some simple tricks and tools to make it real.

It's part of the first climb because it's a challenge. The terrain gets tougher and the steps get shorter. But remember, differentiation isn't about doing *more* work. You're already doing a lot, I know that. It's about doing those great things a bit *differently*, making sure every student is engaged, challenged and supported.

Table 1 contains some further ideas for you to consider.

Table 1: Strategies for implementing differentiation

Strategy	Description
Pre-assess knowledge	Find out what students already know and where they need support. This avoids assumptions and lets you tailor your teaching. Use rating scales or 'traffic light' cards (green = confident, yellow = unsure, red = struggling).
Use choice boards	Give students options for how they engage with content, without creating new lessons for everyone.
Scaffold for success	Adjust the level of support based on where students are in their learning. Sentence starters and graphic organisers help some students organise their thinking.
Leverage technology	Use digital tools to personalise learning and help students work at their own pace without adding more work for you.
Embed reflection	Regularly ask students to reflect on what's working and what's not. This helps you keep improving your strategies. Reflection prompts: *What helped you learn best in this unit?* *What challenges did you face, and how did you overcome them?* *What would you like to see more of in future lessons?*

Why do it?

Differentiation isn't just about making learning more effective; it's about making learning more connected. When students feel that their unique needs and strengths are recognised, they engage more deeply, take greater ownership of their learning, and develop stronger relationships with both their peers and their teachers. This sense of belonging enhances motivation, self-efficacy and academic success (Hattie, 2023).

Differentiation creates a classroom culture where every student is valued, not despite their differences, but because of them (Porta, 2024; Tomlinson & Imbeau, 2023). This shift transforms learning from a passive experience to an active, meaningful journey where students feel empowered to take the next step.

This is about equitable access to learning (Dack et al., 2022). While differentiation might seem like an additional layer of complexity in lesson planning, my hope is that this chapter has given you some additional perspective on this. Research consistently shows that when it's done well, it leads to higher engagement, better learning outcomes and a stronger sense of belonging in the classroom (Tomlinson & Imbeau, 2023).

The fact is, teaching with a one-size-fits-all approach often results in disengagement – some students become frustrated because the content is too difficult, while others become bored because it's too easy (Tomlinson, 2017). By modifying content, process and output, we meet students where they are and push them forward at a pace that fosters growth (Roberts & Inman, 2023).

Learning, like shoes, cannot be 'one-size-fits-all'

All students will benefit from this increased connection to the learning journey, however, significant gains are made when considering students with learning disabilities, gifted students and English language learners (ELLs), as it provides targeted support without lowering expectations (Santangelo & Tomlinson, 2012).

Differentiation, when effective, removes barriers to learning and supports deeper connection to that learning, by providing multiple ways for a student to demonstrate what they have learned (Sobel & Alston, 2021). This ensures that students with diverse needs can participate meaningfully but, more importantly, it creates an inclusive learning environment where all students thrive.

When teachers differentiate, they send a powerful message to students:

"I see you. Your learning matters. You belong here."

This connection fosters a positive learning environment where students feel safe to take risks, ask questions and engage deeply.

The fact is:
- Students in differentiated classrooms report feeling more valued and motivated because instruction is tailored to their needs (Tomlinson, 2017).
- Differentiation helps build stronger relationships between teachers and students, leading to increased trust and engagement.

By investing in differentiation, you take your classroom from traditional to transformative.

Where to next?

Just as a climber continually adjusts to new terrain on the ascent, educators must stay responsive to the shifting needs, interests and readiness levels within their classrooms. Differentiation asks us to be flexible, reflective and open to change – not for the sake of complexity, but to ensure every student is challenged, supported and seen.

The path to effective differentiation isn't linear, and it certainly isn't perfect. The following questions and strategies are designed to guide your ongoing reflection and help sustain a differentiated approach that works for you and your learners.

1. Are students learning at the right level of challenge?

When differentiation is working well, students feel stretched, not stressed. Learning is neither too easy nor overwhelming. Instead, it's engaging, purposeful and just the right amount of challenging. Consider:

- Do students appear motivated and invested, or are they disengaged due to boredom or frustration?
- Are students experiencing success that feels earned, not automatic?
- Am I using formative assessment to adjust the level of challenge for different learners?

2. Is differentiation sustainable in my practice?

Sustainable differentiation feels embedded, not bolted on. It becomes part of your planning rhythm, supported by practical strategies that save time while enhancing learning. Consider:

- Do I have go-to strategies (like choice boards, tiered tasks or flexible grouping) that make differentiation manageable?
- Am I using tools or tech to streamline differentiation, rather than adding to my workload?
- Does differentiation feel like a natural part of my teaching, or something extra?

3. Are students accessing learning in multiple ways?

Differentiation is about more than difficulty; it's also about access. Providing different ways to engage with content and show understanding opens learning for all students. Consider:

- Am I offering varied entry points (visual, auditory, kinaesthetic) to suit different learning preferences?
- Do students have options in how they demonstrate their learning, through writing, speaking, creating or performing?
- Are tasks adaptable to allow for individual strengths and needs?

4. Am I using student feedback to shape differentiation?

Students are the best source of insight into what's working, and what's not. Listening to their voices can help refine and improve your approach. Consider:

- Do I regularly ask students which strategies support their learning best?
- Are students able to reflect on their own learning needs and advocate for adjustments?
- Have I made space in my planning to act on student feedback?

5. What small step can I take next?

Like any journey, differentiation is built on progress, not perfection. Each step forward brings you closer to a classroom where every student can thrive. Consider:

- Is there one aspect of differentiation I can refine, perhaps output options, groupings or scaffolds?
- Can I collaborate with a colleague to share ideas or co-plan a differentiated lesson?
- What is one strategy I can commit to trying or improving in the next few weeks?

TL;DR

Key takeaways

1. **Differentiation builds connection through challenge and support**
   Learning is most powerful when it meets students in the 'just right' zone; challenging enough to promote growth, but supported enough to feel achievable. This isn't just about academic success, it's about fostering a classroom culture where students feel seen, valued and part of the learning journey.

2. **Differentiation transforms diversity into a strength**
   A connected classroom embraces the natural variation in how students learn. When we expect difference and design for it, classrooms become more inclusive, equitable and respectful spaces, not in spite of students' differences, but because of them.

3. **Practical strategies make differentiation doable and sustainable**
   Differentiation doesn't have to mean doing more, it means doing things differently. Approaches like tiered activities, choice boards, flexible groupings and scaffolded supports make it possible to meet a wide range of student needs without adding unnecessary complexity. When differentiation is embedded into everyday routines, it becomes a natural part of effective practice rather than an added burden.

4. **Process and output matter just as much as content**
   Effective differentiation goes beyond what students learn, it includes how they learn and how they show their understanding. Offering multiple pathways to engage with content and demonstrate learning not only boosts access and equity but also builds student agency and motivation.

5. **True differentiation sends a powerful message: you belong here**
   When differentiation is done well, students understand that their learning matters. They feel empowered, trusted and supported to grow at their own pace. This fosters stronger relationships, deeper engagement and a greater sense of ownership.

PART 5
FACING THE VALLEYS

Overcoming challenges to connection

> "The greatest glory in living lies not in never falling, but in rising every time we fall"
>
> — NELSON MANDELA

Every climber knows that the valleys are as much a part of the journey as the peaks. Between every ascent lies a descent – a humbling reminder that progress isn't linear. British climber Joe Simpson, known for his harrowing survival story in the Peruvian Andes, recounts in *Touching the Void* that it was in the lowest, most desperate moments that his determination crystallised. In the valleys, exhaustion sets in, doubts creep up and the next climb can feel impossibly far away. Yet it's in these quiet spaces that resilience is born.

In education, the valley moments arrive without warning. A lesson collapses. A student explodes. A carefully planned sequence goes nowhere. Engagement disappears, tempers rise and the calm we worked so hard to build suddenly feels fragile. These aren't detours – they're the terrain. The real question isn't how to avoid them, but how to move through them with purpose. This part is different. It includes just one chapter – but it goes a little deeper. *Chapter 10: Weathering storms* explores how we navigate the messy, unpredictable, deeply human challenges that come with teaching. It asks what happens to connection when conditions shift – when behaviour disrupts, when students disengage, when the work feels heavier than usual. There is no new climb yet, no new view. This is a moment of pause. A chance to sit in the complexity, look closely at the way we respond to difficulty and decide what kind of teacher we want to be when the conditions aren't ideal.

Because this is where it gets real.

Not every step of the journey is upward. But every step can be meaningful. Part 5 isn't about summiting. It's about staying, listening, learning. Choosing to hold steady when the ground is shifting. Because how we move through the valley determines how (and if) we continue to ascend again.

Let's take a breath, find our balance and begin.

CHAPTER 10
Weathering storms
Traversing classroom challenges

As any climber knows, not every stretch of the mountain is clear skies and steady footing. Some days, the weather changes quickly: clouds roll in, visibility drops and the path ahead becomes hard to see. These are the valley moments, where the climb feels steeper, the footing less stable and progress harder to measure. In teaching, these moments come in the form of disruption, disengagement and behaviour that challenges our calm. Storms are inevitable. But how we respond to them, with frustration or with curiosity, determines whether the experience becomes a moment of disconnection, or a chance to deepen our connection. Classrooms, like mountains, are shaped not just by the terrain, but by how we move through it.

This chapter explores how we can navigate classroom challenges without losing sight of what matters most: connection. Because when conflict arises, when a student disengages or when everything goes off-script, it's not just a test of patience, it's an invitation – an invitation to lead with care, to respond with compassion and to see behaviour not as a problem to fix but as communication to understand. These are the moments where connection either fractures or strengthens. And with the right tools, we can keep climbing – even through the storm.

We've got cows

I'll explain the subtitle above in a moment. But first...

Ever had a bad lesson? I sure have.

Sometimes it's a human 'bad day'-type thing, sometimes it's just a bit of a trash lesson, and we're all lucky we got out when the bell rang. Either way, the classroom dynamic is influenced by these two linked factors and as such we start our exploration of this space here.

Now. Let's quickly talk about *cows*.

In the film *Twister*, there's a moment of unexpected chaos when a cow flies past the storm chasers' vehicle (*"Cow"*) and then loops back again (*"Actually, I think that was the same cow"*). It's sudden, distracting and oddly comical, but it also signals that something much more serious is about to happen. Moments later, the team members find themselves trapped between two massive tornadoes.

This scene captures something many teachers can relate to: the way unforeseen challenges can throw even the best-prepared plans into disarray. In the classroom, these 'flying cow' moments might not be quite as dramatic, but they can still derail the flow of a lesson or the focus of a group in seconds.

One of these in your classroom?
Spilt milk will be the least of your troubles.

A sudden emotional outburst, a tech failure, a student misunderstanding that spirals... these can all act like our metaphorical cows spinning in the storm. Recognising that these moments are part of the teaching experience is key. It's not about preventing every disruption, but being agile enough to respond calmly, support the student/s, refocus the class and avoid being caught in the path of something bigger.

Just like in *Twister*, a cow is (likely) very much out of place in our environment, so as we continue our climb, we want to create predictable and calm conditions for our classes, our students and for ourselves, through even the most challenging moments.

The only reason we will see a cow here on our journey is if we bring it in ourselves or create the conditions in which a student brings it in with them. We need to keep our journey as cow-free as possible so that we can focus on supporting our students' learning, not controlling the herd.

As Bart Simpson, from the animated television show *The Simpsons*, would say:

> "Don't have a cow, man!"

The big two

Our climb through the mountains on The Connection Journey will most certainly come with unexpected obstacles: steep inclines, sudden storms (cow-free) and moments of exhaustion. In the same way, the journey of teaching, particularly in building connection with students, isn't always going to be smooth.

Teachers will inevitably encounter behavioural disruptions, disengagement and curriculum barriers that test their resolve, especially during times of change. However, these difficulties aren't signs of failure, they're simply part of the experience. Just as a climber doesn't abandon their path after a single misstep, educators must learn to adjust, adapt and keep moving forward when challenges arise.

The way we respond to difficulties determines whether they become moments of disconnection or opportunities to reinforce relationships, belonging and meaning. At the heart of this process lie two essential questions:

1. How do we maintain connection when challenges arise?
2. What strategies help address disengagement, conflict and barriers to teaching?

These questions are crucial because they shift our focus from avoiding difficulties to understanding how they can strengthen connections rather than weaken them. These questions challenge the traditional response to difficulty, one that often seeks compliance over understanding, reaction over reflection.

More specifically, we need to ensure that we understand:

- How challenges can either support or deteriorate relationships, depending on how they're handled
- Why moments of disconnection are often opportunities for deeper engagement
- What factors contribute to disengagement and frustration, and how they can be addressed at the source

By shifting our mindset from avoiding challenges to learning from them, we create a classroom culture where setbacks strengthen connection and create optimal conditions for learning (Burden, 2025).

1. How do we maintain connection when challenges arise?

Classroom challenges are inevitable, they will occur. How they impact the classroom depends on how they're supported (James et al., 2021). I'm being very purposeful with the choice of language here. We're dealing with people, emotions and behaviours – each of these three need support, not management or control. Your classroom is where we can rewrite the script on the typical behaviour management story.

Research consistently highlights that punitive approaches to discipline, rigid instructional models and emotionally disconnected learning environments contribute to student alienation (Gregory, Skiba, & Mediratta, 2017; Hudson, 2024). When students feel unheard, unseen or misunderstood, they often respond with withdrawal, defiance or frustration (Hudson, 2024).

> Dr Christopher Hudson states in his book *Leading Positive Classrooms: Adopting an Educative Approach to Behaviour Management in Schools* (2024):
>> "Without positive relationships, the wrong forms of power are relied upon to influence and correct students' off-task behaviours – notably coercive techniques that leverage fear as the driver of influence." (p. 17)
>
> Our job isn't to manage behaviour (and certainly not incite fear) but to foster connection.

Imagine a Year 8 student who suddenly slams their book shut and mutters, *"This is stupid"*, and then leaves the classroom. A traditional response might involve calling out the behaviour, issuing a consequence or demanding compliance. However, this approach often escalates disconnection rather than builds it.

A connection-driven approach instead asks:
- What's behind this reaction?
- Is the student overwhelmed?
- Do they feel unheard?
- Is there something external influencing their mood?

  (Causton & MacLeod, 2020; Porter, 2020)

This shift in perspective transforms challenges from moments of opposition into moments of understanding (Porter, 2020; Wink et al., 2021). It acknowledges that behaviour is often a form of communication, and disconnection can be an invitation to listen rather than control (Brunzell & Norrish, 2021).

We need to approach our classrooms with an understanding that we're all human, and only when we remember this are we able to sustain engagement and support students even when difficulties arise.

Calm, care and considered will be our markers through the challenges of the valley ahead.

2. What strategies help address disengagement, conflict and barriers to teaching?

Just as a climber cannot reach the summit without rest and refuelling, a teacher cannot sustain meaningful connection if they're emotionally depleted. The ability to navigate challenges with patience, empathy and insight requires that teachers themselves feel grounded, supported and resilient (Green, 2022).

This is why maintaining connection isn't only about what students need, but also about what teachers need.

When students disengage, act out or resist learning, it can be emotionally draining for educators. Without the right support, teachers may experience frustration, burnout or detachment, making it even harder to sustain connection (Wang et al., 2024).

The greatest strategy in the classroom is your authentic self. Your students need the best version of you that you can offer on any given day. In a time of great pressure, both internally and externally, how can educators maintain emotional resilience while supporting students?

Is it possible?

To support staff to support students, we need to address the structural and systemic barriers that contribute to student disengagement. We need to alter the design of learning experiences, whether they're lessons, excursions, camps or field trips, so that they support learning and naturally reduce frustration and alienation (Morinaj et al., 2019).

These concepts are so important because they push beyond surface-level solutions and encourage a deeper examination of the root causes of disconnection. Too often, the focus is placed solely on correcting student behaviour rather than examining the systems and structures that shape engagement in the first place (Brunzell & Norrish, 2021; Sobel, 2019).

Difficult moments in the classroom aren't detours from the path of connection; they're part of it. The way we navigate these moments determines whether they become barriers or building blocks in our relationships with students (Brunzell & Norrish, 2021; Hudson, 2024; Sobel, 2019).

There are ways forward and out of the fog in the valleys, but we will only see the summit and the path forwards if we're genuinely willing to address the challenges head-on.

Connection isn't sustained because challenges don't happen, but because we learn how to move through them together.

Unpack your journey

What are you trying to manage?

Modern teachers know behaviour is a multifaceted phenomenon with many potential influences ranging from individual experiences, environmental context and developmental stage (Brunzell & Norrish, 2021; Hudson, 2024; Walker & Graham, 2021). We also know that traditional behaviour management approaches often emphasise control and compliance, focusing on suppressing undesirable behaviours through punitive measures (Porter, 2020; Sobel, 2019).

We know these things, yet we don't see a lot of change. *Undesirable* and *suppressing* are the key words here – and not very positive ones either.

Suppression of behaviour that we, the adults, have deemed undesirable, is the reality. When this is coupled with punitive measures, we fail to not only address the underlying causes, but also the needs of the whole child (Curren, 2020).

> **Five-minute audit**
>
> Look at your mission, vision or values statements. Now look at your behaviour management and other student-based policies.
>
> I'm willing to bet educating the 'whole child' (or similar) features in one of those statements, while punitive measures feature in the frameworks, perhaps demerits or detentions.
>
> If so, the question to ask is: why do our policies not match our desired state?

We need to be very clear here – behaviour is a *form of communication*.

If teachers can recognise, remember and understand this daily, it allows for a clearer interpretation of what's happening in the classroom (Brunzell & Norrish, 2021; Sobel, 2019). When a student (or adult) expresses themselves in this way, it's likely because of unmet needs, emotional distress or responses to past experiences (Mitchell et al., 2019).

It's time to look at the alternatives. Let's start with some big ideas after which we will bring them down to the classroom level.

Big T and little t

A growing component of this thinking is adopting trauma-informed practice. This is an approach that acknowledges the prevalence and impact of trauma on students' learning and behaviour. It involves understanding the effects of trauma on brain development, emotional regulation and social interactions (Brunzell & Norrish, 2021).

Educators adopting a trauma-informed approach strive to create safe, supportive environments that recognise the types and signs of trauma and respond with empathy and understanding (Hudson, 2024). This approach isn't about excusing behaviour but about understanding its origins to support students effectively (NSW Department of Education, 2020).

> **Defining trauma**
>
> Dr Rebecca Ray discusses 'Big T' and 'little t' trauma in her book *Difficult People: Dealing with the Bad Behaviour of Difficult People*.
>
> **Little 't' traumas** are experiences that overwhelm our capacity to cope and disrupt emotional functioning. They aren't inherently life-threatening, but are often ego-threatening, leaving us feeling helpless or emotionally unsettled. For example, financial stress.
>
> **Big 'T' traumas** refer to extraordinary events involving a real or perceived threat to life, safety or bodily integrity. These experiences often leave individuals feeling powerless and unable to regain a sense of control. For example, a natural disaster.

Implementing trauma-informed practices requires a whole-school commitment to fostering a culture of safety, trustworthiness and collaboration, but like our overall focus on connection, it can start with you in your classroom.

Organisations like Berry Street in Australia offer professional development for staff to recognise and respond to trauma, the integration of social-emotional learning into the curriculum, and the establishment of policies that prioritise student wellbeing (Brunzell & Norrish, 2021). Engaging with this learning and demonstrating its impact in your school could have significant impact for your community.

By shifting the focus from behaviour management to behaviour support, educators can create inclusive environments that promote healing and resilience, enabling all students to thrive academically and socially.

Reset, reconnect

Like shifting to a trauma-informed approach, unconditional positive regard (UPR), a concept developed by Carl Rogers (1957), refers to a change in perspective that accepts and values students without judgement, regardless of their behaviour (see Figure 11). In educational settings, UPR stands in stark contrast to traditional punitive behaviour management, which often focuses on compliance through consequences such as detention, isolation or exclusion (Moreno, 2021).

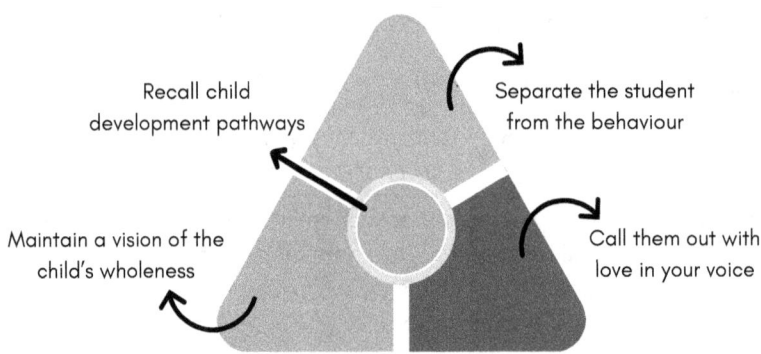

Figure 11: Components of unconditional positive regard

(ADAPTED FROM BERRY STREET, 2018)

I want to stress that I understand why punitive management has persisted; it's been effective in the past, however, the yield is short-term behavioural compliance, most often at the cost of damage to student-teacher relationships and to a student's intrinsic motivation to engage positively (Allen et al., 2018).

In contrast, UPR creates a foundation of trust and psychological safety, enabling students to feel seen and respected even when they struggle. This approach aligns with research we explored earlier, indicating that students are more likely to thrive academically and socially when they feel connected to their teachers (Allen et al., 2018; Moreno, 2021).

Rather than viewing misbehaviour as defiance to be punished, educators using UPR interpret it as a form of communication and respond with curiosity and empathy. This shift supports connection by validating the student's humanity, reducing shame and opening pathways for restorative dialogue (Berry Street, 2018).

A focus on unconditional positive regard fosters an inclusive classroom culture where every student can belong, grow and learn, not because they fear punishment, but because they feel safe enough to be themselves.

The strength of discussion

Cognitive behaviour therapy (CBT) is a psychological approach that helps individuals understand the connection between their thoughts, feelings and behaviours (see Figure 12) (Beck, 2020). While this is typically used by professionals in the mental health field, by understanding its foundations, we can integrate concepts to support students in developing self-awareness and coping strategies.

Figure 12: Cognitive behaviour therapy (CBT)

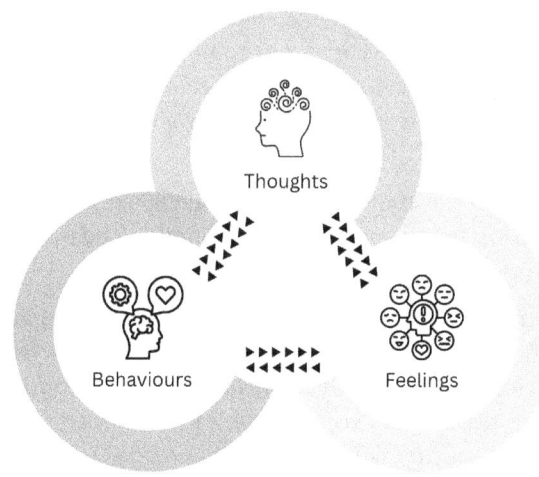

(ADAPTED FROM BECK, 2020)

A focus on CBT principles can be as simple as supporting a student to draw a link between their thoughts, feelings and their behaviour and demonstrating that they're closely aligned (Beck, 2020). This understanding can assist with teaching students to identify negative thought patterns and replace them with more constructive ones, helping them to manage emotions and behaviours more effectively (Beck, 2020).

Now, do I expect you to have a therapy session with every student who has a moment in your classroom? No, of course not.

Teachers aren't placed to intervene cognitively, and this should be left to the professionals such as counsellors and psychologists, but we're able to support behaviourally. To assist with skill-building, there are programs that can be implemented through multiple providers or professional learning sessions that can be run for staff, but ultimately, CBT principles can be integrated into the learning within the classroom through reflection (Tolin, 2024).

Assisting a student to understand their behaviour and the antecedent of that behaviour through a discussion has the potential to not only be powerful learning, but create long-lasting connection also.

You might even argue that it's potential for real *meaningful* learning.

Practice prevention

It might be self-explanatory, but preventative practices in behaviour support focus on creating classroom environments that reduce the likelihood of behavioural issues arising in the first place (Simonsen & Myers, 2025). This involves many of the strategies we've already discussed in this book, such as establishing clear expectations, consistent routines and positive relationships (Hudson, 2024). By proactively teaching and reinforcing desired behaviours, educators can create a culture of respect and responsibility (and keep the cows from the mountain).

Preventative approaches also include designing engaging lessons that cater to diverse learning needs, thereby minimising frustration and disengagement that can lead to behavioural challenges (Barker et al., 2022).

School-wide Positive Behaviour Support (SWPBS) is an example of this type of work (Barker et al., 2022). SWPBS is an evidence-based framework that brings together school communities to develop positive, safe, supportive learning cultures (see Figure 13). SWPBS assists schools in improving social, emotional, behavioural and academic outcomes for children and young people (Barker et al., 2022).

When implemented effectively, SWPBS allows teachers and students to focus more on relationships and classroom instruction, benefitting the entire school community (Department of Education and Training Victoria, 2025).

Implementing preventative practices requires a collaborative effort among educators, administrators and families. It involves ongoing professional development, data-driven decision-making and the use of positive reinforcement to encourage appropriate behaviour (Barker et al., 2022).

By prioritising prevention over punishment, schools can create inclusive environments that support the diverse needs of all students, fostering a sense of belonging and promoting positive behavioural outcomes.

Figure 13: Critical elements of a SWPBS framework

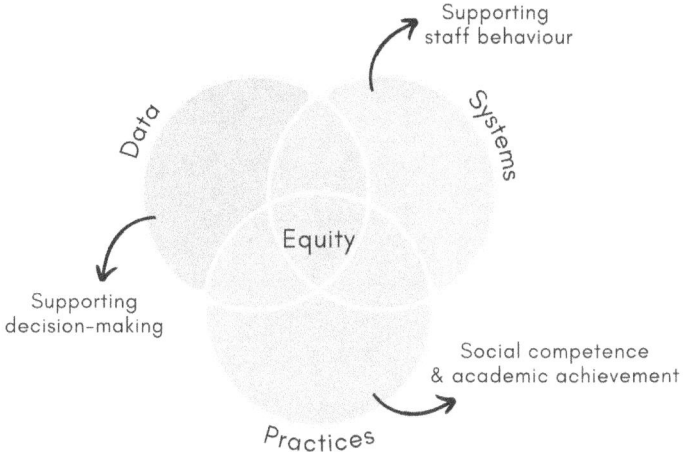

(ADAPTED FROM DEPARTMENT OF EDUCATION AND TRAINING VICTORIA, 2025)

Restore to build stronger

Restorative practices in education emphasise repairing harm and restoring relationships when conflicts occur. Rather than focusing solely on punishment, this approach encourages accountability, empathy and dialogue (Warnick & Scribner, 2020). By involving all parties in the resolution process, restorative practices aim to heal relationships and build a sense of community within the classroom (Lodi et al., 2021).

Restorative practices include strategies such as restorative circles, conferences and informal conversations that provide opportunities for students to reflect on their behaviour, understand its impact and make amends (Kehoe et al., 2018; Lodi et al., 2021). These practices promote a culture of respect and responsibility, encouraging students to take ownership of their actions and develop conflict-resolution skills (see Figure 14 overleaf). By focusing on relationship-building (and re-building), restorative practices contribute to a positive school climate, mirror the real world and reduce the incidence of behavioural issues through understanding (Alonso-Rodríguez et al., 2025).

Implementing restorative practices is a shift in school culture and calls on the commitment of all staff members. It involves professional development to build capacity in restorative approaches, the integration of restorative principles into school policies, and the engagement of students and families in the process (Lodi et al., 2021).

By fostering a restorative culture, schools can create supportive environments where students feel valued, heard and connected, enhancing both academic and social outcomes.

Figure 14: Benefits of restorative practices

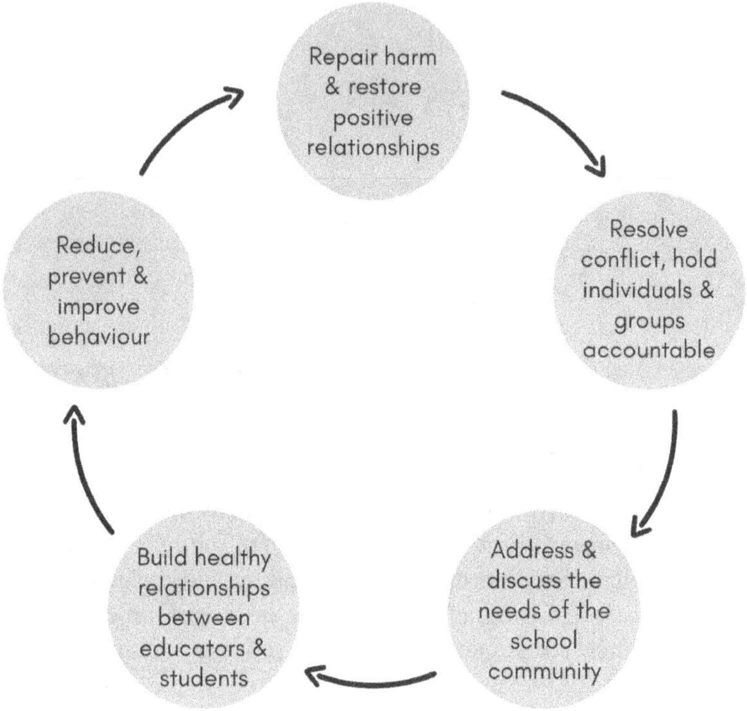

- Repair harm & restore positive relationships
- Resolve conflict, hold individuals & groups accountable
- Address & discuss the needs of the school community
- Build healthy relationships between educators & students
- Reduce, prevent & improve behaviour

(ADAPTED FROM NSW DEPARTMENT OF EDUCATION, 2025)

Securing your own mask, so you CAN help others

Educators' wellbeing, although usually furthest from our own thoughts, is crucial for creating supportive learning environments. It gives me great joy to know this is increasingly becoming an area of focus, but there is much more to do.

High levels of stress, anxiety and burnout among teachers can negatively impact their effectiveness and the overall classroom climate (Agyapong et al., 2022). Addressing these issues broadly requires systemic changes, such as providing adequate resources (social, emotional, mental and physical), professional development and opportunities for collaboration (Benevene et al., 2020).

This is crucial because supporting teacher wellbeing not only benefits educators but also enhances student outcomes, as teachers are better equipped to meet their students' needs when they're well-supported themselves.

Teaching is better when teachers *feel better*.

Research indicates that Australian teachers experience high levels of occupational stress, with the highest contributing factors including excessive workload, lack of resources and challenging student behaviours (Carroll et al., 2022; Heffernan et al., 2022). The impact of student trauma on teachers can also lead to secondary traumatic stress, characterised by symptoms such as acute stress, feelings of helplessness and disturbed sleep (Berger & Nott, 2024). These stressors can lead to burnout, resulting in decreased job satisfaction, increased absenteeism and higher turnover rates (Carroll et al., 2022; Heffernan et al., 2022).

To mitigate stress and prevent burnout, schools must prioritise teacher wellbeing through comprehensive support systems. This includes providing access to mental health resources, fostering a positive school culture and promoting work-life balance (Henrietta, 2023). Professional development opportunities focused on self-care, resilience and stress management can empower teachers to navigate the demands of the profession (Green, 2022).

It should be more obvious than what it currently is, but when schools invest in teacher wellbeing, they not only support their staff but also create environments where students can thrive.

That being said…

Teachers must make changes also. Systemic change is the dream; small individual changes is the reality and the way forward (at this point).

What to do?

Every climber faces obstacles; they're a natural part of the experience. Some of these will be expected and planned for, others more sudden. The difference between those who continue the journey and those who turn back isn't the absence of struggle; it's how they respond to these inevitable challenges.

Is it a bird? Is it a plane?
No, it's just good connective practice

The following five strategies help teachers navigate these challenges while keeping connection intact.

1. Shift from The Punisher to The Repairer

In traditional discipline models, students break a rule, consequences are applied and learning is expected to resume. However, research shows that punitive discipline damages relationships and increases student alienation (Gregory et al., 2017). Instead of repairing harm, it often reinforces separation, making future conflicts more likely.

A restorative approach shifts the focus from punishment to repair, accountability and reintegration. Instead of *"How do I control this student?"* we ask, *"How do we restore connection and responsibility?"*

Table 4 (on page 162) outlines the steps in a restorative conversation.

2. It's always sunny in…

Unconditional positive regard in the classroom is the foundation for strong connection and a sense of safety that allows students to thrive (Moreno, 2021). It means communicating, through both words and actions, that every student is worthy of care, respect and belief, no matter what behaviour they're displaying (Brunzell & Norrish, 2021).

We still teach accountability, but we also show students that their dignity is non-negotiable, and that our belief in their potential doesn't waver when things go wrong. When students know they're accepted even in their most challenging moments, they're more likely to open themselves to connection, regulation and growth (Brunzell & Norrish, 2021).

As educators, we become a secure base from which students can take risks, reflect and recover – something many of them desperately need.

Show them you care!

Here are some ideas for incorporating UPR into your classroom practice:

- *Respond to behaviour with calm consistency, not emotion*
  Handle challenging behaviour with a steady tone and body language. Avoid raising your voice or showing frustration, so students feel safe even as you set boundaries.
- *Routinely repair and reconnect*
  If a rupture occurs, circle back later with a kind word or a fresh start. Show that your care isn't tied to their behaviour.
- *Acknowledge their identity beyond their behaviour*
  Learn about students' interests and strengths and reflect this in conversation and class activities. This shows you see them beyond their behaviour.
- *Praise effort, not just outcomes*
  Highlight effort, like self-control or trying hard, rather than just results. It reinforces growth and internal motivation.

3. Lighten the load

While teachers aren't trained therapists, we're often in a unique position to guide students towards greater self-awareness. By drawing on elements of CBT, teachers can support students to reflect on how their thoughts, feelings and behaviours interact, particularly after a moment of disruption or dysregulation.

We cannot 'fix' students and that really isn't what this is about. It's about walking alongside them as they begin to recognise internal patterns and gain a sense of control over their responses (Alonso-Rodríguez et al., 2025). Creating space for reflective dialogue helps students shift from reactive behaviours to intentional choices.

Over time, these small reflective moments can build essential emotional literacy and resilience, particularly for students who haven't yet developed these skills at home or in other environments (Tolin, 2024).

Partners in climb

Consider these practical ways to support student reflection using CBT principles:

- Use calm, structured debriefs: Wait until the student is calm before talking. Use non-judgemental questions like, *"Can we talk about what happened earlier?"*

- Link thoughts, feelings and actions: Ask questions such as, *"What were you thinking just before?"* or *"How did that thought make you feel?"* to help them see behaviour as a process, not a fixed trait.
- Reframe unhelpful thoughts: When students share defeatist thoughts (like *"Everyone hates me"*), gently explore other views: *"Is it possible they weren't laughing at you?"* or *"What else could that mean?"*
- Encourage their own next steps: After reflecting, help students choose simple, achievable actions for next time, like, *"Take three deep breaths"* or *"Ask for a break".* This builds ownership and follow-through.

4. Better than the cure

Preventing behaviour challenges before they escalate is one of the most effective ways to support student wellbeing and maintain a connected, calm classroom.

Many behavioural issues stem not from defiance but from uncertainty, disconnection or unmet needs (Mitchell et al., 2019). By front-loading expectations, building predictable routines and embedding relational warmth into the flow of the day, we reduce the need for reaction and increase the likelihood of student success (Lester et al., 2017).

Preventative work is often invisible when it's working well, but that is a good thing. That invisible work is the backbone of a thriving learning space.

It's all part of the plan

Let's look at some key preventative practice strategies for your classroom:

- *Teach and revisit behavioural expectations explicitly:* Don't assume students know how to behave. Model respectful listening, role-play transitions and revisit expectations often, not just after issues arise.
- *Use proactive reminders before high-risk moments:* Before challenging times (like group work or lining up), give positive prompts: *"Let's remember to keep hands to ourselves and voices at Level 1 while we move."*
- *Build strong relational routines:* Greet students at the door, check in regularly and create shared rituals like morning circles or weekly reflections. These foster emotional safety and community.
- *Anticipate and plan for triggers:* Think ahead about when or where students might struggle (noisy times, academic stress, late afternoons) and adjust support or structure to lighten the load.

5. Always have fuel in the tank

Connection-driven teaching is deeply relational and emotionally intensive. While it fosters deeper student engagement and trust, it also requires a teacher's emotional presence, patience and adaptability (Green, 2022).

The risk? Teacher burnout.

When educators prioritise student wellbeing without addressing their own, the result is often compassion fatigue – a state where constant emotional labour leads to exhaustion, frustration and, ultimately, disconnection from students (Oberg et al., 2024).

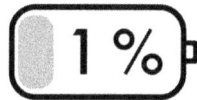

You wouldn't let your phone stay like this for long.
What about your personal battery?

We care about our students, their families and our communities, but we do this in place of ourselves. This chapter has focused on behaviour; again, we must also look within.

Burn bright, not out

Here are some ways to stay at your best, whatever that looks like on any given day:

- *Regulate yourself first*
  Like climbers who need their own oxygen, teachers must regulate their emotions before supporting students.
    - Pause and breathe before reacting to a disruptive student.
    - Name your emotions: *"I'm feeling frustrated because the class isn't engaged. What's a constructive way to handle this?"*
    - Set emotional boundaries, acknowledge struggles without taking them home.
- *Build a professional support network*
  Connection is just as vital for teachers. Schools with peer support and collaboration have lower burnout rates.
    - Micro-debriefs in the staffroom: a quick *"How's your day?"* can release tension.
    - Seek mentorship or coaching for fresh perspectives.
    - Advocate for staff wellbeing programs if they're missing.

- *Focus on what's within your control*
  Systemic issues can make connection-based practices hard. Anchor in what's actionable.
    - Reframe setbacks as data: *"What else can I try?"*
    - Start small, implement restorative practices in your own class first.
    - Celebrate small wins, connection grows over time.

Why do it?

Just because challenge is inevitable, it doesn't mean disconnection has to be.

The real measure of a connected classroom isn't how it functions when everything is calm, but how it responds when things get hard. Calm classrooms are lovely, but calm isn't the point. Connection is. And true connection reveals itself not when things are going smoothly, but when tension rises, when a lesson unravels or when a student's behaviour pushes us to the edge of our patience.

This work, unpacking behaviour, shifting from control to support, listening when it would be easier to shut down, matters because it's in these exact moments that connection is either fractured or deepened. Every classroom challenge presents a fork in the path: we can move towards understanding, or we can fall back into reaction.

And trust me, students don't forget those moments.

They remember the teacher who didn't reduce them to a behaviour. They remember the adult who didn't shame them for struggling. And they remember, perhaps more than anything, the quiet confidence of someone who stayed connected, even when things were messy.

The behaviour is not the student

When we choose to respond with curiosity instead of control, to repair instead of reprimand, we teach far more than content. We model something that is increasingly rare in many students' lives: relational safety. We show them that relationships and belonging don't disappear when behaviour slips. That conflict doesn't mean rejection. That their worth isn't conditional on compliance.

This work builds connection *in the moments it's most at risk* – which is exactly when it matters most.

Why do it? Because connection formed in calm can be meaningful, but connection *maintained in challenge* is transformational.

It's easy to value relationships when things are light and going to plan. It's another thing entirely to keep choosing connection when you're in the middle of a storm or at the bottom of the valley. That is when it becomes more than a strategy. It becomes a philosophy. A way of being.

Because every behaviour tells a story, and if we're willing to pause and listen, we can help young people change the narrative. We can show them that their identity isn't bound to the worst moment of the day but instead shaped by how they're supported through it.

In choosing restoration over reaction, we model the very things we hope our students carry with them: empathy, self-awareness, accountability and compassion. These aren't just 'soft skills', they're the deep infrastructure of a healthy classroom community. They're what create conditions for real learning, not just academic achievement but emotional growth, resilience and meaning.

> In *Hidden Potential: The Science of Achieving Greater Things*, organisational psychologist Adam Grant (2023) reflects:
>
> > "It's often said that where there's a will, there's a way. What we overlook is that when people can't see a path, they stop dreaming of the destination."
>
> It is our job to maintain the path and support their journey as learners.

Classrooms are where young people learn how to be with others, how to be with themselves and how to find meaning even when the climb is steep. This isn't about avoiding challenge. It's about walking through it in a way that strengthens, rather than breaks, the human connections that make learning possible.

We need to make this shift more widespread because when connection is preserved in difficulty, belonging is built.

And when belonging is built, learning becomes more than academic, it becomes personal, powerful and *real*.

Where to next?

Classroom challenges aren't detours from teaching; they *are* teaching. The valleys don't need to be moments of despair; they can be great moments of deep and meaningful learning.

The following questions and strategies are designed to help you reflect on how you respond to challenges and how you might move forward, with connection still at the centre.

1. How am I responding to disruption?

Every classroom disruption is an opportunity, not for punishment, but for understanding. It's not about ignoring behaviour but exploring its roots and responding in ways that preserve dignity and connection. Consider:

- Do I pause to consider what might be behind a student's behaviour, or do I react on instinct?
- Am I able to stay calm and supportive in the moment, even when challenged?
- Are there restorative practices I could use to move from reaction to repair?

2. Am I setting up for prevention, not just response?

Preventative practice often works so well it's invisible. But behind every calm classroom is a foundation of predictability, routine and trust. Consider:

- Have I established clear behavioural expectations, and do I teach them proactively?
- Are routines predictable and supportive for both students and myself?
- Do students know what success looks like socially and emotionally, not just academically?

3. Do my strategies reflect support rather than control?

When we seek compliance, we may get silence, but not connection. True support means guiding students back into learning with care, not coercion. Consider:

- Is my classroom built on mutual respect or a top-down dynamic?
- Am I using strategies that build emotional literacy and self-regulation?
- Do students feel they have agency in how they respond to challenges?

4. Am I protecting my own capacity to connect?

You cannot pour from an empty cup. Your wellbeing isn't an optional extra, it's the foundation of your capacity to stay present, patient and connected. Consider:

- What helps me stay emotionally steady when things get tough?
- Do I have a network of colleagues to debrief and share ideas with?
- Am I clear on what I can control and kind to myself about what I cannot?

5. What's one small shift I can make right now?

Big changes start with small steps. You don't need to redesign everything, just tweak the part of the system that is within reach. Consider:

- Could I try using UPR more consciously tomorrow?
- Is there a moment from today I'd like to revisit or respond to differently?
- What's one preventative structure (a check-in, a clear expectation, a calmer transition) I can embed this week?

Storms will come. Cows may fly. But if we learn to navigate them with compassion and curiosity, we don't just get through the lesson, we grow stronger for it. And more importantly, so do our students.

But wait... there's more!
What if it's not working?

Even with intentional strategies, some students will still disengage, resist or struggle. Instead of seeing this as failure, use these moments as data for adjusting your approach. Table 2 contains a few ideas.

Table 2: Common challenges and solutions

Challenge	Why it happens	How to adjust
Students ignore restorative circles	They're unfamiliar with the process and fear judgement.	Teach why restorative practices matter before implementing them. Model vulnerability by sharing your own reflections.
Choice-based learning leads to avoidance	Some students feel overwhelmed by open-ended tasks.	Provide structured choices with clear expectations, for example, *"Would you rather write a reflection or record an audio response?"*
Engagement strategies don't work on certain students	Students may have deep-rooted mistrust in education.	Build 1:1 relationships first. A small, personal check-in before class can rebuild trust over time.
Restorative practices feel time-consuming	Connection work takes time, but prevents future disruptions.	Invest time upfront in relationship-building; it saves hours of conflict resolution later.

What do I say?

Handling emotionally charged moments with students is challenging. Table 3 provides a few example scripts to maintain connection while setting boundaries.

Table 3: Example scripts for challenging behaviours

Situation	Ineffective	Effective
Dealing with defiance	"You need to stop talking back and do as you're told."	"I can see you're frustrated right now. Let's take a moment. What's going on?"
Addressing a student who says, "This is stupid"	"Sometimes we have to do things we don't like. Just do your work."	"I hear that you're not seeing the point of this lesson. Can we talk about what's making it frustrating?"
Managing a conflict between students	"Both of you need to apologise now and shake hands."	"It seems like there's tension between you. Let's figure out what happened and how we can move forward."

What do I ask?

Supporting a restorative conversation can be nerve-wracking; you are, after all, trying to address strong thoughts, emotions and behaviours. Table 4 has some suggested steps for guiding a restorative conversation after a conflict or behavioural issue.

Table 4: Steps in a restorative conversation

Step	Examples	Purpose
1. Opening the space	"Can we talk for a few minutes about what happened earlier?" "I want to hear your side of the story."	Set a calm tone, show you're not here to punish but to understand.
2. Understanding the student's perspective	"What happened from your point of view?" "How were you feeling at the time?" "What were you needing in that moment?"	Help the student feel heard and valued.

Step	Examples	Purpose
3. Reflecting on impact	"How do you think others were affected?" "What do you think I saw or felt as the teacher?" "How do you think your classmates might have experienced that?"	Build empathy and accountability.
4. Restoring relationships	"What do you think needs to happen to make things right?" "Is there something you would like to say to others involved?" "How can I support you in handling things differently next time?"	Move towards healing and solution, not just consequences.
5. Follow-up plan	Agree on next steps. Set a check-in time if needed.	Reinforce that repair and growth are ongoing processes.

(ADAPTED FROM NSW DEPARTMENT OF EDUCATION, 2025)

TL;DR

Key takeaways

1. **Challenge is inevitable – connection is a choice**
   Every classroom faces disruption, disengagement and the occasional 'flying cow' moment. Connection isn't built by avoiding difficulty – it's built by how we respond when things go wrong. When teachers meet challenges with curiosity, care and calm, those tough moments can become some of the most powerful for building trust and belonging.

2. **Behaviour is communication and connection is the response**
   Traditional behaviour management often seeks compliance through control. Behaviour tells a story – one of stress, unmet needs or disconnection. Trauma-informed approaches and unconditional positive règard help us interpret these stories and respond in ways that restore rather than reprimand.

3. **Preventative practice keeps the storms at bay**
   The best way to manage classroom challenges is to stop them from escalating in the first place. Clear routines, proactive strategies and

emotionally safe learning environments reduce the cognitive, emotional and behavioural overload that leads to disruption.

4. **Teacher wellbeing is essential – not optional**
   Teachers carry emotional, cognitive and relational weight every day – and without support, it's easy to burn out. Prioritising teacher wellbeing isn't self-indulgent, it's strategic. Regulated teachers are more effective at navigating challenges and modelling calm, constructive responses.

5. **In the valley lies the potential for transformation**
   Disconnection doesn't have to be the end of the story – it can be the beginning of a better one. Restorative conversations, student reflection and small shifts in how we approach behaviour can rebuild trust and connection, even after rupture. When we choose connection over control, we show students that they're worthy, seen and valued – even when the cows are flying.

Curiosity

Connection begins with culture.
Celebrate the journey, ask brave questions and imagine what's possible.

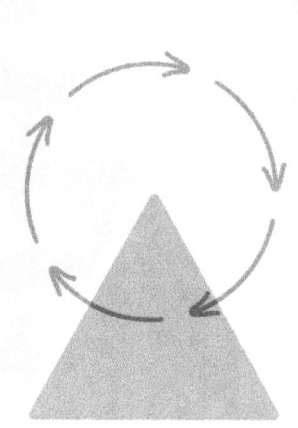

Connection pause

Ask yourself: *What's something I've always wondered about teaching but haven't had the vulnerability to explore?*

Write it down – no pressure to answer it. Just honour the question.

PART 6
THE SUMMIT AND THE NEXT MOUNTAIN

Celebrating the ongoing
pursuit of connection

**"Don't go where the path
may lead, go instead where there
is no path and leave a trail"**

- RALPH WALDO EMERSON

There is a saying among climbers: *"The summit's only halfway."* Reaching the top isn't the end of the journey, it's the beginning of the next one. Sir Edmund Hillary said, *"It's not the mountain we conquer, but ourselves."*

For teachers, this is the moment where we move from *growth* to *influence*. We're not just climbing for ourselves anymore; we're preparing to lead others. The summit's a time for reflection, yes, but also a call to action. It asks: *What will you do with what you've learned? Who else can you bring with you on the next climb?* Part 6 is about legacy and leadership. It explores the quiet courage of educators who don't wait for permission to lead. Who reflect deeply, act intentionally and extend the connection movement beyond their own classrooms. We're no longer building connection in isolation; we're building momentum across a community. We begin in *Chapter 11: Planting the flag*, where we reflect not only on how far we've come, but what it means to carry that experience forward. True reflection isn't nostalgia – it's preparation. We then move to *Chapter 12: Acting with courage*, where we explore the next step, sharing the climb. Here, we unpack what it means to lead without a title, to influence culture through action and to start building a movement of connection that reaches beyond individual classrooms.

Leadership isn't a badge; it's a mindset. A practice. A habit of courage.

Together, these chapters are a turning point. From reflection to action. From self to system. From summit to new trail. The view may be stunning, but the journey isn't done. The next mountain calls – and now, you're ready to answer.

Don't leave it too long.

CHAPTER 11
Planting the flag
Reflecting on progress and growth

Reaching a summit is a moment for celebration, but it's also a time for reflection. The view offers perspective, a chance to look back over the path travelled and to glimpse the mountains still to come. It's tempting to pause too long, to stay wrapped in the satisfaction of progress. But the summit's not the end. It's a milestone and a reminder that growth isn't about arriving but continuing. True reflection is the art of standing still just long enough to take stock: to understand what brought us here, what holds us here and what will move us forward. Reflection is a vital discipline, shaping our next steps with greater intention, deeper connection and renewed purpose.

This chapter explores how reflection deepens growth, not only for students but for teachers themselves. Reflection fuels leadership from within, not through titles or positions, but through habits of awareness, adaptability and action. When we reflect meaningfully, we stay grounded in the present, honour the lessons of the past and chart a more deliberate course into the future. Because at the summit, the real question is never, *"Are we there yet?"*, it's always, *"Where to next?"*

The big two

The power of reflection in teaching and leadership

Reflection is a funny concept. We typically think reflection is about looking back. But the mirror doesn't replay our past, nor does it reflect our future. What we see in the mirror is a presentation of our current state. The mirror is a tool for making small refinements to that current state or cleaning up remnants of the past.

Perhaps I'm being too philosophical, or a bit pretentious. Too literal? Definitely.

Reflection is a concept that is confusing, though. Not because it's exceptionally complex but because it's deceptively simple. Simple can be moulded to suit different purposes. I've mentioned it many different times myself throughout this book and likely framed it to suit the purpose of the chapter it's used within. I'm potentially guilty of adding to that confusion, too.

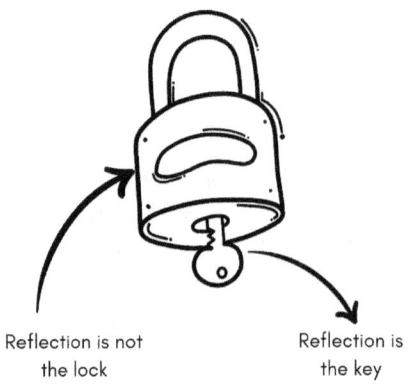

Reflection is not the lock

Reflection is the key

Reflection is not a compulsory process.
It is a voluntary behaviour

Schools have selectively absconded with reflection as both a term and a practice, and so I want to be clear on what I mean when I discuss it. Reflection is taking stock of the present, looking at the past that has informed it and crafting something actionable for use in the near future (Chang, 2019).

Now, then and *forward with purpose.*

The most effective educators I've worked with do more than review what has worked in their classrooms; they use those insights to refine their practice, enhance student learning and drive meaningful change. They do this on their own. Not in a staff meeting or a professional learning session. They do it when they finish a lesson, when they are planning; they likely do it when they're in the middle of a lesson, too. The best time to reflect is *constantly*.

Dwelling on a poor lesson, a tough conversation or some less than constructive feedback isn't reflection. Reflection is working with the data you have with a critical but positive frame of mind. *Forward* with purpose. You cannot move forward if you're always looking over your shoulder.

For too long (and in too many publications), reflection has been framed primarily as a student or early career exercise (Brookfield, 2017). A tool for self-assessment and personal responsibility in learning. But reflection is just as critical for experienced teachers, serving as a key to:

- **Professional growth** – understanding what works and why
- **Stronger decision-making** – refining teaching practices based on real experiences
- **Leadership development** – expanding influence beyond the classroom

    (Zepeda, 2019)

Teachers who engage in continuous self-assessment, who evaluate their impact, adjust their approaches and set new goals model the very habits they seek to instil in their students (Mathew et al., 2017; Moayeri & Rahimiy, 2019). At the heart of this discussion lie two essential questions:

1. How can reflection fuel both student and teacher growth?
2. How does personal reflection empower teachers to lead from within?

Here at the summit, these questions help us explore why reflection matters, not just for improving instruction, but for fostering a mindset of continuous growth, leadership and connection. Because we *cannot* stay here.

At the start of our journey the goal was to build connection in our classroom, yes, but always with the goal of spreading the connection wider.

Reflection is essential to the journey onwards and the trails to *the next mountains*.

1. How can reflection fuel both student and teacher growth?

Reflection is often seen as a tool for student learning, but it's a fundamental driver of growth for both students and teachers (Moayeri & Rahimiy, 2019). We cannot expect to grow without a deep and thorough understanding of the conditions that support that growth (Tomlinson & Imbeau, 2023). Reflection is fundamental to organic and authentic learning, but we often treat it as a data-collection method in our classroom. It's become the mandatory component at the end of the assessment rather than a genuine part of the process.

> **For students, reflection promotes:**
> - *Deeper learning* – encouraging them to think critically about their progress.

- *Self-awareness* – helping them identify strengths, challenges and areas for growth.
- *Greater independence* – allowing them to take ownership of their learning.

(Chang, 2019)

Similarly, we can apply these principles to teachers (again, teachers are human). For school staff, reflection is the bridge between experience and growth. Without it, teaching becomes static rather than adaptive, and we fail to address the core need of connection.

A reflective teacher:
- *Assesses their impact* – examining what strategies are working and what needs adjustment.
- *Identifies patterns in student engagement and success* – looking beyond surface-level outcomes to understand deeper learning trends.
- *Adjusts instruction based on evidence* – moving beyond intuition and making informed decisions about teaching methods.

(Danielson, 2024)

This process isn't about self-criticism; it's about continuous refinement. The best teachers don't wait for external directives to tell them what needs improvement; they actively refine their craft based on their own observations and insights.

2. How does personal reflection empower teachers to lead from within?

Teachers who engage in deep reflection aren't just improving their own practice, they're shaping school culture, influencing colleagues and driving systemic change (Kruse & Louis, 2008).

To reflect deeply you must have a clear sense of what meaningful education looks and feels like, you need to know how to create it and do what you can to make that a reality. You must have the ability and humility to modify your practice based on real-world challenges you experience and, ultimately, a mindset that is geared towards sharing insights and seeking out learning from others.

To me this reads quite simply: a reflective teacher is a *leader*.

Those qualities are clearly *vision*, *adaptability* and *collaboration* – three essential values of an effective educational leader.

At the summit and looking out over the next mountains to climb, we need to look not only at individual growth but also the power of reflection to foster collective improvement. Schools thrive when educators share their insights, challenge assumptions and work to build a school-wide commitment to growth (Tschannen-Moran, 2014).

We need to be aware of what's working and why, so we can encourage our students to do the same and convince other staff to come along on the next climb with us.

If we put in the work, reflection can become a habit rather than an occasional (or enforced) exercise, then, and only then, does it become a catalyst for innovation and transformation (Tschannen-Moran, 2014). Teachers no longer see professional development as something imposed upon them but as something they drive from within.

By embedding reflection into daily practice, teachers lead from within, not because of a title, but because of the mindset they cultivate.

Unpack your journey

Tool of the trade

Reflection is no doubt a part of the educational lexicon. We know of it, we take part in it, we prescribe it and we speak on it. It's a tool and one that has probably become a little blunt.

When reflection is at its best, for students it's a means for them to assess their learning and set future goals; for teachers it's an essential leadership skill that strengthens decision-making, drives innovation and fosters collective growth within the school community (Bono et al., 2022; Brookfield, 2017). We're going to prioritise this for the moment.

To put it lightly, teaching is a complex and dynamic profession, and the ability to critically examine and refine your practice is what will set you and your colleagues apart – you know it, I know it and the research supports it (Morgan, 2019). By engaging in intentional reflection, teachers can lead from within their classrooms, influencing colleagues, students and the broader school culture without waiting for formal leadership roles or external directives.

Here is where we start to think about your ability to influence connection in the classroom, but also more widely.

Decisions, decisions and metacognitions

At its core, reflection is an exercise in metacognition or thinking about one's thinking. John Flavell (1979), who pioneered the concept of metacognition, argued that when individuals engage in self-awareness regarding their cognitive processes, they become better decision-makers and problem-solvers.

In the classroom, this means that teachers who reflect on their instructional strategies, student engagement and learning outcomes are more adept at making real-time adjustments that enhance their effectiveness (Hargreaves & Fullan, 2012).

Metacognition enables educators to become proactive rather than reactive. Instead of merely responding to classroom challenges as they arise, teachers who engage in regular reflection develop the foresight to anticipate potential obstacles and adjust their approach accordingly (Lin et al., 2018).

Research supports the idea that reflective practitioners are more adaptive and resilient (Schön, 1983). Donald Schön's concept of 'reflection in action' and 'reflection on action' (see Figure 15) highlights how skilled professionals, including teachers, continuously assess their decisions both during and after instructional moments. This iterative process allows for refined decision-making and improved student outcomes over time (Schön, 1983).

Figure 15: Schön's 'reflection in action' and 'reflection on action'

Reflection in action
Reflecting as something happens
Consider the situation
Decide how to act
Act immediately

Reflection on action
Reflecting after something happens
Reconsider the situation
Think about what needs changing for the future

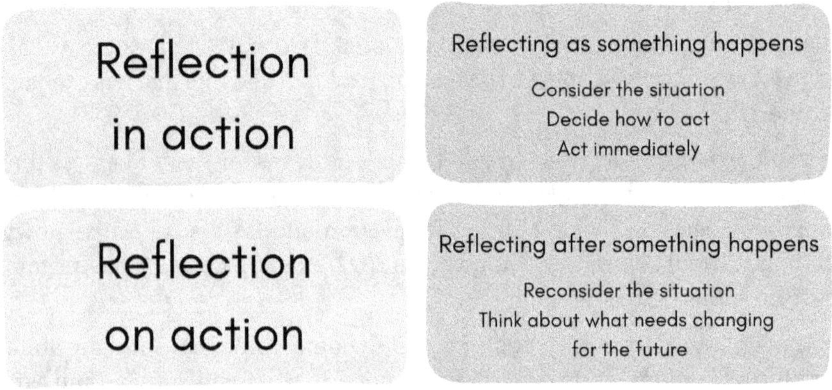

(ADAPTED FROM SCHÖN, 1983)

Reflection also fosters self-regulation – a critical skill for both teachers and students. Dr Shyam Barr (2024), in his book *Educate to Self-Regulate: Empowering Learners for Lifelong Success*, emphasises that self-regulated learners set goals, monitor progress and adjust their strategies as needed.

> **Barr (2024) states:**
> "Autonomous learning empowers learners to take charge of their educational journey, fostering self-direction and personal responsibility… It places a strong emphasis on critical thinking, problem-solving and the ability to independently seek and use resources." (p. 120)

The same self-regulation benefits apply to teachers who engage in reflective practice. Through analysis of their instructional choices, assessment of student responses and refinement of their methodologies, educators enhance their professional efficacy and deepen their leadership potential (Barr, 2024).

Be the inspiration

Reflective educators naturally contribute to a culture of professional learning (Tuli, 2017; Zepeda, 2019), as their commitment to self-improvement often extends beyond personal practice and into collaborative discussions with peers. They want to improve and want you to improve alongside them.

When teachers openly share their reflections, whether through informal conversations, professional learning communities or written documentation, they provide valuable insights that benefit their colleagues (Admiraal et al., 2021; McPherson & Asghar, 2023).

Don't treat your reflections like your lunch in the staff room fridge — share it with your colleagues

Research by Visible Learning Meta[x] (2024) suggests that collective teacher efficacy - the shared belief among educators in their ability to impact student learning - is one of the most significant factors in improving student outcomes (it currently has an effect size of 1.12!).

Reflection serves as a key driver of this efficacy, as it encourages teachers to engage in meaningful discussions about challenges, successes and strategies for improvement.

It is genuine connection in action.

A reflective teacher so openly demonstrates this essential practice, that it can inspire students to adopt similar habits (Brookfield, 2017). When educators model self-assessment, goal setting and a commitment to growth, students internalise these behaviours, leading to increased autonomy and resilience in their learning journeys (Gorelova, 2025). In this way, the impact of reflection extends beyond the individual teacher, creating echoes of influence throughout the classroom and school community.

It creates the start of a *connection movement*.

What to do?

Reflection only becomes powerful when it moves from passive contemplation into deliberate action. Too often, teachers are encouraged to reflect but aren't given concrete strategies to make that reflection meaningful and transformative.

The goal is to go beyond simply acknowledging what worked, and what didn't, towards a structured approach that refines teaching practice, strengthens belonging and fosters shared learning. Here are three strategies to turn reflection into a habit, an external influence and an action plan.

1. Habit your way

Reflection is most effective when it becomes a regular routine, rather than an afterthought at the end of a staff meeting. Just as we build habits for lesson planning and classroom management, structured reflection should be embedded in our practice.

> James Clear (2018), author of *Atomic Habits: An Easy & Proven Way to Build Good Habits & Break Bad Ones*, captures this idea:
>
> > "All big things come from small beginnings. The seed of every habit is a single, tiny decision. But as that decision is repeated, a habit sprouts and grows stronger." (p. 22)
>
> If we want reflection to stick, it needs structure and time to grow.

One simple way to formalise self-reflection is through journalling. Writing clarifies thoughts, reveals patterns and ensures insights don't get lost in the school day's chaos (Barr, 2024; Clear, 2018).

Personally, I'm always jotting down thoughts, whether in my phone's notes app, recording voice memos on a street corner while walking the dog, or even with my arm out of the shower (does anyone else get a lot of ideas mid-shower?). My notes might be messy, but revisiting them weekly helps me spot the insights worth carrying forward.

> Consider using the following prompts in a weekly reflection journal:
> - What worked well this week? (Instructional strategies, student engagement.)

- What would I change if I could teach this week again?
- How did I foster connection this week?
- What's one small action I can take next week to improve my teaching?

Research backs this up: Farrell (2018) found that reflective writing enhances teacher awareness and evidence-based practice. Even a short weekly routine can lead to significant growth over time. And when teachers model reflection, students learn to self-reflect, too, building metacognition and ownership of their learning (Zimmerman et al., 2017).

Encouraging students to assess their engagement and progress can be as simple as incorporating quick reflective routines:

- **Exit tickets** – students write one thing they learned and one question they still have.
- **Self-assessment rubrics** – a checklist where students rate their effort, participation and understanding.
- *Think-Pair-Share* **reflection** – discussing learning challenges and successes with peers before sharing with the class.

When teachers and students reflect together, it normalises reflection as a core part of learning.

2. Make the internal, external

Reflection is often seen as a private act, but its real power emerges when shared. Schools that foster collective reflection, where teachers openly discuss, question and challenge one another, build a culture of growth and collaboration that goes beyond the token *"chat with the person next to you"* moment in staff meetings (Admiraal et al., 2021).

As time becomes scarcer, it seems like the informal chats in staffrooms and yards are disappearing. Yet these quick conversations are vital for reflection and mental health – no one can carry it all alone! While we might need to start with a more structured approach, the aim is to recapture this informal magic and turn it into intentional action.

Informally formal formation

Since it's unlikely that 'informal conversation time' will be scheduled in, it's up to us to create these opportunities until they start to appear on their own:

- *Reflection partnerships* – pair with a colleague for a quick weekly debrief.
- *Professional learning communities* – structured discussions around teaching challenges and wins.

- *Shared digital spaces* – Google Docs or discussion boards for ongoing reflective dialogue.

Sharing reflections makes them a part of collective learning, not just personal growth. It also creates valuable qualitative data that complements student test scores or evaluations. Reflecting on how our development impacts our communities is essential for authentic progress.

Building a space to share reflections requires trust. If your school has invested in creating psychological safety, collaborative reflection can be a powerful tool for change (Edmondson, 2018).

Consider the following when establishing a collaborative self-reflection effort:
- *Track themes over time* – look for patterns in challenges and growth.
- *Compare reflections with student feedback* – offers a balanced view of instructional impact.
- *Use reflections as evidence in professional development discussions* – can provide valuable insights for goal setting.

When teachers see reflection as collective learning, it builds relationships, breaks down cliques and strengthens belonging (Clarà et al., 2019).

3. Make tracks

Reflection shouldn't be an end point, but it so often is.

Reflect at the end of a unit.

Reflect at the end of a year.

Reflect at the end of a contract or even a career.

That was much more Dr Seuss than I intended.

Reflection becomes most effective when paired with incremental, ongoing action (Collier & Williams, 2023). Rather than feeling pressured to change everything at once, focus on one small adjustment each week.

Be the tortoise, not the hare

Here's a simple plan to turn reflections into action:
- *Identify a single strategy to tweak* – maybe group work, formative assessment or a new questioning technique.
- *Implement the change and observe its impact.*
- *Reflect at the end of the week* – what worked? What needs refining?

Hattie and Zierer (2019) found that small, evidence-based tweaks lead to big improvements over time. This one-step-at-a-time approach also makes sharing easier – find a peer to discuss your experiments, host informal reflection meet-ups or weave reflection into mentoring.

By treating reflection as an ongoing cycle, teachers can build a culture of continuous improvement, normalise collaboration and celebrate growth (Tuli, 2017).

So, find a colleague. Observe each other's lessons. Reflect together. Support one another to climb further.

Why do it?

I'd love to be in a situation in which connection was something we could simply wish into existence. But it's not. It requires change and effort. It's commonly left to chance encounters or to linger in the margins of a busy classroom, but we can change this. Reflection is one key practice that makes this change possible. Without reflection, I fear connection risks becoming performative rather than transformative.

When we reflect, we deepen our understanding not only of what we do, but why we do it. It features here at the summit as we look across the journey we've taken, but also equally, the mountains in the ranges to come, because this 'why' is the foundation of meaningful and sustainable connection.

It's the flag we proudly plant at the summit for all to see.

In classrooms, students are quick to detect authenticity. They will be impacted by this metaphorical flag. They will know when your actions are aligned with a deeper purpose and when they're simply going through the motions. Through reflective practice, teachers strengthen their alignment between intention and action, making every interaction more genuine, more personal and more impactful (Brookfield, 2017; Hall & Simeral, 2017).

Young people have a fine-tuned bull**** detector

Reflection helps us to notice the small moments that build relationships, the quiet encouragement offered after a setback, the check-in with a student who seemed off-task, the respectful listening that shows students they're heard and valued. These moments might otherwise pass us by in the rush of the day. Reflection makes them visible, meaningful and replicable. Over time, these accumulated small acts of awareness create an environment where belonging can thrive.

Beyond individual relationships, reflection supports the construction of a shared classroom culture where connection is embedded into the learning experience (Tuli, 2017; Zepeda, 2019). When teachers reflect on the relational dynamics in their classrooms – who feels included, who's on the fringes, what power structures are at play – they can consciously design environments that are more equitable and inclusive (Morgan, 2019).

Reflection moves us from assumptions to informed action, enabling us to be responsive rather than reactive.

Importantly, the influence of reflection doesn't end within the four walls of the classroom. A reflective practitioner naturally models openness, vulnerability and a commitment to growth – the very qualities that drive positive change across a school community (Brookfield, 2017). Reflection shifts connection from being a personal act to a collective habit.

At its core, reflection ensures that connection isn't left to chance. It makes connection conscious. It strengthens our relationships with students, with colleagues and with ourselves. It empowers us to build classrooms and schools that aren't just effective, but humane; not just successful, but meaningful.

This is why we do it.

We reflect not merely to improve, but to connect more authentically, more deeply and more enduringly. Reflection is the act that turns the classroom from a place of instruction into a community of belonging, and turns a school from a workplace into a living, breathing ecosystem of growth.

Reflection isn't an add-on to connection; it's the *lifeblood* of it.

Where to next?

Reflection isn't a task to be checked off after a project, unit or year, it's a mindset, a daily habit and an essential tool for both professional growth and meaningful connection. Like an experienced climber who constantly adjusts their footing on the mountain, reflective educators continuously recalibrate their practice, always with a clear view towards the next peak.

The following questions and strategies are designed to guide your ongoing reflection and help embed reflective practice into the core of your teaching and leadership journey.

1. Am I making reflection a regular habit?

True reflection isn't something that happens once a year in a review meeting, it's a consistent practice that sharpens insight, fosters growth and strengthens connection. Consider:

- Have I built time into my week for structured reflection?
- Am I capturing reflections (through journalling, voice notes or conversations) before they slip away?
- Do I treat reflection as essential or something I'll get to 'if I have time'?

2. Am I moving from reflection to action?

Reflection is powerful when it leads to action. Insights without follow-through risk becoming just good intentions. Consider:

- After reflecting, do I identify one small, practical change to implement?
- Am I using reflection to set intentional, achievable goals for myself and my students?
- How am I tracking and reviewing the impact of changes I make?

3. Am I sharing reflection with others?

Reflection is even more powerful when it becomes a shared practice. Discussing insights, challenges and strategies creates a culture of growth and collective efficacy. Consider:

- Do I have a trusted colleague or team with whom I regularly share reflective conversations?
- Have I helped foster a culture where it's normal to talk about both successes and struggles?
- Am I open to learning from others' reflections as well as offering my own?

4. Am I modelling reflective practice for my students?

If we want students to become reflective learners, we must first model reflection ourselves – openly, authentically and consistently. Consider:

- Do my students see me reflecting on my practice, my choices and my learning?
- Am I building regular reflection into classroom routines for students, not just as an end-of-unit add-on?
- How am I helping students connect reflection to their own growth and success?

5. What small step can I take next?

Reflective practice is built step by step, not by giant leaps. Even the smallest act of intentional reflection can set new growth in motion. Consider:

- What's one reflective routine I could commit to this week – journalling, peer discussion, student feedback?

- Could I start or join a reflection partnership or learning community?
- What's one aspect of connection or teaching practice I could refine through purposeful reflection?

Reflection fuels connection. It builds leadership from within. It creates the pathways to our next summits.

The view from here is beautiful, but the journey continues.

TL;DR

Key takeaways

1. **Reflection is now, not just then**
   The best educators don't wait for formal reviews to reflect; they refine their practice constantly, in small and purposeful ways. Reflection grounds us in now, then and forward with purpose, helping both teachers and students move beyond dwelling to growing.

2. **Reflective practice fuels growth – for everyone**
   Reflection isn't only for students. It's a core driver of both student and teacher growth. When teachers reflect deeply, they strengthen their impact, improve their decision-making and model leadership from within the classroom.

3. **Leadership starts in the classroom**
   Reflective teachers naturally lead by example, shaping school culture through adaptability, collaboration and a commitment to growth. By embedding reflection into daily practice, teachers expand their influence beyond the classroom, inspiring colleagues and fostering collective improvement across the school.

4. **Reflection must move beyond the self**
   Informal conversations, collaborative reflection groups and peer learning communities build a culture where growth is normalised and connection is strengthened. Schools thrive when reflection shifts from an individual act to a collective habit.

5. **Small, reflective actions drive big change**
   Reflection becomes transformative when it leads to deliberate, sustained action. Reflective teachers aren't passengers in their professional journey; they're drivers of continuous improvement and deeper connection.

CHAPTER 12
Acting with courage
Celebrating progress and inspiring greater change

Every ascent demands strength, but also courage. At the summit, we pause, not just to celebrate, but to consider what lies beyond. The journey upward is focused, singular, often fuelled by a clear goal. But from the summit, the terrain opens. Possibilities multiply. And with them comes uncertainty. This is where courage becomes essential, not the dramatic kind, but the quiet, deliberate kind. The kind that asks you to move when it would be easier to stay where it's safe.

The summit's not an ending, but a threshold. In that space between achievement and what comes next, you're faced with a choice: will you carry your insights down into the world below and lead others up their own paths? Or will you remain, content but still? This chapter explores what it means to act with courage in education, to initiate rather than wait, to influence from within, to model change rather than ask for it. It's an invitation to lead not from a title, but from your values. Because the real work doesn't begin at the summit. It begins when you step beyond it into the unknown, with clarity, conviction and the courage to go first.

The big two

Don't just teach, lead!

The summit's a place of raw emotion. No matter the difficulties of the climb, the length of the journey or the depth of the valleys, it's a place of celebration. And you absolutely must celebrate every summit, no matter the context of the mountain or its terrain. Every climb is worth a moment of enjoyment.

The challenge at this point is over. Your goal is achieved; you made it! All that is left now is to start making your way down, but it's not as easy as it sounds. Every actual trail I've been fortunate to walk, from the Everest Base Camp trek and the Annapurna Circuit to the hike up Mount Kinabalu or the expedition to Machu Picchu, each of these has had its own challenges and, for many of them, the walk from the summit or the historical landmark, the reason for being there, is just as difficult.

Towards the summit, you have a clear end point. At the summit, you have a multitude of directions and possibilities. It's easy at the summit and on the way down to call it a day and hang up the boots and the pack. You successfully summited on our journey up the first mountain of connection.

The challenge from the summit is to celebrate without finality – there is much work still to be done. Your goal is now to create a connection movement where there was none before. You took up this journey because you couldn't wait for the expedition to start formally. It's time for you to lead – there are many more mountains in the range. The key is to take a larger party to the next mountain and the next summit.

It's your time

Teachers often feel powerless when it comes to creating school-wide change (Lockton & Fargason, 2019). It happens to them, not by their hand. I can understand this. There is a lingering belief that meaningful transformation must come from leadership and that policies, directives and top-down initiatives are the only ways to shift school culture (Lipscombe et al., 2019). However, this assumption isn't only limiting but also inaccurate.

Teachers, through their daily actions, interactions and choices, wield significant influence over their colleagues, students and, ultimately, the entire school environment (Gningue et al., 2022). Culture isn't built solely through policy (I'd argue it's not built through policy at all), it's shaped by the collective actions of the people within it.

At the heart of this reality lie two final essential questions:

1. How can teachers influence school-wide change without waiting for leadership?
2. What are practical ways to lead from within the classroom?

These questions challenge the idea that leadership is reserved for those with formal authority and instead highlight how everyday teaching practices can spark transformation on The Connection Journey.

1. How can teachers influence school-wide change without waiting for leadership?

Leadership in education is often viewed as hierarchical, with influence flowing from the top down (Lipscombe et al., 2019). It's viewed this way, well, because it is this way. It's been like this for a very long time and at a certain point a few decades ago, it was very successful.

However, research consistently shows that grassroots change, that is, change driven by passionate, engaged educators, is often more effective and sustainable than top-down mandates (Hargreaves & Fullan, 2012).

I wonder if you would agree.

Schools are some of the most dynamic ecosystems within the community, and within them is most likely a strong reliance on relationships, trust and peer influence to shape both how teachers teach and how students learn. A single teacher's approach to connection, rather than these three in isolation, can create waves of engagement and belonging, bringing meaning to curriculum and changing the cultural make-up throughout the entire school.

A teacher-led shift in culture happens through:
- *Modelling relational and connection-driven teaching* – when students thrive in an engaging, supportive classroom, others take notice.
- *Demonstrating student impact* – improved engagement, fewer behavioural challenges and stronger academic outcomes make a compelling case for change.
- *Challenging assumptions* – When teachers introduce new ways of thinking about student relationships and instructional approaches, they disrupt outdated norms.

(Nguyen, 2022; Reinius et al., 2022)

Teachers hold a unique advantage in influencing school-wide change because they often hold insights that school leaders lack (Drago-Severson & Blum-DeStefano, 2018). These insights are gained from the interactions between students, families and their peers, providing first-hand data on what's working and what's not. Teachers also shape school culture from the inside out, influencing students, colleagues and, ultimately, the broader educational environment (Reinius et al., 2022).

If you're a leader and reading this: your teachers are your strength. They're your compass. They're your changemakers. Let them go.

Teachers, rather than waiting for permission to implement meaningful change, you can lead a movement towards whole-school connection through action now – one lesson, one conversation and one relationship at a time.

2. What are practical ways to lead from within the classroom?

Every day you step into your classroom, you're a leader in my opinion. The assumption that leadership is tied to an official position is a fallacy and one that too often holds teachers back from recognising how significant their influence on their community is (Scroggins, 2017). Leadership isn't about title or authority; it's about impact. The title or the badge don't automatically increase your impact.

When teachers view their daily practice as a vehicle for transformation, they redefine leadership as something that happens through action, not position (Wilkinson & Kemmis, 2016). You may not be the leader of a school, but you can certainly be the leader of the change, especially because so many of the former leaders aren't taking the first steps.

Leading from within the classroom starts with three fundamental shifts in mindset:

- From waiting to initiating – recognising that teachers don't need leadership approval to start making small, meaningful changes.
- From individual practice to collective influence – understanding that teacher-led change grows through collaboration, not isolation.
- From compliance to advocacy – seeing teaching as an active role in shaping not just student learning but also school culture.

  (Jakavonytė-Staškuvienė & Barkauskienė, 2023; Reinius et al., 2022)

When educators embrace these shifts, they not only improve their own teaching but also inspire change in those around them.

You become the leader this journey requires.

You foster the connection your community is desperately in need of.

Unpack your journey

Leading from where you are

The transformational leadership connection required happens not through formal mandates but through action and influence (Wilkinson & Kemmis,

2016). This simple fact means a teacher's ability to model, inspire and engage directly within their classroom and among their peers is one of the most powerful drivers of school-wide change, and it's a power you can access and utilise right now.

The first step: *stop waiting!*

There are plenty of times when you will be told what to do in your role within a school. Connection cannot be part of this 'wait and see approach'.

The only leadership badge you need

Transformational leadership isn't about waiting for an official role to drive change; it's about modelling the practices that shape school culture from within the classroom. Burns (1978) introduced the concept of transformational leadership as a process where "leaders and followers raise one another to higher levels of motivation and morality" (p. 20).

In schools, this means that teachers who embed connection-based practices, such as focusing on strong relationships, belonging and meaningful engagement, become catalysts for broader change (Molla & Nolan, 2020).

Modelling is a leadership tool, as it influences colleagues to experiment with similar strategies. Research supports this, showing that teachers who experience new pedagogical approaches as observers in their own school are significantly more likely to adopt them (Darling-Hammond et al., 2017).

Which makes sense – we often don't see the conversations in the boardroom, but we see each other's classrooms. Leading from within aligns with the idea that educational change doesn't start in those board meetings, it begins at the classroom level.

Peer influence over policy institution

While educational policies provide overarching frameworks for schools, research consistently shows that teachers are more likely to adopt new strategies from colleagues they respect than from formal mandates (Leithwood et al., 2021). This is because trust and shared experience play a crucial role in professional learning. When a fellow teacher models an effective connection-based practice, it feels more relevant and attainable than a prescribed policy handed down from leadership.

The concept of *situated learning* (Lave & Wenger, 1991) explains why peer influence is so powerful in schools. Learning doesn't happen in isolation, it occurs within communities of practice, where professionals interact, share insights and refine their craft together (Nicolini et al., 2022). Schools function as these communities, where the strongest professional learning happens informally through collaboration, observation and shared problem-solving (Prenger et al., 2021).

This idea challenges the traditional notion that educational change must be driven by external directives. Instead, it highlights that transformation is most effective when teachers take ownership of best practices and spread them through natural peer interactions – it creates a feeling of attainable change, gradually shifting the school's instructional culture (Reinius et al., 2022).

Shaping the future

Teachers who prioritise connection-based learning influence change not only through their colleagues but also their students.

Your actions can create *emissaries of connection*; a classroom of students who are experiencing connection daily and building trust, respectfulness and increasing their engagement, creating a shift in their overall attitude towards school in general (Banks & Smyth, 2021). This, in turn, can impact how they interact with their peers, other teachers and the wider school community.

This is where the research on student-teacher relationships, which we discussed earlier, can be framed to be a more critical factor for whole-school change.

When students feel connected to their teachers, they're more likely to exhibit prosocial behaviours and engage in the learning process, creating a school environment that fosters academic success and wellbeing (Roorda et al., 2017).

As these benefits accumulate, the school culture starts to evolve. A single teacher implementing connection-based strategies can influence how students engage throughout the school day. When multiple teachers adopt these approaches, the shift becomes even more pronounced, shaping a school-wide culture where positive relationships and engagement become the norm (Weiner & Higgins, 2017).

It's time to take ownership of your professional impact.

What to do?

Knowing that leadership is an action rather than a title, the next step is putting this understanding into practice. Creating a shared experience of connection starts with intentional choices in the classroom, but it doesn't end there. By modelling connection-based teaching, fostering collaboration among colleagues and strategically influencing leadership, teachers can shape school culture from the ground up. The following three strategies will show you the way.

1. Strike a pose

The most effective form of leadership is leading by example – you must be *the model*.

Some of the most influential professional learning sessions I've participated in throughout my career were run by my brilliant colleagues. They're the ones that stick often because we know, trust and are connected to the person sharing them, not just as a presenter, but as a professional in our context.

When colleagues witness a classroom where students are engaged, behaviour issues are reduced and relationships thrive, they're naturally drawn to the methods that create such an environment – this is called *behavioural diffusion* (Rogers, 2003).

Much of our professional learning is based on imagining the destination. When a colleague shows how they have arrived at this destination, rather than simply talking about being there, the potential for change is increased dramatically.

> **Look at me!**
>
> One of the simplest yet most powerful ways to spread connection-based teaching is through informal peer observation. Unlike formal evaluations, this is about professional sharing, giving colleagues a window into connection in action. While teachers might feel vulnerable at first, these visits create opportunities for organic learning.
>
> When introducing it to your peers, consider the following:
>
> - *Clarify purpose* – make it clear that it's about growth, not evaluation. Frame it as a learning opportunity, not a judgement.
> - *Offer first* – invite them to observe your class before suggesting a return visit. This shows trust and reduces pressure.
> - *Agree on a focus* – keep it manageable by choosing one area (for example, questioning, transitions, student engagement).
> - *Normalise it* – present it as part of a collaborative teaching culture or a professional learning initiative, not a one-off.

- *Co-design the process* – involve them in deciding what to observe, when and how feedback is shared. Autonomy builds comfort.
- *Use constructive feedback tools* – use prompts like *"I noticed…"*; *"I wondered…"*; *"What went well?"*; *"What might be tried differently?"*
- *Highlight benefits* – reinforce the value: new strategies, better student outcomes, stronger professional relationships, reduced isolation.
- *Follow up informally* – reflect together shortly after the observation in a low-key conversation.
- *Use a shared framework* – a neutral tool (like a checklist or protocol) can help focus and depersonalise feedback.

(Adapted from British Council, 2012).

If all this feels too big to start, harness the magic of the 'come see this' – a spontaneous invite to a passing colleague, encouraging them to observe a quick, powerful example of connection in practice.

2. Be the opportunist

While leading by example is a crucial start, sustainable change requires collective effort. Schools that foster teacher collaboration see greater professional growth, increased innovation and a stronger sense of community (Admiraal et al., 2021). Connection-based practices flourish when teachers have spaces to share, support and learn from each other.

The challenge here is that meeting schedules are often bloated without room to introduce flexibility. As a teacher who's likely a member of multiple teams, it falls to you to push for a shift in how those meetings are conducted.

One of the most effective ways to embed connection-based practices is to integrate them into existing structures (such as meeting schedules) rather than re-create the wheel. Lesson planning and professional learning community time can become admin heavy, so advocating for structured coaching time within the agenda, where teachers can focus on connection-building strategies, ensures that these discussions move beyond isolated efforts and become part of the school culture (Osterman, 2023).

This shift won't happen overnight, but key to making this work is acknowledging progress, no matter how small, to reinforce positive changes.

It also might save us all from another meeting that could have been an email.

Put me in coach!

To secure initial buy-in from a team leader, start small with something inviting, *peer coaching*.

Informal peer coaching, where teachers support each other through shared observations, idea exchanges or casual chats, is a low-pressure way to spread best practice (Smala et al., 2025).

Start with ten minutes using this framework:

1. *Pair up* – choose a trusted colleague or someone you're keen to learn from.
2. *Set a focus (1 minute)* – one person names a specific area for feedback (for example, student engagement, questioning, clear instructions).
3. *Share context (2 minutes)* – briefly explain what happened, what you aimed for and what you're unsure about.
4. *Coach responds (4 minutes)* – the listening partner:
   - Asks open-ended questions.
   - Uses prompts like:
     - "What did you notice?"
     - "What surprised you?"
     - "What options are you considering?"
   - Avoids advice unless asked.
5. *Reflection and takeaway (3 minutes)* – the speaker reflects on what they've gained or might try next. Keep it practical and future focused.

   (Adapted from Harvard College, 2015)

Key principles:
- Keep it confidential, non-evaluative and respectful.
- Listen more than you speak.
- Focus on the teacher's thinking, not fixing the problem.

3. Permission granted

Many teachers hesitate to advocate for change because they assume leadership must initiate it (Lockton & Fargason, 2019). This may be true in certain areas (policy, for example), but surprisingly not in most.

How often, realistically, does a leader inquire or involve themselves in your classroom?

You're trusted to lead your space and with a small re-frame of that thinking, you can apply this permission towards becoming an influencing factor in your wider school community.

This is true even in schools where leadership is hesitant to adopt new approaches. Many leaders I've worked with have made decisions with the purpose of protecting teachers, their time, their workload and their health.

The nature of decision-making is that not all of these have the desired effect, most likely because they aren't grounded in the day-to-day realities of the modern teacher (Postholm, 2018).

You have this knowledge, you live it, breathe it and embrace it every day you arrive at school. Be confident in the fact that you're an expert and through that expertise you can find ways to influence decision-making and create meaningful shifts that extend far beyond your classroom door.

> **Lead 'below the radar' (initially)**
>
> Often, when leaders see positive results, they become more open to change.
>
> Start collecting tangible evidence – student engagement surveys, behaviour reflections and other qualitative feedback can be powerful advocacy tools. When teachers can show that these practices improve student outcomes, it's hard for leaders to ignore.
>
> Start small, avoid overwhelm and share when you can.

An additional thought: find allies

Sustaining change is difficult in isolation. Find like-minded educators within your school to create momentum. This informal network serves as a support system, providing encouragement, idea-sharing and reinforcement.

We're stronger together and often, as I say to my students, many of us are probably thinking the same thing. To find the hidden allies within your community, start with small conversations and leverage your existing relationships.

Mention connection strategies, activities and benefits whenever and wherever you can. Just as student engagement spreads within a classroom, connection-based teaching spreads when educators collaborate and support one another (Id-Deen & Nalu, 2024).

Remember: to connect is *human*. Somewhere, perhaps deep down for some, we all need it to be our best.

Why do it?

Impact is one of the biggest drivers of school change. Schools are constantly looking for it, with mixed results. Leading from the classroom isn't just about professional fulfilment, it's a contributor to that real, measurable impact we're searching for.

Schools that prioritise relationships, belonging and meaning create environments where both educators and students thrive (Pitman, 2024). I truly believe that when teachers take initiative, modelling and spreading connection-based practices, they contribute to an echo-like effect down the mountain that has the potential to transform school culture.

Pass it down

Contemporary schools and school leadership are tied down in administrative tasks and policy. Leaders may not have the same capacity to drive whole-school change that once existed in the past. Even though research has demonstrated that meaningful and lasting change doesn't come from policy directives alone (Sharples et al., 2019), departmental mandates and pressure somewhat driven by the media has leaders with their hands bound.

While leadership plays an important role, top-down mandates often face resistance or fade over time because they lack grassroots buy-in (Fullan, 2011). Who could blame a teacher for not embracing the latest changes to a code of conduct they had no word in influencing?

Connection is the way forward and teachers are in the driver's seat. From this position, the adoption of new ideas happens more organically and spreads more sustainably.

It *lands*.

It *sticks*.

It *works*.

This is because culture in a school isn't dictated by a mission statement or a set of policies, it's built through the daily interactions between teachers, students and colleagues (Lindsey et al., 2018). Your work builds this culture, not a piece of paper. Without your action, your daily commitment to your work, the words on any policy document are just ink.

A school's culture is essentially the sum of its connections. When teachers create relational, student-centred classrooms, those values spill over into the broader school environment. Students who feel a strong sense of belonging in one class are more likely to carry that feeling into other spaces. Staff who have a sense of meaning in their work will shape others through their words and actions.

Over time, these shifts contribute to a broader transformation, where connection, trust and collaboration become embedded into the way the school operates (Jefferson & Anderson, 2017).

Schools with strong professional relationships among teachers have higher retention rates, greater job satisfaction and increased collaboration (Kraft & Falken, 2020).

Teachers can start immediately, and change can be made tomorrow with the smallest consideration of practice, which could influence their peers and demonstrate that meaningful change is possible from the ground up. In other words, they can instantly start to build *professional capital*.

> Renowned educational researchers Andy Hargreaves and Michael Fullan (2012), in their book *Professional Capital: Transforming Teaching in Every School*, describe *professional capital* as the collective knowledge, experience and relationships that educators build over time.
>
> The more teachers take ownership of their impact, rather than deferring to leadership, the stronger this professional capital becomes.

The idea of leading change and building professional capital can feel overwhelming, but it doesn't require sweeping reforms. Micro-movements, small, intentional actions repeated over time, are often the most powerful drivers of change. A single teacher incorporating connection-based practices in their classroom can be the start of something greater.

Studies on behavioural diffusion (Rogers, 2003) show that when new ideas are easy to observe and implement, they spread faster. The key is to start with *doable* actions such as:

- Inviting a peer to observe a classroom routine that fosters connection
- Sharing student feedback on the impact of relationship-building strategies
- Encouraging collaborative discussions about what works in different classrooms
- Advocating for professional learning focused on engagement and connection

Each of these small acts contributes to a larger cultural shift. As more teachers join the movement, connection-based teaching becomes not just an individual practice, but a shared expectation within the school.

Don't get stuck looking at the view from the summit, look for where the next path leads and make a start.

Where to next?

For educators, courage is the quiet, repeated decision to show up, speak up and step forward even when the path is uncertain. It's the kind of leadership that grows not from position, but from purpose.

The following questions and strategies are designed to help you build courageous habits into the heart of your professional practice, so that leading from within doesn't feel like an exception, but the expectation.

1. Am I acting before I'm invited?

One of the biggest myths in schools is that change must be led from the top. But some of the most powerful transformations start from teachers who decide not to wait. Consider:

- Do I believe I have to be asked to lead, or do I see leadership as something I already embody?
- Where am I already leading through action, without a formal title?
- What change could I initiate tomorrow, without needing permission?

2. Am I modelling the change I want to see?

Leadership isn't a role, it's a mirror. The way you connect, the risks you take and the way you respond when things don't go to plan are noticed by more people than you think. Consider:

- What message do my actions send to students and colleagues about what matters most?
- Do I demonstrate connection-based practices clearly and consistently?
- Where could I be more visible in modelling relational leadership?

3. Am I creating allies, not just ideas?

Courageous change rarely happens alone. While individual actions matter, it's shared action that truly shifts culture. Influence expands when it's carried by many voices. Consider:

- Who in my school shares similar values around connection, belonging and impact?

- Have I taken time to build relationships with colleagues who might be open to co-leading change?
- What's one small collaboration I could invite a peer into this week?

4. Am I using what I know to influence what could be?

Teachers sit on a goldmine of insight, about students, learning, barriers and what works. When this wisdom stays locked in the classroom, school improvement slows. Consider:

- Have I shared stories or data from my classroom that demonstrate what connection looks like in action?
- How might I frame my experience as evidence, not just anecdote?
- What leadership conversations could I influence by showing rather than telling?

5. What small courageous step can I take next?

Courage doesn't have to roar. Sometimes, it whispers: *"Just try this."* Tiny actions build momentum. One brave step leads to another. Consider:

- Could I try one connection-based strategy this week and reflect on its impact?
- Could I invite someone into my classroom or step into theirs?
- What's one assumption about leadership I'm ready to let go of?

Courage fuels change. It redefines what leadership looks like in schools. It creates space for new voices, new ideas and new ways of being.

The summit shows us what's possible, but courage is what gets us to the next one.

The journey isn't over. In fact, this is where it *really begins*.

TL;DR

Key takeaways

1. **The summit's not the end – it's the launchpad**
   Reaching a summit's worth celebrating, but it's not where the journey stops. The challenge now is to lead others towards the next mountain. The courage to keep going, to guide, inspire and grow the movement of connection is what transforms individual wins into collective progress.

2. **Leadership doesn't wait for a title**
   Real leadership in schools starts in the classroom. It's not about having a badge or being in a leadership team, it's about acting. Teachers shape

culture through their daily practice, not policy. Courage means stepping up without waiting for permission and leading from where you are.

3. **Modelling change matters more than mandates**
Connection-based teaching spreads through action, not announcements. When teachers model strong relationships, engagement and belonging, others take notice. Influence grows when practice is visible from *"come see this"* moments to everyday collaboration. Behaviour is contagious.

4. **Peer influence outweighs policy**
Professional growth thrives on trust, not directives. Teachers learn most from each other, not from the top down. Building a culture of peer observation, informal coaching and shared reflection drives real, lasting change. Connection grows when we move together.

5. **Courage is a muscle – use it daily**
Change doesn't require a revolution. It starts with micro-movements: inviting a peer in, sharing what works, taking one step without waiting. Courageous leadership is built through small, consistent actions that echo across classrooms and communities. Don't just admire the view, find the next path and lead on.

Conclusion

"The world is moved along, not only by the mighty shoves of its heroes, but also by the aggregate of the tiny pushes of each honest worker"
– Helen Keller

This truth, from the brilliant author, educator and disability rights advocate, Helen Keller, sits at the heart of teaching. While we often celebrate the standout moments or exceptional educators, it's the daily, deliberate actions of teachers, the tiny pushes, that truly move education forward.

The greeting at the door.

The patient pause before reacting.

The extra check-in.

These moments rarely earn headlines, but they shape lives. They change classrooms. Over time, they shift entire cultures.

Every mountain climber understands that reaching a summit's not the end of the expedition. It's a point of perspective; a chance to reflect, recalibrate and prepare for what lies beyond. Teaching is no different. The work of building connection doesn't conclude with a strategy, a successful lesson or a breakthrough with a student. It's a continuous climb. Ongoing. Messy. Incomplete. And entirely worth it.

Rather than write a large conclusion, unpacking and re-packing everything you've just read, I hope to leave you with an inspiring set of thoughts. If you want to revisit components of the journey, I hope the TL;DR sections at the end of each chapter can assist, but it doesn't feel right to end this book with a bulleted summary.

It doesn't feel to me how journeys end and lead into the next. I want this to be like the chats by the fire on the first night back from the summit. A recap of ideas, told like stories. Tales and provocations to inspire the next leg of the journey from me to you.

While I have made every effort to find the most relevant research to support this, I cannot claim to have found it all. When I have added my own experience and my own spin, perhaps I have it wrong. My perspective may change in the future, or new research come to light. In any case, connection is my passion, my mission, my focus and I hope that, at the very least, that has been positively represented here.

Throughout this book, I hope that I have given you a sense of direction, a sense of momentum. Together, we've walked/climbed/scrambled across the terrain of the mountainous connection journey to address the challenge of The Connection Conundrum head-on. From the call to climb, through valleys that challenge and the shared relief of summits reached, we've explored how connection isn't simply a method, it's a mindset. It's not something that happens as an afterthought; it's tied to everything we do.

And now, as we reach the final steps on this leg of the journey, we don't conclude, we reflect on the one truth that remains:

Connection isn't a destination. It's a practice.

A daily one. A deliberate one. A *human* one.

The real work of education

Educational change doesn't begin in an agenda. It begins in moments, small, human, often unplanned. It happens when a teacher notices a student's silence and pauses. When a colleague offers support without fanfare. When a lesson shifts direction to meet a need instead of a timeline. These aren't grand gestures. They're daily decisions that shape culture.

In schools across Australia and beyond, we're facing an unspoken crisis, not just of attendance or outcomes, but of disconnection. It shows up in subtle ways: student apathy, behavioural outbursts, staff attrition, a general sense that education feels more draining than sustaining. But these symptoms have a common root.

We've drifted from connection.

And yet, teachers remain our most powerful agents of change. You don't need permission to build relationships, foster belonging or help students find meaning. You already have the tools. What's needed now is *belief in yourself*, in *your impact* and in the importance of this work.

The teacher as a cultural leader

You don't need a title to lead. Leadership in education isn't defined by hierarchy but by influence, and the most influential person in any school is the staff member in the classroom, working face-to-face with students, moment by moment.

Teachers shape lives in real time. They build trust in seconds and repair it in days. They hold space for anger, grief, growth, joy, sometimes all within the same lesson. You may not always *see* the results, but you must trust that they're taking root.

If you know me, or have read *The Connection Curriculum*, you may not be surprised that I believe one of the clearest illustrations of this quiet power comes from an animated television show: *The Simpsons*.

In Season 2, Episode 19, *Lisa's Substitute*, Lisa, an intelligent, socially awkward 8-year-old, meets Mr Bergstrom – a substitute teacher who sees her in ways others haven't. He listens. He affirms. He challenges her to think more deeply and love learning again. When he must leave, Lisa is devastated. She begs him to stay. Instead, he gives her a simple note that says:

> *You are Lisa Simpson.*

No big speech. No promises. Just one powerful sentence. It tells her: *"You matter. You're enough. And even when I'm gone, you have what you need."*

Imagine if that wasn't rare. Imagine if every student left school not just with grades or content knowledge, but with a deeper sense of identity, of being seen, valued and believed in.

That is the work of connection. It's the answer to the *Conundrum*. And it begins with *you*.

What sustained connection looks like

Connection isn't built in a moment, and it doesn't last without care. What we build on day one can be lost by week five. A student who once felt secure can suddenly feel unsafe again. A colleague who was open can shut down. A culture of inclusion can harden into compliance. That is why connection is a *sustained* practice, not a quick win.

It's found in the way we show up when we're exhausted. In how we repair after a mistake. In the rituals and routines that remind people they belong.

Sustainable connection isn't always exciting. Sometimes it's a quiet check-in with a withdrawn student. Sometimes it's adjusting expectations to meet someone where they are. Sometimes it's simply staying.

And it's especially important during those long stretches of the year: Term 3 fatigue, report season or the final weeks of Term 4, when energy is low and disconnection creeps in. That is when connection work matters most.

Veteran teachers know this. They know that the small gestures in those moments, a quick *"I see you"* or a patient redirect, are what students remember long after the year ends.

From individual impact to collective movement

We've spoken a lot in this book about metaphors – mountains, climbers, weather – and they're not just rhetorical tools. They matter because they capture how this work *feels*. Some days, we climb easily. Other days, the fog sets in and every step feels uncertain.

But here is what matters most: you're *not climbing alone*.

The summit's not the goal. The goal is the movement.

A movement of teachers who lead with presence.

A movement of schools that see connection as core, not optional.

A movement of students who feel safe, seen and capable of growth.

That kind of culture doesn't start with government or systems. It starts with individuals, like you, who decide that connection is worth the climb.

And the more of us that lead that way, the easier it becomes for others to follow.

What happens next?

As you finish this book, you may be wondering: what now?

You don't need a grand plan. But you do need a first step. A commitment. A change in how you move through the terrain of your school.

So, here are some questions to carry with you:
- How will I make connection visible in my classroom?
- How can I influence the culture of my school through small, daily actions?
- What support do *I* need to sustain this work?
- Who around me is already doing this and how can we climb together?
- How will I embrace *culture, communication, collaboration* and *curiosity* in my day-to-day work?

Your classroom, your daily presence, is where the journey begins.

A tale from my journey

I'm no Mr Bergstrom, but before we part ways, I want to share one story.

A few years ago, I taught a student we will call Alex. Bright, perceptive, but withdrawn. They rarely spoke in class and avoided group work. Most days, they sat quietly and completed just enough to pass.

I decided to start with small connection rituals. A greeting at the door. A comment on their recent writing. Slowly, they opened up. Not quickly. Not dramatically. But over weeks, their posture changed. The best way to describe it is they went from folding themselves into their chair to sitting up, tall and alert. They began to offer to read aloud and stayed back once or twice to ask a question.

Then, one afternoon, they stopped short of the door, waited for everyone to leave and said:

"Thanks for helping me. This is the first time I've felt smart in school. You're a good teacher."

I still remember that moment. Not because it was extraordinary, or because it was an ego boost, but because it reminded me that *nothing* about this work is wasted. Even when we cannot see the impact right away. Even when we're tired. Even when the student never says a word.

Connection makes a difference. Even when it's invisible.

So, you must keep climbing.

There is always another mountain. A new student. A tougher week. A challenging conversation. But there is also another moment of trust. Another burst of laughter. Another breakthrough.

Some days will be steep. Some will be still. But through it all, one truth remains:

Connection is worth the climb.

Because when students feel safe, seen and valued, they learn.

When teachers feel supported, connected and fulfilled, they stay.

And when schools build a culture of relationships, belonging and meaning, education becomes what it was always meant to be: *a space for human potential to thrive.*

So, take the next step. Keep leading. Keep listening. Keep climbing.

The future of education isn't written by policy; it's shaped by the teachers who choose to lead with heart.

And you're one of them.

Onward!

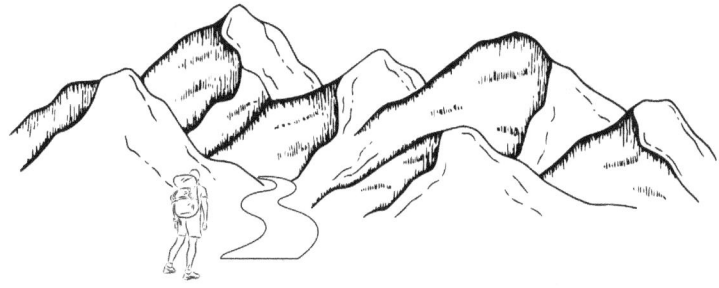

References

Adeoye, M. A., Prastikawati, E. F., & Abimbowo, Y. O. (2024). Empowering Learning: Pedagogical Strategies for Advancing 21st Century Skills and Quality Education. *Journal of Nonformal Education, 10*(1).

Admiraal, W., Schenke, W., De Jong, L., Emmelot, Y., & Sligte, H. (2021). Schools as professional learning communities: what can schools do to support professional development of their teachers? *Professional Development in Education, 47*(4), 684-698.

Agyapong, B., Obuobi-Donkor, G., Burback, L., & Wei, Y. (2022). Stress, Burnout, Anxiety and Depression among Teachers: A Scoping Review. *International Journal of Environmental Research and Public Health, 19*(17), 10706.

Akintayo, O. T., Eden, C. A., Ayeni, O. O., & Onyebuchi, N. C. (2024). Inclusive curriculum design: Meeting the diverse needs of students for social improvement. *International Journal of Applied Research in Social Sciences, 6*(5), 770-784.

Akinyemi, A. F., Rembe, S., & Nkonki, V. (2020). Trust and Positive Working Relationships among Teachers in Communities of Practice as an Avenue for Professional Development. *Education Sciences, 10*(5), 136.

Albrecht, J. R., & Karabenick, S. A. (2018). Relevance for learning and motivation in education. *The Journal of Experimental Education, 86*(1), 1-10.

Aldridge, J. M., & McLure, F. I. (2024). Preparing Schools for Educational Change: Barriers and Supports – A Systematic Literature Review. *Leadership and Policy in Schools, 23*(3), 486-511.

Allen, J. L., Bird, E., & Chhoa, C. Y. (2018). Bad Boys and Mean Girls: Callous-Unemotional Traits, Management of Disruptive Behavior in School, the Teacher-Student Relationship and Academic Motivation. *Frontiers in Education, 3*, 108.

Allen, K.-A., & Boyle, C. (2022). School Belonging and Student Engagement: The Critical Overlaps, Similarities, and Implications for Student Outcomes. In *Handbook of Research on Student Engagement* (pp. 133-154). Springer.

Allen, K.-A., Kern, M. L., Rozek, C. S., McInerney, D. M., & Slavich, G. M. (2021). Belonging: a review of conceptual issues, an integrative framework, and directions for future research. *Australian Journal of Psychology, 73*(1), 87-102.

Allen, K.-A., Kern, M. L., Vella-Brodrick, D., Hattie, J., & Waters, L. (2018). What Schools Need to Know About Fostering School Belonging: a Meta-analysis. *Educational Psychology Review, 30*(1), 1-34.

Allport, G. W. (1954). *The nature of prejudice*. Addison-Wesley.

Alonso-Rodríguez, I., Pérez-Jorge, D., Pérez-Pérez, I., & Olmos-Raya, E. (2025). Restorative practices in reducing school violence: a systematic review of positive impacts on emotional wellbeing. *Frontiers in Education, 10*, 1520137.

Amerstorfer, C. M., & von Münster-Kistner, C. F. (2021). Student Perceptions of Academic Engagement and Student-Teacher Relationships in Problem-Based Learning. *Frontiers in Psychology, 12*, 713907.

Archbell, K. A., & Coplan, R. J. (2022). Too anxious to talk: Social anxiety, academic communication, and students' experiences in higher education. *Journal of Emotional and Behavioral Disorders, 30*(4), 273-286.

Atkinson, R. C., & Shiffrin, R. M. (1968). Human Memory: A Proposed System and its Control Processes. In K. W. Spence & J. T. Spence (Eds.), *The Psychology of Learning and Motivation* (Vol. 2, pp. 89-195). Academic Press.

Australian Education Research Organisation [AERO]. (2023a). *How students learn best*. https://www.edresearch.edu.au/sites/default/files/2023-11/how-students-learn-best-aa_0.pdf

Australian Education Research Organisation [AERO]. (2023b). *Positive teacher-student relationships: Their role in classroom management*. https://www.edresearch.edu.au/summaries-explainers/explainers/positive-teacher-student-relationships-their-role-classroom-management

Australian Institute for Teaching and School Leadership [AITSL]. (2021). *Spotlight: Classroom Management: Standards-aligned evidence-based approaches*. https://www.aitsl.edu.au/research/spotlights/classroom-management-standards-aligned-evidence-based-approaches

Australian Institute for Teaching and School Leadership [AITSL]. (2023). *Spotlight: Australia's Teacher Workforce Today*. https://www.aitsl.edu.au/research/spotlights/australia-s-teacher-workforce-today

Australian Institute for Teaching and School Leadership [AITSL]. (2024). *Strengthening parent engagement to improve student outcomes*. https://www.aitsl.edu.au/research/spotlights/strengthening-parent-engagement-to-improve-student-outcomes

Australian Institute of Health and Welfare [AIHW]. (2023). *Primary and secondary schooling*. https://www.aihw.gov.au/reports/australias-welfare/primary-and-secondary-schooling

Baehr, J. (2022). *Deep in Thought: A Practical Guide to Teaching for Intellectual Virtues*. Harvard Education Press.

Bălănescu, E. O. (2024). The Role of Learning Targets in Raising Student Achievement. *Analele Universității din Craiova, Seria Științe Filologice, Limbi Străine Aplicate*, (1), 35-42.

Bandura, A. (1977). Self-efficacy: Toward a unifying theory of behavioral change. *Psychological Review, 84*(2), 191-215.

Bandura, A. (1986). *Social Foundations of Thought and Action: A Social Cognitive Theory*. Prentice-Hall.

Banks, J., & Smyth, E. (2021). "We Respect Them, and They Respect Us": The Value of Interpersonal Relationships in Enhancing Student Engagement. *Education Sciences, 11*(10), 634.

Barker, K., Poed, S., & Whitefield, P. (Eds.). (2022). *School-Wide Positive Behaviour Support: The Australian Handbook*. Taylor & Francis.

Barr, S. (2024). *Educate to Self-Regulate: Empowering learners for lifelong success*. Amba Press.

Baumeister, R. F., & Leary, M. R. (1995). The need to belong: Desire for interpersonal attachments as a fundamental human motivation. *Psychological Bulletin, 117*(3), 497-529.

Beck, J. S. (2020). *Cognitive Behavior Therapy: Basics and Beyond*. Guilford Publications.

Benevene, P., De Stasio, S., & Fiorilli, C. (2020). Well-being of School Teachers in Their Work Environment. *Frontiers in Psychology, 11*, 1239.

Berger, E., & Nott, D. (2024). Predictors of compassion fatigue and compassion satisfaction among Australian teachers. *Psychological Trauma, 16*(8),1309-1318.

Berlyne, D. E. (1960). *Conflict, arousal, and curiosity*. McGraw-Hill.

Berry Street. (2018). Linking Unconditional Positive Regard and Teacher Wellbeing. https://www.berrystreet.org.au/news/linking-unconditional-positive-regard-and-teacher-wellbeing

Bono, G., Duffy, T., & Moreno, S. (2022). Gratitude in School: Benefits to Students and Schools. *Handbook of Positive Psychology in Schools*, 118-134.

Botha, M., & Cage, E. (2022). "Autism research is in crisis": A mixed method study of researcher's constructions of autistic people and autism research. *Frontiers in Psychology, 13*, 1050897.

Bottiani, J. H., Duran, C. A., Pas, E. T., & Bradshaw, C. P. (2019). Teacher stress and burnout in urban middle schools: Associations with job demands, resources, and effective classroom practices. *Journal of School Psychology, 111*(5), 827-844.

British Council. (2012). *A Guide to Continuing Professional Development – Formal observations*. https://www.teachingenglish.org.uk/sites/teacheng/files/2025-06/c226_cpd_formal_observations_report_v4_1_0.pdf

Bronfenbrenner, U. (1981). *The Ecology of Human Development: Experiments by Nature and Design*. Harvard University Press.

Brookfield, S. D. (2017). *Becoming a Critically Reflective Teacher*. John Wiley & Sons.

Brooks, A. W., & John, L. K. (2018, May-June). *The Surprising Power of Questions*. Harvard Business Review. https://hbr.org/2018/05/the-surprising-power-of-questions

Brown, B. (2018). *Dare to Lead: Brave Work. Tough Conversations. Whole Hearts*. Random House.

Brown, C., White, R., & Kelly, A. (2023). Teachers as educational change agents: what do we currently know? Findings from a systematic review. *Emerald Open Research, 1*(3).

Brown, L., & Bartlett, A. (2024). Safety and predictability. In *Trauma-Informed Teaching in Your Elementary Classroom* (pp. 85-98). Routledge.

Brown, P. C., Roediger, H. L., & McDaniel, M. A. (2014). *Make it stick: The science of successful learning*. Belknap Press.

Brunzell, T., & Norrish, J. (2021). *Creating Trauma-Informed, Strengths-Based Classrooms*. Jessica Kingsley.

Bryk, A. S., & Schneider, B. L. (2002). *Trust in Schools: A Core Resource for Improvement*. Sage.

Budak, A. (2022). *Becoming a Changemaker: Transform Your Career, Your Community, and the World*. Hachette.

Burden, P. R. (2025). *Classroom Management: Creating a Successful K-12 Learning Community*. John Wiley & Sons.

Burger, J., Newman, K., & Stevens, D. (2024). Student Engagement – Pre and Post COVID-19 Pandemic. *Canadian Journal of School Psychology, 39*(1), 53-71.

Burner, T. (2018). Why is educational change so difficult and how can we make it more effective? *Forskning og Forandring, 1*(1), 122-134.

Burns, J. M. (1978). *Leadership*. Harper & Row.

Cai, Y., Yang, Y., Ge, Q., & Weng, H. (2023). The Interplay between Teacher Empathy, Students' Sense of School Belonging, and Learning Achievement. *European Journal of Psychology of Education, 38*(3), 1167-1183.

Carroll, A., Forrest, K., Sanders-O'Connor, E., Flynn, L., Bower, J. M., Fynes-Clinton, S., York, A., & Ziaei, M. (2022). Teacher stress and burnout in Australia: examining the role of intrapersonal and environmental factors. *Social Psychology of Education, 25*(2), 441-469.

CAST. (2018). *Universal Design for Learning Guidelines version 2.2*. http://udlguidelines.cast.org

Causton, J., & MacLeod, K. (2020). *From Behaving to Belonging: The Inclusive Art of Supporting Students Who Challenge Us*. ASCD.

Century. (2022). *What is Cognitive Load Theory and how it can help teaching?* https://www.century.tech/news/cognitive-load-theory-and-how-it-can-help-teaching

Chang, B. (2019). Reflection in Learning. *Online Learning, 23*(1), 95-110.

Chapman, C., & Muijs, D. (2014). Does school-to-school collaboration promote school improvement? A study of the impact of school federations on student outcomes. *School Effectiveness and School Improvement, 25*(3), 351-393.

Chiu, T. K. (2022). Applying the self-determination theory (SDT) to explain student engagement in online learning during the COVID-19 pandemic. *Journal of Research on Technology in Education, 54*(1), S14-S30.

Christidamayani, A. P., & Kristanto, Y. D. (2020). The Effects of Problem Posing Learning Model on Students' Learning Achievement and Motivation. *Indonesian Journal on Learning and Advanced Education, 2*(2), 100-108.

Clarà, M., Mauri, T., Colomina, R., & Onrubia, J. (2019). Supporting collaborative reflection in teacher education: a case study. *European Journal of Teacher Education, 42*(2), 175-191.

Clark, C., Dyson, A., & Millward, A. (Eds.). (2018). *Towards Inclusive Schools?* Routledge.

Clear, J. (2018). *Atomic Habits: An Easy & Proven Way to Build Good Habits & Break Bad Ones*. Avery.

Coffey, S. (2023). Differentiation in theory and practice. In J. Dillon & M. Maguire (Eds.), *Becoming a Teacher: Issues in Secondary Education* (6th Edition. ed., pp. 197-209.). Open University Press.

Collaborative for Academic, Social, and Emotional Learning [CASEL]. (n.d.). *What Does the Research Say?* https://casel.org/fundamentals-of-sel/what-does-the-research-say

Collier, P. J., & Williams, D. R. (2023). Reflection in Action: The Learning–Doing Relationship. In *Learning Through Serving* (pp. 95-111). Routledge.

Cornelius-White, J. (2007). Learner-Centered Teacher-Student Relationships are Effective: A Meta-Analysis. *Review of Educational Research, 77*(1), 113-143.

Curren, R. (2020). Punishment and motivation in a just school community. *Theory and Research in Education, 18*(1), 117-133.

Dack, H., Chiles, E., Kathman, L., Poessnecker, A., & Strohl, E. (2022). The Key to Equitable Differentiation. *Middle School Journal, 53*(5), 15-32.

Damon, W., & Malin, H. (2020). The development of purpose. *The Oxford Handbook of Moral Development: An Interdisciplinary Perspective*, 110-127.

Danielson, C. (2024). *Enhancing Professional Practice: The Framework for Teaching* (3rd Edition). ASCD.

Darling-Hammond, L., & Cook-Harvey, C. M. (2018). *Educating the Whole Child: Improving School Climate to Support Student Success*. Learning Policy Institute.

Darling-Hammond, L., Flook, L., Cook-Harvey, C., Barron, B., & Osher, D. (2020). Implications for educational practice of the science of learning and development. *Applied Developmental Science, 24*(2), 97-140.

Darling-Hammond, L., Hyler, M. E., Gardner, M. (2017). *Effective Teacher Professional Development*. Learning Policy Institute.

Das, D. (2011). 4C Model: A New Approach to Determine and Measure Organizational Effectiveness. Available at SSRN 1879413.

De Neve, D., Bronstein, M. V., Leroy, A., Truyts, A., & Everaert, J. (2023). Emotion Regulation in the Classroom: A Network Approach to Model Relations among Emotion Regulation Difficulties, Engagement to Learn, and Relationships with Peers and Teachers. *Journal of Youth and Adolescence, 52*(2), 273-286.

Deng, J. (2024). The Role of Class Collective Consciousness in Shaping Students' Psychological Sense of Belonging: The Application of Group Dynamics Theory in Education. *Applied & Educational Psychology, 5*(7), 102-108.

Department of Education and Training Victoria. (2025). School-wide Positive Behaviour Support. https://www.vic.gov.au/school-wide-positive-behaviour-support

Dolbier, S. Y., Dieffenbach, M. C., & Lieberman, M. D. (2025). Open-mindedness: An integrative review of interventions. *Psychological Review, 132*(1), 204-238.

Doran, G. T. (1981). There's a S.M.A.R.T. way to write management's goals and objectives. *Management Review, 70*(11), 35-36.

Dörnyei, Z., & Muir, C. (2019). Creating a motivating classroom environment. In *Second Handbook of English Language Teaching*, 719-736.

Drago-Severson, E., & Blum-DeStefano, J. (2018). *Leading Change Together: Developing Educator Capacity Within Schools and Systems*. ASCD.

Dweck, C. S. (2006). *Mindset: The new psychology of success*. Random House.

Dweck, C. S. (2017). *Mindset: Changing the way you think to fulfil your potential* (Updated ed.). Robinson.

Dwivedi, R., & Srivastava, S. (2021). Developing Leadership Skills in Secondary Students. *Journal of Educational Planning and Administration, 35*(1), 35-46.

Edmondson, A. C. (1999). Psychological Safety and Learning Behavior in Work Teams. *Administrative Science Quarterly, 44*(2), 350-383.

Edmondson, A. C. (2018). *The Fearless Organization: Creating Psychological Safety in the Workplace for Learning, Innovation, and Growth*. John Wiley & Sons.

Edmondson, A. C., & Bransby, D. P. (2023). Psychological Safety Comes of Age: Observed Themes in an Established Literature. *Annual Review of Organizational Psychology and Organizational Behavior, 10*(1), 55-78.

Engel, S. (2015). *The Hungry Mind: The Origins of Curiosity in Childhood*. Harvard University Press.

Epstein, J. L. (2018). *School, Family, and Community Partnerships: Preparing Educators and Improving Schools*. Routledge.

Erenrich, S. J., & Wergin, J. F. (Eds.). (2017). *Grassroots Leadership and the Arts for Social Change*. Emerald.

Fabris, M. A., Settanni, M., Longobardi, C., & Marengo, D. (2024). Sense of Belonging at School and on Social Media in Adolescence: Associations with Educational Achievement and Psychosocial Maladjustment. *Child Psychiatry & Human Development, 55*(6), 1620-1633.

Farrell, T. S. C. (2018). Reflective Practice for Language Teachers. In J. I. Liontas (Ed.), *The TESOL Encyclopedia of English Language Teaching* (pp. 1-6). Wiley.

Fayed, I., & Cummings, J. (2021). *Teaching in the post COVID-19 era*. Springer.

Flavell, J. H. (1979). Metacognition and cognitive monitoring: A new area of cognitive–developmental inquiry. *American Psychologist, 34*(10), 906-911.

Fletcher, J. (2019, May 7). Philosophical Chairs: A Framework for Whole-Class Discussions. Edutopia. https://www.edutopia.org/article/framework-whole-class-discussions

Frey, N., Fisher, D., & Smith, D. (2019). *All Learning is Social and Emotional: Helping Students Develop Essential Skills for the Classroom and Beyond*. ASCD.

Frommert, C. (2024, March 21). Bringing the Harkness Method to Math Classes. Edutopia. https://www.edutopia.org/article/using-harkness-methond-math-class

Fullan, M. (2011). *Change Leader: Learning to Do What Matters Most*. Jossey-Bass.

Fullan, M. (2016). *The New Meaning of Educational Change* (5th ed.). Teachers College Press.

Gan, Z., An, Z., & Liu, F. (2021). Teacher Feedback Practices, Student Feedback Motivation, and Feedback Behavior: How Are They Associated With Learning Outcomes? *Frontiers in Psychology, 12*, 697045.

García-Moya, I. (2020). Barriers and Facilitators for Student-Teacher Connectedness: The Case of Classroom Management and Authority. In *The Importance of Connectedness in Student-Teacher Relationships* (pp. 65-91). Springer.

Gheyssens, E., Coubergs, C., Griful-Freixenet, J., Engels, N., & Struyven, K. (2022). Differentiated Instruction: The Diversity of Teachers' Philosophy and Praxis to Adapt Teaching to Students' Interests, Readiness and Learning Profiles. *International Journal of Inclusive Education, 26*(14), 1383-1400.

Gningue, S. M., Peach, R., Jarrah, A. M., & Wardat, Y. (2022). The Relationship between Teacher Leadership and School Climate: Findings from a Teacher-Leadership Project. *Education Sciences, 12*(11), 749.

Göktaş, E., & Kaya, M. (2023). The Effects of Teacher Relationships on Student Academic Achievement: A Second Order Meta-Analysis. *Participatory Educational Research, 10*(1), 275-289.

Gorelova, V. (2025). Promoting Self-Regulation and Motivation in the Classroom: Theory-Based Practices for Effective Learning. ResearchGate. https://www.researchgate.net/publication/391395764_Promoting_Self-Regulation_and_Motivation_in_the_Classroom_Theory-Based_Practices_for_Effective_Learning

Goss, P., Sonnemann, J., & Griffiths, K. (2017). *Engaging students: creating classrooms that improve learning*. Grattan Institute. https://grattan.edu.au/wp-content/uploads/2017/02/Engaging-students-creating-classrooms-that-improve-learning.pdf

Grant, A. (2023). *Hidden Potential: The Science of Achieving Greater Things*. Penguin Random House.

Green, A. (2022). *Teacher Wellbeing: A Real Conversation for Teachers and Leaders*. Amba Press.

Greenwood, L., & Kelly, C. (2019). A systematic literature review to explore how staff in schools describe how a sense of belonging is created for their pupils. *Emotional and Behavioural Difficulties, 24*(1), 3-19.

Gregory, A., Skiba, R. J., & Mediratta, K. (2017). Eliminating Disparities in School Discipline: A Framework for Intervention. *Review of Research in Education, 41*(1), 253-278.

Griful-Freixenet, J., Struyven, K., Vantieghem, W., & Gheyssens, E. (2020). Exploring the interrelationship between Universal Design for Learning (UDL) and Differentiated Instruction (DI): A systematic review. *Educational Research Review, 29*, 100306.

Haelermans, C. (2022). The Effects of Group differentiation by students' learning strategies. *Instructional Science, 50*(2), 223-250.

Hall, P., & Simeral, A. (2017). *Creating a Culture of Reflective Practice: Capacity-Building for Schoolwide Success*. ASCD.

Hammack, M. N., Moore, C. R., & Offord, E. C. (2020). The Critical Role of Social-Emotional Learning in Building Resilience within School Communities. Clemson University ThinkShops™. https://thinkshops.org/assets/file/research-resources/critical-role-of-sel-white-paper.pdf

Hammond, Z. (2015). *Culturally Responsive Teaching and the Brain: Promoting Authentic Engagement and Rigor Among Culturally and Linguistically Diverse Students*. Corwin.

Hamre, B. K., & Pianta, R. C. (2006). Student-teacher relationships. In G. G. Bear & K. M. Minke (Eds.), *Children's needs III: Development, prevention, and intervention* (pp. 59-71). National Association of School Psychologists.

Han, J., Way, N., Yoshikawa, H., & Clarke, C. (2025). Interpersonal Curiosity and its Association with Social and Emotional Skills and Well-Being During Adolescence. *Journal of Adolescent Research, 40*(3), 636-668.

Han, K. (2021). Fostering Students' Autonomy and Engagement in EFL Classroom Through Proximal Classroom Factors: Autonomy-Supportive Behaviors and Student-Teacher Relationships. *Frontiers in Psychology, 12*, 767079.

Hargreaves, A. (2001). Emotional geographies of teaching. *Teachers College Record, 103*(6), 1056-1080.

Hargreaves, A. (2023). *Leadership From the Middle: The Beating Heart of Educational Transformation*. Routledge.

Hargreaves, A., & Fullan, M. (2012). *Professional Capital: Transforming Teaching in Every School*. Teachers College Press.

Harris, A. (2013). *Distributed Leadership Matters: Perspectives, Practicalities, and Potential*. Corwin.

Harris, A., Jones, M., & Huffman, J. B. (2017). *Teachers Leading Educational Reform: The Power of Professional Learning Communities*. Routledge.

Harvard College. (2015). Coaching Conversation Planning Guide. https://visiblybetter.cepr.harvard.edu/files/visibly-better/files/coaching-conversation-planning-guide.pdf

Hastuti, I. D., Supangken, S., Sutarto. S, & Dafik, D. (2020). The Effect of Guided Inquiry Learning in Improving Metacognitive Skill of Elementary School Students. *International Journal of Instruction, 13*(4), 315-330.

Hattie, J. (2009). *Visible Learning: A Synthesis of Over 800 Meta-Analyses Relating to Achievement*. Routledge.

Hattie, J. (2023). *Visible Learning: The Sequel: A Synthesis of Over 2,100 Meta-Analyses Relating to Achievement*. Routledge.

Hattie, J., & Timperley, H. (2007). The Power of Feedback. *Review of Educational Research, 77*(1), 81-112.

Hattie, J., & Yates, G. (2013). *Visible Learning and the Science of How We Learn*. Routledge.

Hattie, J., & Zierer, K. (2019). *Visible Learning Insights*. Routledge.

Heffernan, A., Bright, D., Kim, M., Longmuir, F., & Magyar, B. (2022). 'I cannot sustain the workload and the emotional toll': Reasons behind Australian teachers' intentions to leave the profession. *Australian Journal of Education, 66*(2), 196-209.

Heinsch, M., Agllias, K., Sampson, D., Howard, A., Blakemore, T., & Cootes, H. (2020). Peer Connectedness during the Transition to Secondary School: A Collaborative Opportunity for Education and Social Work. *Australian Educational Researcher, 47*, 339-356.

Henrietta, H. M. (2023). A Comprehensive Review on Human Health, Promoting the Well-Being of Teaching Professionals. *International Journal of Environment, Engineering and Education, 5*(2), 79-86.

Hofkens, T. L., & Pianta, R. C. (2022). Teacher-Student Relationships, Engagement in School, and Student Outcomes. In *Handbook of Research on Student Engagement* (pp. 431-449). Springer.

Hofkens, T. L., Pianta, R. C., & Hamre, B. (2023). Teacher-Student Interactions: Theory, Measurement, and Evidence for Universal Properties That Support Students' Learning Across Countries and Cultures.

In *Effective Teaching Around the World: Theoretical, Empirical, Methodological and Practical Insights* (pp. 399-422). Springer.

Holzer, A., & Daumiller, M. (2025). Building trust in the classroom: perspectives from students and teachers. *European Journal of Psychology of Education, 40*(62).

Hudson, C. (2024). *Leading Positive Classrooms: Adopting an Educative Approach to Behaviour Management in Schools*. Amba Press.

Hultberg, P., Calonge, D. S., & Lee, A. E. S. (2018). Promoting Long-Lasting Learning Through Instructional Design. *Journal of the Scholarship of Teaching and Learning, 18*(3).

Hunt, J. (1954). *The Ascent of Everest*. Hodder & Stoughton.

Ibarra, B. N. (2022). Understanding SEL to Create a Sense of Belonging: The Role Teachers Play in Addressing Students' Social and Emotional Well-Being. *Current Issues in Education, 23*(2).

Id-Deen, L., & Nalu, N. (2024). Belonging Matters: Amplifying Teachers' Voices in Schools. *Mathematics Teacher Educator, 12*(3), 185-194.

Jakavonytė-Staškuvienė, D., & Barkauskienė, A. (2023). Transformative teacher leadership experiences in schools in creating an innovative educational culture: The case of Lithuania. *Cogent Education, 10*(1), 2196239.

James, D. M., Fisher, S., & Vincent, S. (2021). Challenging behaviour around challenging behaviour. *Journal of Applied Research in Intellectual Disabilities, 34*(4), 1166-1179.

Jefferson, M., & Anderson, M. (2017). *Transforming Schools: Creativity, Critical Reflection, Communication, Collaboration*. Bloomsbury.

Kahan, S. (2010). *Getting Change Right: How Leaders Transform Organizations from the Inside Out*. Jossey-Bass.

Kashdan, T. B., Sherman, R. A., Yarbro, J., & Funder, D. C. (2013). How are curious people viewed and how do they behave in social situations? From the perspectives of self, friends, parents, and unacquainted observers. *Journal of personality, 81*(2), 142-154.

Kaufman, E. M., & Killen, M. (2022). Children's Perspectives on Fairness and Inclusivity in the Classroom. *The Spanish Journal of Psychology, 25*, e28.

Kehoe, M., Bourke-Taylor, H., & Broderick, D. (2018). Developing student social skills using restorative practices: A new framework called H.E.A.R.T. *Social Psychology of Education, 21*, 189-207.

Khattak, S., Shah, S., & Saeed, H. (2025). The Role of Emotional Intelligence and Empathy in Reducing Prejudice. *Research Journal of Psychology, 3*(1), 390-397.

Khatter, A., Thalaachawr, K., & Blyth, M. (2024). Student engagement and fostering ownership of learning. *Journal of Applied Learning and Teaching, 7*(1). https://doi.org/10.37074/jalt.2024.7.1.38

Killion, J. (2015). High-quality collaboration benefits teachers and students. https://learningforward.org/wp-content/uploads/2015/10/high-quality-collaboration-benefits-teachers-and-students.pdf

Klepsch, M., & Seufert, T. (2020). Understanding instructional design effects by differentiated measurement of intrinsic, extraneous, and germane cognitive load. *Instructional Science, 48*(1), 45-77.

Knowles, E. (Ed.). (2005). *Oxford Dictionary of Phrase and Fable* (2nd ed.). Oxford University Press.

Kong, Y. (2021). The Role of Experiential Learning on Students' Motivation and Classroom Engagement. *Frontiers in Psychology, 12*, 771272.

Korpershoek, H., Canrinus, E. T., Fokkens-Bruinsma, M., & De Boer, H. (2020). The relationships between school belonging and students' motivational, social-emotional, behavioural, and academic outcomes in secondary education: a meta-analytic review. *Research Papers in Education, 35*(6), 641-680.

Kotter, J. P. (2012). *Leading Change*. Harvard Business School Press.

Kraft, M. A., & Falken, G. T. (2020). Why School Climate Matters for Teachers and Students. *State Education Standard, 20*(2), 33.

Krumrei-Mancuso, E. J., Haggard, M. C., LaBouff, J. P., & Rowatt, W. C. (2020). Links between intellectual humility and acquiring knowledge. *The Journal of Positive Psychology, 15*(2), 155-170.

Kruse, S. D., & Louis, K. S. (2008). *Building Strong School Cultures: A Guide to Leading Change*. Corwin.

Kunwar, R., & Adhikari, S. (2023). An exploration of the conceptualization, guiding principles, and theoretical perspectives of inclusive curriculum. *Journal of Contemporary Research in Social Sciences, 5*(1), 1-13.

Larmer, J., & Mergendoller, J. R. (2015). *Gold Standard PBL: Essential Project Design Elements* [White paper]. Buck Institute for Education.

Lave, J., & Wenger, E. (1991). *Situated learning: Legitimate peripheral participation*. Cambridge University Press.

Leithwood, K., Jantzi, D., & Steinbach, R. (2021). Leadership and other Conditions which Foster Organizational Learning in Schools. In *Organizational Learning in Schools* (pp. 67-90). Taylor & Francis.

Lester, R. R., Allanson, P. B., & Notar, C. E. (2017). Routines are the Foundation of Classroom Management. *Education, 137*(4), 398-412.

Lieberman, A., Campbell, C., & Yashkina, A. (2016). *Teacher Learning and Leadership: Of, By, and For Teachers*. Routledge.

Lin, X., Schwartz, D. L., & Hatano, G. (2018). Toward Teachers' Adaptive Metacognition. In *Computers as Metacognitive Tools for Enhancing Learning* (pp. 245-255). Routledge.

Lindsey, R. B., Nuri-Robins, K., Terrell, R. D., & Lindsey, D. B. (2018). *Cultural Proficiency: A Manual for School Leaders*. Corwin.

Lipscombe, K., Tindall-Ford, S., & Kirk, M. (2019). Leading a top down directive from the bottom up: A school and university partnership. *Leading and Managing, 25*(1), 29-43.

Lockton, M., & Fargason, S. (2019). Disrupting the Status Quo: How Teachers Grapple with Reforms That Compete with Long-Standing Educational Views. *Journal of Educational Change, 20*(4), 469-494.

Lodi, E., Perrella, L., Lepri, G. L., Scarpa, M. L., & Patrizi, P. (2021). Use of Restorative Justice and Restorative Practices at School: A Systematic Literature Review. *International Journal of Environmental Research and Public Health, 19*(1), 96.

Longobardi, C., Settanni, M., Lin, S., & Fabris, M. A. (2021). Student–teacher relationship quality and prosocial behaviour: The mediating role of academic achievement and a positive attitude towards school. *British Journal of Educational Psychology*, 91(2), 547-562.

Lubicz-Nawrocka, T., & Bao, X. (2025). Partnership in the Classroom: Engaging Students Through Inclusive Student-Teacher Relationships to Advance Social Justice. *Social Sciences*, 14(2), 75.

Mackey, M., Takemae, N., Foshay, J., & Montesano, A. (2023). Experience-Based UDL Applications: Overcoming Barriers to Learning. *International Journal of Instruction*, 16(3), 1127-1146.

Madison, E. (2023). *Raising Empowered Learners: Cultivating Students' Curiosity, Character, and Confidence*. Rowman & Littlefield.

Maeda, J. (2017). Self-Efficacy Reduces Impediments to Classroom Discussion for International Students. *IAFOR Journal of Education*, 5(2), 93-109.

Malin, H. (2021). *Teaching for Purpose: Preparing Students for Lives of Meaning*. Harvard Education Press.

Malone, T. W., & Lepper, M. R. (2021). Making Learning Fun: A Taxonomy of Intrinsic Motivations for Learning. In *Aptitude, learning, and instruction* (pp. 223-253). Routledge.

Marzano, R. J., Marzano, J. S., & Pickering, D. J. (2003). *Classroom Management That Works: Research-Based Strategies for Every Teacher*. ASCD.

Maslow, A. H. (1943). A theory of human motivation. *Psychological Review*, 50(4), 370-396.

Mathew, P., Mathew, P., & Peechattu, P. J. (2017). Reflective Practices: A Means to Teacher Development. *Asia Pacific Journal of Contemporary Education and Communication Technology*, 3(1), 126-131.

McPherson, H., & Asghar, A. (2023). Professional learning communities: the journey from 'do we HAVE to go there' to 'teachers getting together and being colleagues'. *Professional Development in Education*, 1-17.

Meyer, A., Rose, D. H., & Gordon, D. (2014). *Universal Design for Learning: Theory and Practice*. CAST Professional Publishing.

Meyer, K., Sears, S., Putnam, R., Phelan, C., Burnett, S., Warden, S., & Simonsen, B. (2021). Supporting students with disabilities with positive behavioral interventions and supports in the classroom: Lessons learned from research and practice. *Beyond Behavior*, 30(3), 169-178.

Mitchell, B. S., Kern, L., & Conroy, M. A. (2019). Supporting students with emotional or behavioral disorders: State of the field. *Behavioral Disorders*, 44(2), 70-84.

Moayeri, M., & Rahimiy, R. (2019). The Significance of Promoting Teacher Reflection: A Review Article. *Latin American Journal of Content & Language Integrated Learning*, 12(1).

Molla, T., & Nolan, A. (2020). Teacher agency and professional practice. *Teachers and Teaching*, 26(1), 67-87.

Mora-Ruano, J. G., Heine, J.-H., & Gebhardt, M. (2019). Does Teacher Collaboration Improve Student Achievement? Analysis of the German PISA 2012 Sample. *Frontiers in Education*, 4, 85.

Moreno, G. (2021). Stemming exclusionary school discipline: implementing culturally attuned positive behavior practices. *Emotional and Behavioural Difficulties*, 26(2), 176-186.

Morgan, A. (2019). Cultivating critical reflection: educators making sense and meaning of professional identity and relational dynamics in complex practice. In *Teaching in Alternative and Flexible Education Settings* (pp. 1-55). Routledge.

Morinaj, J., Marcin, K., & Hascher, T. (2019). School alienation and its association with student learning and social behavior in challenging times. In *Motivation in education at a time of global change: Theory, research, and implications for practice* (pp. 205-224). Emerald.

Muijs, D., & Harris, A. (2006). Teacher led school improvement: Teacher leadership in the UK. *Teaching and Teacher Education*, 22(8), 961-972.

Murphy, M. C., & Zirkel, S. (2015). Race and Belonging in School: How Anticipated and Experienced Belonging Affect Choice, Persistence, and Performance. *Teachers College Record*, 117(12), 1-40.

Naz, F. L., Afzal, A., & Khan, M. H. N. (2023). Challenges and Benefits of Multicultural Education for Promoting Equality in Diverse Classrooms. *Journal of Social Sciences Review*, 3(2), 511-522.

Nguyen, D. (2022). Developing a Model of Establishing Receptivity to Teacher-Led Change in Schools. In *The Palgrave Handbook of Teacher Education Research* (pp. 1-22). Springer.

Nicolini, D., Pyrko, I., Omidvar, O., & Spanellis, A. (2022). Understanding communities of practice: Taking stock and moving forward. *The Academy of Management Annals*, 16(2), 680-718.

NSW Department of Education. (2020). *Trauma-informed practice in schools: An explainer*. https://education.nsw.gov.au/about-us/education-data-and-research/cese/publications/research-reports/trauma-informed-practice-in-schools

NSW Department of Education. (2025). *What is Restorative Practice?* https://education.nsw.gov.au/schooling/school-community/attendance-behaviour-and-engagement/behaviour-support-toolkit/support-for-teachers/restorative-practices/restorative-practices

Oberg, G., Macmahon, S., & Carroll, A. (2024). Assessing the interplay: teacher efficacy, compassion fatigue, and educator well-being in Australia. *Australian Educational Researcher*, 1-25.

O'Keefe, P. A., Lee, H. Y., & Chen, P. (2021). Changing students' beliefs about learning can unveil their potential. *Policy Insights from the Behavioral and Brain Sciences*, 8(1), 84-91.

Oranga, J., & Matere, A. (2022). Post COVID-19 education strategies: Envisaging learning in a post COVID-19 pandemic world. *Research Journal in Advanced Social Sciences*, 3(2).

Organisation for Economic Co-operation and Development [OECD]. (2019). *Teaching and Learning International Survey (TALIS): Teachers and School Leaders as Lifelong Learners*. OECD Publishing.

Osterman, K. F. (2023). Teacher Practice and Students' Sense of Belonging. In *Second International Research Jandbook on Values Education and Student Wellbeing* (pp. 971-993). Springer.

Pantić, N., Galey, S., Florian, L., Joksimović, S., Viry, G., Gašević, D., Knutes Nyqvist, H., & Kyritsi, K. (2022). Making sense of teacher agency for change with social and epistemic network analysis. *Journal of Educational Change, 23*(2), 145-177.

Parker-Shandal, C. A. (2023). Relational Connections in Classroom Curriculum: Power and Privilege in Diverging Perspectives. In *Restorative Justice in the Classroom: Liberating Students' Voices Through Relational Pedagogy* (pp. 167-196). Springer.

Patrick, H., & Kaplan, A. (2022). Promoting students' growth motivation: Mastery-structured classrooms. In *Handbook of Positive Psychology in Schools* (pp. 295-308). Routledge.

Paul, R., & Elder, L. (2019). *The Thinker's Guide to Socratic Questioning*. Rowman & Littlefield.

Pendergast, D., Allen, J., McGregor, G., & Ronksley-Pavia, M. (2018). Engaging Marginalized, "At-Risk" Middle-Level Students: A Focus on the Importance of a Sense of Belonging at School. *Education Sciences, 8*(3), 138.

Picione, R. D. L., & Lozzi, U. (2021). Uncertainty as a constitutive condition of human experience: Paradoxes and complexity of sensemaking in the face of the crisis and uncertainty. *International Journal of Psychoanalysis and Education: Subject, Action & Society, 1*(2), 14-53.

Pink, D. H. (2009). *Drive: The Surprising Truth About What Motivates Us*. Riverhead Books.

Pitman, M. (2024). *The Connection Curriculum: Igniting Positive Change in Schools Through Sustainable Connection*. Amba Press.

Porges, S. W. (2011). *The Polyvagal Theory: Neurophysiological Foundations of Emotions, Attachment, Communication, Self-Regulation*. W.W. Norton & Company.

Porta, T. (2024). *The Dance of Differentiation: Choreographing Inclusive Learning in Schools*. Amba Press.

Porter, L. (2020). *Student Behaviour: Theory and practice for teachers*. Routledge.

Post, T., & van der Molen, J. H. W. (2018). Do children express curiosity at school? Exploring children's experiences of curiosity inside and outside the school context. *Learning, Culture and Social Interaction, 18*, 60-71.

Postholm, M. B. (2018). Teachers' professional development in school: A review study. *Cogent Education, 5*(1), 1522781.

Prenger, R., Poortman, C. L., & Handelzalts, A. (2021). Professional learning networks: From teacher learning to school improvement? *Journal of Educational Change, 22*(1), 13-52.

Priestley, M., Biesta, G., & Robinson, S. (2015). *Teacher Agency: An Ecological Approach*. Bloomsbury.

Puntambekar, S. (2022). Distributed scaffolding: Scaffolding students in classroom environments. *Educational Psychology Review, 34*(1), 451-472.

Reeve, J. (2024). *Understanding Motivation and Emotion*. John Wiley & Sons.

Reeves, D. B. (2009). *Leading Change in Your School: How to Conquer Myths, Build Commitment, and Get Results*. ASCD.

Reimers, F. M. (2020). *Educating Students to Improve the World*. Springer Nature.

Reinius, H., Kaukinen, I., Korhonen, T., Juuti, K., & Hakkarainen, K. (2022). Teachers as transformative agents in changing school culture. *Teaching and Teacher Education, 120*, Article 103888.

Reinke, W. M., Herman, K. C., & Stormont, M. (2013). Classroom-level positive behavior supports in schools implementing SW-PBIS: Identifying areas for enhancement. *Journal of Positive Behavior Interventions, 15*(1), 39-50.

Roberts, J. L., & Inman, T. F. (2023). *Strategies for Differentiating Instruction: Best practices for the classroom*. Routledge.

Robinson, C. D. (2022). A framework for motivating teacher-student relationships. *Educational Psychology Review, 34*(4), 2061-2094.

Rogers, C. R. (1957). The necessary and sufficient conditions of therapeutic personality change. *Journal of Consulting Psychology, 21*(2), 95-103.

Rogers, E. M. (2003). *Diffusion of Innovations (5th Edition)*. Free Press.

Rohm, A. J., Stefl, M., & Ward, N. (2021). Future Proof and Real-World Ready: The Role of Live Project-Based Learning in Students' Skill Development. *Journal of Marketing Education, 43*(2), 204-215.

Ronfeldt, M., Farmer, S. O., McQueen, K., & Grissom, J. A. (2015). Teacher Collaboration in Instructional Teams and Student Achievement. *American Educational Research Journal, 52*(3), 475-514.

Roorda, D. L., Jak, S., Zee, M., Oort, F. J., & Koomen, H. M. Y. (2017). Affective Teacher-Student Relationships and Students' Engagement and Achievement: A Meta-Analytic Update and Test of the Mediating Role of Engagement. *School Psychology Review, 46*(3), 239-261.

Rosenthal, R., & Jacobson, L. (1968). *Pygmalion in the classroom: Teacher expectation and pupils' intellectual development*. Holt, Rinehart & Winston.

Ryan, R. M., & Deci, E. L. (2020). Intrinsic and extrinsic motivation from a self-determination theory perspective: Definitions, theory, practices, and future directions. *Contemporary Educational Psychology, 61*, Article 101860.

Sabol, T. J., & Pianta, R. C. (2012). Recent trends in research on teacher–child relationships. *Attachment & Human Development, 14*(3), 213-231.

Saborío-Taylor, S., & Rojas-Ramírez, F. (2024). Universal Design for Learning and artificial intelligence in the digital era: Fostering inclusion and autonomous learning. *International Journal of Professional Development, Learners and Learning, 6*(2).

Santangelo, T., & Tomlinson, C. A. (2012). Teacher Educators' Perceptions and Use of Differentiated Instruction Practices: An Exploratory Investigation. *Action in Teacher Education, 34*(2), 309-327.

Schaefer, M. B., Pennington, S. E., Divoll, K., & Tang, J. H. (2024). A Systematic Review of Literature on Student Voice and Agency in Middle Grade Contexts. *Education Sciences, 14*(11), 1158.

Schein, E. H. (2004). *Organizational Culture and Leadership*. Jossey Bass.

Schein, E. H. (2018). *Humble Inquiry: The Gentle Art of Asking Instead of Telling*. Berrett-Koehler.
Schoem, D., Modey, C., & John, E. P. S. (Eds.). (2023). *Teaching the Whole Student: Engaged Learning With Heart, Mind, and Spirit*. Taylor & Francis.
Schön, D. (1983). *The Reflective Practitioner: How Professionals Think in Action*. London: Temple Smith.
Schunk, D. H., & Zimmerman, B. J. (Eds.) (2023a). Self-regulation in education: Retrospect and prospect. In *Self-regulation of Learning and Performance* (pp. 305-314). Routledge.
Schunk, D. H., & Zimmerman, B. J. (Eds.) (2023b). Self-regulation of self-efficacy and attributions in academic settings. In *Self-regulation of Learning and Performance* (pp. 75-99). Routledge.
Scroggins, C. (2017). *How to Lead when You're Not in Charge: Leveraging Influence when You Lack Authority*. Zondervan.
Sharples, J., Albers, B., Fraser, S., & Kime, S. (2019). *Putting Evidence to Work: A School's Guide to Implementation. Guidance Report*. Education Endowment Foundation.
Sharratt, L., & Planche, B. (2016). *Leading Collaborative Learning: Empowering Excellence*. Corwin Press.
Siegel, D. J. (2011). *The Whole-Brain Child: 12 Revolutionary Strategies to Nurture Your Child's Developing Mind*. Delacorte Press.
Siegel, D. J. (2020). *The Developing Mind: How Relationships and the Brain Interact to Shape Who We Are*. Guilford Publications.
Simonsen, B., & Myers, D. (2025). *Classwide Positive Behavioral Interventions and Supports: A Guide to Proactive Classroom Management*. Guilford Publications.
Sinek, S. (2009). *Start with Why: How Great Leaders Inspire Everyone to Take Action*. Portfolio.
Singh, A., & Manjaly, J. A. (2022). Using Curiosity to Improve Learning Outcomes in Schools. *SAGE Open, 12*(1), 21582440211069392.
Skaalvik, E.M., & Skaalvik, S. (2021). Collective teacher culture: exploring an elusive construct and its relations with teacher autonomy, belonging, and job satisfaction. *Social Psychology of Education, 24*, 1389-1406.
Smala, S., McLay, K., & Gillies, R. M. (2025). Teacher relationships and social connectedness. *Teachers and Teaching*, 1-24.
Sobel, D. (2019). *Leading on Pastoral Care*. Bloomsbury.
Sobel, D., & Alston, S. (2021). *The Inclusive Classroom: A new approach to differentiation*. Bloomsbury.
Sofoluke, R. (2024). *Together We Thrive: How to find your tribe, build a community and create the dream network*. Random House.
St-Amand, J., Girard, S., & Smith, J. (2017). Sense of Belonging at School: Defining Attributes, Determinants, and Sustaining Strategies. *IAFOR Journal of Education, 5*(2), 105-119.
Steinmayr, R., Weidinger, A. F., Schwinger, M., & Spinath, B. (2019). The Importance of Students' Motivation for Their Academic Achievement – Replicating and Extending Previous Findings. *Frontiers in Psychology, 10*, 464340.
Stoll, L. (2015). Three greats for a self-improving school system – pedagogy, professional development and leadership. *National College for Teaching & Leadership*.
Sull, D., & Sull, C. (2018, June 5). With Goals, FAST Beats SMART. *MIT Sloan Management Review*. https://sloanreview.mit.edu/article/with-goals-fast-beats-smart
Swain, N. (2024). *Harnessing the Science of Learning: Success Stories to Help Kickstart Your School Improvement*. Routledge.
Sweller, J. (1988). Cognitive Load During Problem Solving: Effects on Learning. *Cognitive Science, 12*(2), 257-285.
Systems Innovation. (2023, January 17). *Systems thinking is a framework for seeing interrelationships rather than things, for seeing patterns of change rather than static 'snapshots'.* [Tweet]. X. https://x.com/Sys_innovation/status/1615257750929375235
Thibodeaux, T., Harapnuik, D., & Cummings, C. (2019). Student Perceptions of the Influence of Choice, Ownership, and Voice in Learning and the Learning Environment. *International Journal of Teaching and Learning in Higher Education, 31*(1), 50-62.
Tikkanen, L., Anttila, H., Pyhältö, K., Soini, T., & Pietarinen, J. (2022). The role of empathy between peers in upper secondary students' study engagement and burnout. *Frontiers in Psychology, 13*, 978546.
Tolin, D. F. (2024). *Doing CBT*. Guilford Publications.
Tomlinson, C. A. (2017). *How to Differentiate Instruction in Academically Diverse Classrooms* (3rd ed.). ASCD.
Tomlinson, C. A. (2022). *Everybody's Classroom: Differentiating for the Shared and Unique Needs of Diverse Students*. Teachers College Press.
Tomlinson, C. A., & Imbeau, M. B. (2023). *Leading and Managing a Differentiated Classroom*. ASCD.
Tomlinson, C. A., & Jarvis, J. M. (2023). Differentiation: Making curriculum work for all students through responsive planning & instruction. In *Systems and Models for Developing Programs for the Gifted and Talented* (pp. 599-628). Routledge.
Tomlinson, C. A., & Murphy, M. (2018). The Empathetic School. *Educational Leadership, 75*(6), 20-27.
Tschannen-Moran, M. (2014). *Trust Matters: Leadership for Successful Schools*. John Wiley & Sons.
Tuli, F. (2017). Teachers Professional Development in Schools: Reflection on the Move to Create a Culture of Continuous Improvement. *Journal of Teacher Education and Educators, 6*(3), 275-296.
UNESCO. (2015). Global citizenship education: topics and learning objectives. UNESCO.
Valente, S., Lourenço, A. A., Dominguez-Lara, S., Derakhshan, A., Németh, Z., & Almeida, L. S. (2022). Teachers' Emotion Regulation: Implications for Classroom Conflict Management. *Australian Journal of Teacher Education, 47*(8).
Van Geel, M., Keuning, T., Frèrejean, J., Dolmans, D., van Merriënboer, J., & Visscher, A. J. (2019). Capturing the complexity of differentiated instruction. *School Effectiveness and School Improvement, 30*(1), 51-67.

Van Orden, K.A., Bower, E., Lutz, J., Silva, C., Gallegos, A.M., Podgorski, C.A., Santos, E.J., & Conwell, Y. (2021). Strategies to Promote Social Connections Among Older Adults During "Social Distancing" Restrictions. *The American Journal of Geriatric Psychiatry, 29*(8), 816-827.

Van Pham, S. (2024). The Influence of Social and Emotional Learning on Academic Performance, Emotional Well-Being, and Implementation Strategies: A Literature Review. *Saudi Journal of Humanities and Social Sciences, 9*(12), 381-391.

Visible Learning Meta[x]. (2024). Teacher-student relationships. Corwin. https://www.visiblelearningmetax.com/influences/view/teacher-student_relationships

Vygotsky, L. S. (1978). *Mind in society: The Development of Higher Psychological Processes*. Harvard University Press.

Wachtel, T. (2016). *Defining Restorative*. International Institute for Restorative Practices. https://www.iirp.edu/images/pdf/Defining-Restorative_Nov-2016.pdf

Wahyuni, A. (2018). The Power of Verbal and Nonverbal Communication in Learning. In *1st International Conference on Intellectuals' Global Responsibility (ICIGR 2017)*, (pp. 80-83). Atlantis Press.

Walker, S., & Graham, L. (2021). At risk students and teacher-student relationships: student characteristics, attitudes to school and classroom climate. *International Journal of Inclusive Education, 25*(8), 896-913.

Walton, G. M., & Brady, S. T. (2017). The Many Questions of Belonging. In Elliot, A. J., Dweck, C. S., & Yeager, D. S. (Ed.), *Handbook of Competence and Motivation: Theory and Application* (2nd Ed., pp. 272-293). Guilford Press.

Wang, M.-T., & Eccles, J. S. (2013). School context, achievement motivation, and academic engagement: A longitudinal study of school engagement using a multidimensional perspective. *Learning and Instruction, 28*, 12-23.

Wang, X., Yang, L., Chen, K., & Zheng, Y. (2024). Understanding teacher emotional exhaustion: exploring the role of teaching motivation, perceived autonomy, and teacher–student relationships. *Frontiers in Psychology, 14*, 1342598.

Warnick, B. R., & Scribner, C. F. (2020). Discipline, Punishment, and the Moral Community of Schools. *Theory and Research in Education, 18*(1), 98-116.

Weiner, J. M., & Higgins, M. C. (2017). Where the two shall meet: Exploring the relationship between teacher professional culture and student learning culture. *Journal of Educational Change, 18*, 21-48.

Wigfield, A., & Eccles, J. S. (2000). Expectancy–Value Theory of Achievement Motivation. *Contemporary Educational Psychology, 25*(1), 68-81.

Wilkinson, J., & Kemmis, S. (2016). Practice Theory: Viewing leadership as leading. In *New Directions in Educational Leadership Theory* (pp. 36-52). Routledge.

Williams, M. A. (2023). *The Connected Species: How the Evolution of the Human Brain Can Save the World*. Rowman & Littlefield.

Willingham, D. T. (2021). *Why Don't Students Like School?: A Cognitive Scientist Answers Questions About How the Mind Works and What it Means for the Classroom*. John Wiley & Sons.

Wink, M. N., LaRusso, M. D., & Smith, R. L. (2021). Teacher Empathy and Students with Problem Behaviors: Examining Teachers' Perceptions, Responses, Relationships, and Burnout. *Psychology in the Schools, 58*(8), 1575-1596.

Wisniewski, B., Zierer, K., & Hattie, J. (2020). The Power of Feedback Revisited: A Meta-Analysis of Educational Feedback Research. *Frontiers in Psychology, 10*, 487662.

Wolff, M., Stojan, J., Buckler, S., Cranford, J., Whitman, L., Gruppen, L., & Santen, S. (2020). Coaching to improve self-directed learning. *The Clinical Teacher, 17*(4), 408-412.

Wubbels, T., Brekelmans, M., Den Brok, P., Wijsman, L., Mainhard, T., & Van Tartwijk, J. (2014). Teacher–Student Relationships and Classroom Management. In *Handbook of Classroom Management* (pp. 363-386). Routledge.

Xie, F., & Derakhshan, A. (2021). A Conceptual Review of Positive Teacher Interpersonal Communication Behaviors in the Instructional Context. *Frontiers in Psychology, 12*, 708490.

Yeager, D. S., & Dweck, C. S. (2020). What Can Be Learned from Growth Mindset Controversies? *American Psychologist, 75*(9), 1269-1284.

Yi, C., Nasri, N. B. M., & Jiao, J. (2023). Exploration and Analysis of Middle School Teachers' Classroom Questioning Methods from the Perspective of Dialogue Education. *Journal of Law and Sustainable Development, 11*(6), e834-e834.

Yulianti, K., Denessen, E., Droop, M., & Veerman, G. J. (2021). Transformational Leadership for Parental Involvement: How Teachers Perceive the School Leadership Practices to Promote Parental Involvement in Children's Education. *Leadership and Policy in Schools, 20*(2), 277-292.

Zepeda, S. J. (2019). *Professional Development: What Works*. Routledge.

Zimmerman, B. J., Schunk, D. H., & DiBenedetto, M. K. (2017). The role of self-efficacy and related beliefs in self-regulation of learning and performance. *Handbook of Competence and Motivation: Theory and Application, 313*, 41-50.

Zuma, B. (2014). Contact theory and the concept of prejudice: Metaphysical and moral explorations and an epistemological question. *Theory & Psychology, 24*(1), 40-57.

www.ingramcontent.com/pod-product-compliance
Lightning Source LLC
Chambersburg PA
CBHW052023070526
44584CB00016B/1872